AF608242

ASIAN LAW SERIES
School of Law
University of Washington
Number 10

ASIAN LAW SERIES

School of Law

University of Washington

The Asian Law Series was initiated in 1969, with the cooperation of the University of Washington Press and the Institute for Comparative and Foreign Area Studies (now the Henry M. Jackson School of International Studies), in order to publish the results of several projects under way in Japanese, Chinese, and Korean law. The members of the editorial committee are Donald C. Clarke, Daniel H. Foote, John O. Haley, Nicholas R. Lardy, and Dan Fenno Henderson (chairman).

1. *The Constitution of Japan: Its First Twenty Years, 1947–67,* edited by Dan Fenno Henderson
2. *Village "Contracts" in Tokugawa Japan,* by Dan Fenno Henderson
3. *Chinese Family Law and Social Change in Historic and Comparative Perspective,* edited by David C. Buxbaum
4. *Law and Politics in China's Foreign Trade,* edited by Victor H. Li
5. *Patent and Know-how Licensing in Japan and the United States,* edited by Teruo Doi and Warren L. Shattuck
6. *The Constitutional Case Law of Japan: Selected Supreme Court Decisions, 1961–70,* by Hiroshi Itoh and Lawrence Ward Beer
7. *Japan's Commission on the Constitution: The Final Report,* translated and edited by John M. Maki
8. *Securities Regulations in Korea: Problems and Recommendations for Feasible Reforms,* by Young Moo Shin
9. *Order and Discipline in China: The Shanghai Mixed Court 1911–27,* by Thomas B. Stephens
10. *The Economic Contract Law of China: Legitimation and Contract Autonomy in the PRC,* by Pitman B. Potter
11. *Japanese Labor Law,* by Kazuo Sugeno, translated by Leo Kanowitz
12. *Constitutional Systems in Late Twentieth Century Asia,* edited by Lawrence W. Beer

The Economic Contract Law of China

Legitimation and Contract Autonomy in the PRC

PITMAN B. POTTER

University of Washington Press
Seattle and London

To my parents,
the late Dalton Potter and
Jane Huntington Potter

Printed in the United States of America

Library of Congress Cataloging-in-Publication Data
Potter, Pitman B.
The economic contract law of the PRC : legitimation and contract autonomy in China / Pitman B. Potter.
p. cm. — (Asian law series ; no. 10)
Includes bibliographical references and index.
ISBN 0–295–97127–4
1. Liberty of contract—China. 2. Contracts—China. I. Title. II. Series.
KNQ858.3.P68 1992
346.51'02—dc20
[345.1062] 91-36749
CIP

The paper used in this publication meets the minimum requirements of American National Standard for Information Sciences—Permanence of Paper for Printed Library Materials, ANSI Z39.48–1984. ♾

Contents

Acknowledgments

Throughout the course of the project, I received invaluable assistance from many people. As this book grew out of my Ph.D. dissertation, I would first like to thank my dissertation committee, comprised at various times of James R. Townsend (Chair), Daniel Lev, Elizabeth Perry, Peter Rohn, and Geunther Roth, with Roland Hjorth acting as graduate observer. These individuals gave generously of their time during the preparation of the dissertation, and provided numerous helpful comments and suggestions. Jim Townsend in particular has been extremely helpful throughout the preparation of the dissertation and in the preparation of this volume. He has been a valued counselor and friend.

My dissertation field research in Hong Kong and China was funded in part by a fellowship from the Social Science Research Council in concert with the American Council of Learned Societies under grants from the Ford Foundation and the Mellon Foundation, for which I am deeply grateful. Dr. Sophie Sa at the Social Science Research Council provided constant encouragement and support during the period of my field research. Funding for both research and writing of the dissertation was also provided under a National Resource Fellowship, for which I am also very grateful.

In Hong Kong, John Dolfin generously made available to me the excellent resources of the Universities Service Centre. Suzanne Pepper provided very helpful comments on the techniques and problems of interviewing Chinese emigrés. The USC staff was extremely helpful, as was the staff at the Union Research Institute. The East Asia College of the Chinese University of Hong Kong generously acted as my sponsor in Hong Kong, and made office and library facilities available to me. In particular, I would like to thank Joseph Cheng, Byron Weng, and Peter Lee for their kind assistance and encouragement.

My research in China was helped significantly through the generous efforts of the late Senator Henry Jackson and his staff, particularly

Dorothy Fosdick. Leon Slawecki at the U.S. Embassy in Beijing was exceedingly generous with his time, particularly as liaison with Chinese governmental organizations. Jack Dull at the University of Washington was also helpful in arranging research opportunities for me in Beijing.

During the process of preparing my dissertation and this volume, I benefited from the comments and suggestions of a number of China and East Asia area specialists, each of whom helped increase my understanding of law and society in China. At the University of Washington Law School, I received constant encouragement and useful guidance from John Haley, Dan Henderson, and Paul Liu. At the University of Michigan, Michel Oksenberg provided many helpful comments, as well as warm hospitality during my stay at Ann Arbor. Whitmore Gray was also a source of many useful insights. Ramon Myers was very helpful at the Hoover Library. Lowell Dittmer and Robert Scalapino were generous in making time available to me at Berkeley. William C. Jones provided extended useful comments on civil law structures during one of his visits to Hong Kong, for which I am particularly grateful. Others who provided helpful comments and encouragement include Rosser Brockman, Timothy Cheek, Jerome Alan Cohen, Steven Connor, Anthony Dicks, James Feinerman, Karl Herbst, Stanley Lubman and James Spear. I owe a particular debt of gratitude to Dorothy Solinger and to an anonymous reviewer for insightful comments on an earlier draft.

During the period of my field research, I received assistance from several important university libraries. I would like to thank the staff of the East Asian Library and the Law School Library at the University of Washington. I would also like to thank the staff of the libraries at the University of Michigan, the University of California at Berkeley, and the Hoover Center at Stanford University for their kind assistance and support.

I would like to thank the editors and staff at the University of Washington Press, particularly Naomi Pascal, Julidta Tarver, and Margery Lang for their helpful and patient editing. The law firms of LeSourd and Patten in Seattle and Graham & James in San Francisco, Beijing, Hong Kong, and elsewhere were extraordinarily generous in making word processing facilities available to me and in supporting my use of time to work on this book. I would also like to thank Victoria Ching for her patient typing of an earlier version of the manuscript at the Graham & James office in Beijing.

Finally, I am forever in debt to my wife, Vicki, for her unfailing support for my work on this project. Not only did she provide tireless assistance in typing and proofreading the dissertation, and later the manuscript, but she provided constant encouragement throughout the process that resulted in this volume.

Space limitations prohibit my naming the many other classmates, colleagues, and friends who provided useful comments, suggestions, and encouragement in connection with this book. These individuals and their contributions are not forgotten. I only wish I could thank each of them properly.

Despite the widespread and generous assistance that I received in the course of writing this book, numerous faults undoubtedly remain, for which I alone am responsible.

The Economic Contract Law of China
Legitimation and Contract Autonomy in the PRC

Introduction

The Economic Contract Law of the People's Republic of China (hereinafter, referred to as the ECL) was the cornerstone of the regulatory framework for the economic reform policies that emerged from the Third Plenum (hereafter, the Third Plenum) of the Eleventh Central Committee of the Chinese Communist party (hereafter, CCP).[1] The ECL was applied to virtually all types of economic transactions in China, and thus represented an important focal point of the interaction between legal and economic reform. The effectiveness of the ECL, however, is a function of its ability to acquire legitimacy in the perception of Chinese economic actors. This study examines the ability of the ECL to acquire legitimacy and promote contract autonomy.

The Economic Contract Law and Chinese Economic Policy Reforms

The ECL was enacted in December 1981, and went into effect in June 1982. At this time, the contract responsibility system in agriculture, adopted at the Third Plenum, had been in effect for over a year, granting to farming families, and then to individual farmers, greater autonomy in production and sales activities.[2] The responsibility system had not yet been introduced in the commercial and industrial sectors, but discussion had been underway on this since the time of the Third Plenum.[3] These policies reflected the consensus of the Chinese leadership that certain transactions should be separated from the mechanism of state planning in order to rely more fully on local market forces. These new policies and their impact on contract regulation and activity may be understood best in comparison to pre-existing policy conditions.

Contracts Prior to 1978

Prior to the Third Plenum, the role of contracts in Chinese economic activity had depended on the economic policies of the time. Following the establishment of the People's Republic in 1949, the government enacted contract regulations that specified the types of economic transactions permitted, the parties permitted to engage in economic activity, the rules governing economic transactions, and the rules for enforcement of economic agreements, all of which depended on the changing policies of the new regime.[4]

Limited private contract activities were permitted in the early 1950s as the Chinese government sought to consolidate the economy following the disruption of war and revolution.[5] During the mid-1950s, laws on economic transactions reflected the conflicting views of the Chinese leadership as to how to proceed toward full socialism. During the high-tide of collectivization in 1955–56, and again during the Great Leap Forward in 1959–60 the rules governing economic transactions emphasized collectivism and state control. During the period preceding the Great Leap, and again during the early 1960s, greater emphasis was placed on autonomy of economic activity based on market requirements. During the Cultural Revolution decade of 1966–76, economic policy again emphasized state control and collective action.[6] The alternative policy priorities of state-centric and market-oriented contract activities gave rise to different types of contract behavior.

When the state-centric model was emphasized, primarily during the 1958–60 period and during the Cultural Revolution, most economic transactions were subject to comprehensive state planning.[7] The State Planning Commission's national plan would be subdivided and sent down to the various provinces, municipalities, and autonomous regions, and then again to the district and county levels, and ultimately to each individual working unit. The products produced, the raw materials used, the transportation and sale of finished and semifinished goods, all were controlled according to the state plan. In the course of this activity, documents termed "contracts" were used to record various transactions.[8] However, the parties to these transactions had little, if any, authority to control the terms. Rather the contracts tended to be commands issued by planning departments or related units in the planning process to be performed by other units. These contracts served later as records of the extent to which various plan quotas were performed.

During the periods when market-oriented economic policies held sway, production and marketing units were permitted broader degrees of autonomy in forming contracts based on market conditions but within the broad parameters of planning targets. The parties to these agreements had limited negotiating autonomy on issues of price and specifications for goods.[9] These market-oriented contracts were used primarily during the mid 1950s and early 1960s, but were shelved during the Cultural Revolution and until after the Third Plenum policies took hold.

Economic Contract Law and Third Plenum Reform Policies

The Third Plenum's emphasis on private economic activity represented a reversal of the collectivist economic policies of the Cultural Revolution, and a recommencement of the market-oriented policies of the early 1960s. In addition, the Third Plenum also resulted in a legal reform effort that emphasized the role of laws and legal institutions in regulating social and economic activity.[10] The ECL was part of this effort, and represented the use of legislation to codify the policy decisions of the Third Plenum.

In line with the Third Plenum policies, the ECL promoted the autonomy of economic actors to engage in increasingly diverse economic transactions. The ECL emphasized the rights of the contracting parties to a greater degree than previously evident in China,[11] and complemented the Third Plenum reform policies imposing on economic actors greater responsibility for economic activity. The ECL encouraged transactional autonomy by reducing the power of units unrelated to the contracting parties to supervise contract formation. The ECL also strengthened the enforceability of contracts through its emphasis on compulsory dispute settlement and monetary remedies for nonperformance of contracts. Each of these and other provisions of the ECL was consistent with the thrust of the Third Plenum's economic reform policies to provide more autonomy to economic actors.

This use of legislation to express policy priorities revealed new confidence in the longevity of the policies themselves, and represented an effort to insulate them from policy reversals. Past policy decisions, to the extent they were formalized at all, generally were implemented through administrative regulations. Administrative regulations could be revised or canceled without the need for National People's Congress review, whereas such review was required for amendment or cancellation of the ECL and other formal legislation. Thus, the use of the ECL to express formally the autonomy of economic actors granted under the Third Plenum policies of economic reform held the promise of greater permanence of these policies and their implementation.

The durability of the ECL in turn was intended to encourage popular assimilation of the norms expressed by this law, as economic actors come to accept and rely upon them. An unintended consequence of this assimilation is that it may extend to autonomy in other spheres.[12] Thus, the recognition of contract autonomy under the ECL has potentially great significance for the future of law and economic regulation in China generally.

The ECL and Legitimacy

The ECL's ability to foster the recognition and enforcement of contract autonomy depends on the ability of the law to acquire legitimacy.[13] The law was enacted, not through a process of popular consultation and ratification, but rather through decree by the political leadership. As imposed law, the ECL depends on more than the government's protestations as to the law's importance—particularly in the context of China's traditional ambivalence toward law. Rather, those economic actors who are subject to the law must accord it legitimacy by accepting the validity of its provisions and by relying upon them in practice. Although the prospects for the ECL to gain legitimacy may be viewed by reference to the process of the legitimation of law generally, distinctions must be made between legitimation in the Western tradition and legitimation of imposed law.

Abstract Legitimation of Law in the European Tradition:

Although the wide differences between the European and Chinese cultural and philosophical traditions bar strict comparison of the legitimation of law in these two types of society, an understanding of the legitimation of European law is instructive. The legitimacy of law in societies of the European tradition has been seen as dependent on the ability of law to replace other social mechanisms for enforcing norms.[14] Max Weber traced law's legitimacy to the lawmaking process.[15] Emile Durkheim emphasized that it was law's expression of the collective social conscience, the lowest common denominator of social norms, which enables the state to employ law as an instrument of social control.[16] Departing from Marx's instrumentalist approach to analyzing law merely as a tool of bourgeois domination, Gramsci used the term "hegemony" to explain society's acceptance of normative values that served to reinforce society's subservience to such domination.[17]

Whether analyzed in terms of the distillation of social conscience or as the imposition of norms conducive to bourgeois dominance, the acceptance by Western society of legal rationality as a legitimate basis for the regulation of behavior reveals an ideology of law peculiar to the Western historical experience. At the root of this ideology is the concept of natural law that grew from a rhetorical device employed by the merchant classes and the church in pursuit of autonomy from monarchical authority to a normative concept infusing egalitarian standards on the doctrines of law.[18]

The legitimacy of law in societies of the European tradition also may be assessed in terms of the law's ability to satisfy the ideological expectations of society that are derived from social norms. Under Weber's rational-legal typology, the legitimacy of law depends on the extent to which the lawmaking process acquires legitimacy by its accord with the expectations of Western legal ideology.[19] More contemporary scholars have focused on the ideals expressed in substantive law as the source of law's legitimacy. Balbus contends, for example, that the legitimacy of the legal order depends on society's acceptance of the ideals of formality and generality that are embodied in legal doctrine even if they are not realized fully in practice.[20] Trubek argues that the acceptance of law's legitimacy depends on the concept that law represents a mechanism for reconciling the conflict between egalitarian social ideals and the hierarchical character of social structures.[21]

In sum, law can be seen as gaining legitimacy in societies of the European tradition by virtue of its ability to satisfy society's ideological expectations. That such expectations are ideological rather than material allows law to gain legitimacy by expressing an accepted set of ideals even if such ideals are not realized in practice. This kind of legitimacy may be termed *abstract legitimacy.* The abstract legitimacy of law in these societies also carried with it practical utility in encouraging economic growth and development, strengthening the legitimacy of the law as a regulator of economic activity. Nonetheless, the foundation for the acceptance of law as a regulator of economic and social life was the abstract legitimacy of the law.

Legitimation of Imposed Law: Practical Legitimacy

In many societies, however, legalization follows a process by which the elite imposes on society rules that do not necessarily reflect local norms. But since the codification of law in such societies does not represent the institutionalization of social norms, resulting rules cannot be assumed automatically to receive abstract legitimacy. In societies where law is imposed by a ruling elite, the legitimacy of law may in fact conflict with customary norms. The obstacles to the legitimation of imposed law derive from the conflicts between the norms of imposed law and pre-existing norms.

Although the subjects of imposed law may accept its inherent validity in the abstract, legitimacy of imposed law is manifested by reliance on the law in practice.[22] And while authoritarian regimes have the power to compel minimal compliance with legal regulations, the acceptance of law as an effective replacement for pre-existing norms must be largely voluntary to be effective. Thus, the legitimacy of imposed law depends on whether the subjects of the law accept in practice the law's utility as a regulatory mechanism. This acceptance may be termed "practical legitimacy," as distinguished from legitimacy in the abstract. The legitimacy of imposed law requires both abstract and practical legitimacy.

The legitimacy of imposed law requires a conscious acceptance by the subjects of the law that it is preferable to pre-existing customary norms. Inherent in this acceptance is the conflict between the norms of imposed law and the pre-existing norms with which the law competes for acceptance. Analysis of this conflict requires an assessment of the resiliency of pre-existing norms, a task made difficult by the use of the vocabulary of formal legalism to express what may in fact be customary norms.[23]

Once pre-existing norms have been identified and their nature as an obstacle to the legitimacy of imposed law understood, the examination must focus on the process by which economic actors identify the norms of imposed law. To accept the norms of imposed law, the subjects of the law must identify these norms and then "recognize" value in them.[24] Since both recognition and legitimacy are functions of perception, examination of the legitimacy of imposed law must focus on how it is perceived by the subjects of law.[25]

Insights as to the perception of law by its subjects are obtained by examination of its doctrine and operation. The doctrine includes not only the statutory language, but also official and nonofficial interpretations of such language. The practical application of the law may be examined by reference to its operational record. Thus, the potential for imposed law to acquire abstract and practical legitimacy may be determined from examination of the law's doctrine and practice in light of pre-existing norms and their impact.

The Economic Contract Law and the Challenge of Legitimacy

To be an effective basis for economic regulation, and for the emergence of contract autonomy, the ECL must achieve both abstract and practical legitimacy. The abstract legitimacy of the ECL lies in the extent to which the economic actors who are subject to the law recognize their own parochial values in its content. The ability of the ECL to achieve practical legitimacy depends in part on the extent to which the operation of the law is consistent with its doctrinal principles. The potential for the ECL to acquire abstract and practical legitimacy depends also on the ability to overcome a variety of attitudinal and operational obstacles.

Obstacles to Legitimacy of the ECL

The primary obstacles to the ECL's attaining legitimacy involve preexisting attitudes toward the role of law as a mechanism for economic regulation, as well as the various operational difficulties related to the interpretation and application of the ECL itself.

Attitudinal obstacles to the ECL's legitimacy derive from traditional Chinese ambivalence toward private law, engendered both by the Chinese legal tradition and by the use of law in post-1949 China.

Traditional Chinese Law. In traditional China, the role of formal law was limited mainly to the maintenance of public order.[26] The Confucian ethic of personal rectification resulted in the courts placing greater emphasis on confession, even if achieved through torture, than on factually based findings of guilt or innocence. Further, the view was often held that the very existence of a criminal accusation meant that the Confucian social order had been disrupted, and that punishment was due. As a result, involvement with law and legal institutions was seen as something to be avoided by all members of society.

To the extent that formal law played a role in governing economic activity, the focus was primarily on regulating various public relationships rather than the private relationships that characterize typical commercial contract transactions.[27] Thus, state regulations were used to enforce government monopolies, to enforce licensing rules for special occupations, and to ensure collection of taxes on economic transactions.[28]

Private commercial transactions, on the other hand, were governed by informal customary law rules. Although written contracts were used to express transactional terms and conditions, these generally did not receive formal recognition from the state but were supported by private guarantees enforced through informal organizations centered on the family and guild.[29] Thus, contract relationships were formed and enforced in the context of larger personal and organizational relationships in which the parties operated. Accordingly, the rights of contract parties were dependent on relationships external to the contract transaction, and the conduct of contracting parties was influenced mainly by these external relationships, rather than by formal law or transactionally based contract rules.

As a result, economic actors in traditional China paid only limited attention to the role of formal law in recognizing and enforcing economic rights. External personal and organizational relationships were of greater significance in governing the conduct of contracting parties.

Law in the People's Republic. The importance of external relationships was also evident in the role of law in post-1949 China. Following the Communist revolution, law was given a Marxist-Leninist orientation, and was used mainly as an instrument for enforcing the domination of the ruling class.[30] The class orientation of the Chinese Communists meant that the substance and application of law depended on class relations, rather than on a universal set of rules and principles. The law was an instrument of the state, under the leadership of the party, which purported to espouse the interests of the ruling proletariat class. In the public sector, law was used to suppress counterrevolutionaries, rightists, and other elements considered hostile to the interests of the ruling proletarian class, as represented by the Communist party.[31] Law was also used to set the rules for the taking of property by the state in pursuit of returning the means of production to the proletariat. The critical point in these activities was not the relationship between the parties to a particular transaction, but rather the relationship of the parties to the rest of society. This external relationship dictated the nature of the parties' rights, and the rules governing enforcement of these rights.

In the economic sphere, the status and conduct of economic units depended on their relationships with other units in the bureaucratic hierarchy.[32] The economic function of any particular unit rested on its relationship to other units in the state planning process. The operational status of economic units rested on their administrative relationship to the system of state ministries or commissions. Accordingly, economic transactions were part and parcel of a larger administrative whole to which transacting parties were organizationally tied. As a result, economic transactions were dictated by the external organizational relationships of the parties, rather than by the terms and rules specific to the transactions themselves.

Similarly, the rules governing economic transactions were specified by external relations rather than by the parties involved. In contrast to the European and Anglo-American concepts of contracts as agreements by which the parties set the rules governing their specific transactions,[33] Chinese economic actors had little authority to set these rules themselves. Rather they were dependent on administrative regulations to formulate transactional terms and conditions. These regulations in turn reflected the policy priorities of the state (in theory, the collective priorities of the community). Thus, with the exception of brief periods during the mid-1950s and early 1960s, the norms governing economic transactions prior to enactment of the ECL were subject to external factors that set the terms and conditions of such transactions.

The emphasis on external factors in contract relationships that characterized both the customary rules of traditional China and socialist law of Communist China reflected the primacy of collectivist norms. For it is the recognition of the priority of the collective interests of the community that requires contract relationships to be subjugated to factors external to the transaction. The ability of the ECL to gain practical legitimacy will depend in large part on whether economic actors perceive that the norm of autonomy granted under the ECL is more desirable than the collectivist norms that obtained previously.

In addition to the attitudinal obstacles posed by pre-existing norms to the legitimacy of the ECL, certain challenges of interpretation and application of the ECL also must be overcome. The legitimation of law requires that before the process can begin of recognition of valued norms, the subjects of law must be able to identify those norms. With regard to the ECL, such identification requires consistent interpretation and application of the doctrine espoused in the law.

The ECL must be interpreted by a host of governmental and legal entities, each with differing policy and organizational priorities. The extent to which these various entities are able to formulate a consistent doctrine of the ECL will affect the legitimacy granted the law by economic actors. Doctrinal consistency will support legitimation as economic actors perceive the doctrine as unified and widely supported by the governmental authorities. Doctrinal differences, on the other hand, whether derived from genuine conceptual debate or from political and organizational rivalries, would call into question the reliability of various doctrinal viewpoints. This would tend to undermine the legitimacy of the law generally, as economic actors come to question which of the various competing views is correct and whether any have sufficient governmental support to be effective.

In addition, the application of the ECL in practice must be consistent with the doctrinal principles. Such consistency is difficult in the face of varying and complex factual situations. In addition, doctrinal differences born of disagreements as to underlying policy cannot but lead to operational inconsistencies among those charged with implementing the law. The pattern that had obtained in the past of contract regulations being subservient to economic policy may cause implementing officials and economic actors alike to view the ECL as but an appendage of a transitory economic policy that does not warrant long-term, consistent support. These and other factors raise the potential that inconsistencies of doctrine and disparities of doctrine and practice will cause economic actors to doubt the validity of the doctrinal norms themselves. Such doubt hampers a committed obedience to doctrine and undercuts practical legitimacy, as economic actors question whether the doctrinal norms have any practical significance.

Thus, the critical challenge to the legitimacy of the ECL concerns achieving consistency of doctrine and practice. Doctrinal and operational consistency permit economic actors to identify the ECL's norms of autonomy, to rely on these in practice, and to weigh their relative benefits against those derived from pre-existing norms of collectivism. The extent to which such consistency can be achieved, although not in itself a guarantee of legitimation of the ECL, will have an important effect on the legitimacy of this law.

Doctrinal and Operational Issues and the ECL

Certain issues underlying the ECL are particularly instructive regarding the potential for the law to acquire legitimacy. These are (1) the role of contracts and contract law; (2) supervision over contract formation and performance; and (3) institutions and methods for dispute resolution. Doctrinal discussions and the operational record concerning these issues prior to and following the enactment of the ECL reveal tensions between the norms of autonomy and collectivism that are the focus of the ECL's quest for legitimacy.

Contracts and Contract Law

The role of contracts and contract law are central issues relating to the economic policies that the ECL was intended to support. The function of contracts in the Chinese economy is inextricably tied to the policy issue of whether economic conduct should be based on collectivist central planning or upon more autonomous market-oriented decision making by economic actors themselves. Although contracts had been used previously to document various stages of fulfillment of the state economic plan,[34] the critical question related to the ECL concerned the use of contracts outside the plan.[35]

Doctrinal discussion of the proper role of contracts and contract law in China has tended to fall along a spectrum embracing the following typologies:

1. When there is planning without contracts or contract law, no independent economic actors exist and all economic transactions are directed by the planning bureaucracy. In addition, the concentration of economic decision-making authority within the state planning bureaucracy denies the role of autonomous contract relationships. The resulting economic transactions are purely public relationships by which the state plan is implemented. This model embodies the circumstances of Chinese contract practice prior to the Third Plenum, and can be viewed as one of the pre-existing norms with which the ECL competes for acceptance.

2. Planning with contracts as a supplement to plan directives permits limited contract autonomy, subject to general planning guidelines. Although administrative planning regulations dominate economic decision-making, specialized private contracts may be formed in the fulfilling of state plan directives. These specialized contracts are then subject to transactionally specific contract rules based on and supported by a generalized contract law. For example, a manufacturing enterprise may be responsible under the state plan for a certain level of output, but may also sign independently contracts with unrelated parties for supply of raw materials necessary to fulfill its output requirements under the plan. In such cases, administrative orders issued under the state plan would dictate the manufacturing enterprise's planned output quota, and thus would influence the terms and conditions of the raw materials supply contract. The terms and conditions for the supply contract not directly related to the manufacturing enterprise's planning directives could be negotiated independently between the manufacturing enterprise and its supplier. Thus, the raw material sup-

ply contract would contain provisions conditioned by the state plan obligations of the manufacturer, and also would contain rules specific to the transaction and subject to the general provisions of a state contract law. This typology is consistent with Article 4 of the ECL that requires that contracts not be in conflict with the plan, but does not insist that all contracts be plan contracts.

3. As contracts gradually supersede the plan, they become subject only to the requirements of contract law. This typology foresees the gradual elimination of state planning altogether, as economic actors have autonomy to select independently the parties and contents of contracts. Under such circumstances, contract transactions would contain only transactionally specific rules set by the parties themselves, but subject to the general rules set forth in a national contract law. The rights and obligations of the contracting parties would derive primarily from the terms of the contract and would be largely independent from state economic policies.

Doctrinal discussions of the role of contracts and contract law reveal preferences regarding the dichotomy of autonomy and collectivism, while the record of operations reveals the extent to which the doctrine is carried out in practice. Contracts signed pursuant to transactions outside the plan encourage autonomous decision making by economic actors, as these actors must determine how to arrange their economic activity and decide the terms of their transactions without state guidance or direction. Plan contracts, on the other hand, simply document the administrative obligations of economic units to implement plan targets within the general organizational framework. Thus, the terms of such contracts and the character of the economic activity underlying them are determined by external bureaucratic and organizational factors. Accordingly, support for expanded use of nonplan contracts may be seen as support for expanded autonomy in economic activity, whereas support for the primacy of state plan contracts represents continued insistence on the collectivist ethic embodied in the state plan system.

The role of contract law is an important issue relating to whether contract laws and regulations, including the ECL, are intended primarily to be an instrument of collectivist policy management or a set of norms for autonomous transactions. Doctrinal positions supporting the role of contract law solely as an instrument for enforcing the state plan or other state economic policies may be interpreted as support for the collectivist view of economic actors as components in the national economic administrative system. On the other hand, doctrinal positions supporting the role of the contract law as aimed at governing the rights and obligations of economic actors in specific transactions reveals support for the autonomy of economic actors based on protections derived from the ECL and related regulations.

Consistency of doctrine and practice in the implementation of contracts and contract law will reveal much about the potential for the ECL to acquire legitimacy. Consistency, or the lack thereof, in doctrinal positions on the role of contracts and contract law will determine whether economic actors are afforded the opportunity to recognize the norms offered under the ECL as a precursor to extending abstract legitimacy. Consistency of practice with doctrine will help determine whether economic actors will be afforded the opportunity to assess the operation of such norms as a precursor to extending practical legitimacy. Thus, the issues of the role of contracts and contract law are important focal points for this study.

Institutions and Methods of Contract Supervision

Supervision over contract formation and fulfillment entails several sensitive issues with significance for contract activity in China. The major issue concerning the methods of contract management is whether supervision should be exercised within the context of existing bureaucratic hierarchies, or exercised from outside these hierarchies. The institutions charged with supervision over contracts range from contract management offices within economic enterprises to interagency organs such as the State Administration for Industry and Commerce (hereafter, referred to as SAIC) and to the Notarial Offices under the Ministry of Justice.

Doctrinal positions concerning contract supervision reveal different views as to the proper relationship between contracting parties and other units. Where supervision is exercised by units that are organizationally related to the contracting parties, it may be considered as "internal supervision." In such circumstances, the contracting parties are inseparable from the larger bureaucratic organization to which they are attached and their rights and obligations are subject to factors external to the contract transaction itself, such as the collective policies and relationships of the parent. In contrast to internal supervision, supervision exercised by units that are organizationally independent from the contracting parties may be considered as "external supervision." In such instances, the contracting parties enjoy greater autonomy, and their contract rights and obligations depend more on the terms of the contract than on external factors.

Doctrinal preferences regarding the use of external or internal methods of contract supervision reveal support for or opposition to the expansion of autonomy in the formation of contracts. The operational reality of contract supervision reveals the extent to which the doctrinal views are carried out in practice. Doctrinal consistency regarding contract supervision is critical to the ability of economic actors to recognize, and perhaps grant abstract legitimacy to, the norms embodied in the ECL concerning supervision of contracts. Consistent application of the doctrine in practice is essential to afford economic actors the chance to experience the norms of the ECL in operation, as a precursor to extending practical legitimacy.

Institutions and Methods for Dispute Resolution

The institutions and methods used for dispute settlement reflect varying priorities as to the compulsory enforcement of contract rights and obligations. Such enforcement is furthered by the availability of compulsory dispute resolution. Compulsory dispute resolution may be viewed as supporting the autonomy of contract transactions, as the enforceability of contract rights and obligations is focused on the contract transaction itself, rather than on relationships, policies, or other factors external to the transaction.

In China, dispute resolution has taken one of several forms, mediation, arbitration, and adjudication, comprising a spectrum between consensual and compulsory dispute settlement. Submission to mediation and compliance with mediation decisions are voluntary, and such voluntariness has been presented as consistent with Chinese traditional collectivist norms favoring compromise and avoidance of confrontation.[36] Arbitration and adjudication, on the other hand, result in decisions with which compliance is compulsory. Submission to arbitration is voluntary whereas submission to adjudiction is not.

The institutions available for dispute settlement include administrative departments related to the contracting parties, interagency bodies, and organizationally separate judicial institutions. This spectrum of dispute settlement organs with varying ties to the disputants is similar in its implications to the spectrum of internal and external methods of contract supervision. Just as contract transactions may become increasingly autonomous as contract supervision becomes increasingly external, so too the autonomy of contract rights enforcement may be expected to expand as dispute resolution is handled by institutions independent from the disputants. Such organizational independence permits dispute settlement organs to be disinterested in the outcome of particular disputes, and permits the dispute resolution process to be increasingly free of outside influences.

The ECL links strengthened enforceability of contract rights and obligations with increased use of compulsory dispute settlement by organizationally independent organs, and thus suggests further support for the autonomy of contract relationships. This approach stands in contrast to pre-existing collectivist norms that favored consensual dispute settlement. However, as a result of the Third Plenum economic reform policies requiring economic actors to take responsibility for their own profits and losses, including losses resulting from other parties' nonperformance of contracts, the practical interests of economic actors may stimulate a greater willingness to insist on contract enforcement, even at the expense of the traditional collectivist norms.

An examination of doctrinal consistency concerning dispute resolution is useful to explain the potential for economic actors to recognize new norms concerning contract dispute resolution as a step in the process of abstract legitimation. Comparison of doctrine and practice will reveal the extent to which the new norms concerning dispute resolution are put into operation, a prerequisite to achieving practical legitimacy.

Organization of the Volume

The focus of this study is whether the new norms of autonomy offered under the ECL can overcome various attitudinal and operational obstacles to abstract and practical legitimacy, and thus possibly create a basis for recognition and enforcement of autonomous contracts. The volume is organized to present in order (1) the normative conflict between the ECL and pre-existing contract norms; (2) the doctrinal discussions regarding the issues concerning the role of contracts and contract law, contract supervision, and dispute resolution; (3) the practice of contract formation; and (4) the practice of contract dispute resolution.

Chapter 1 offers a comparison of the provisions of the ECL with pre-existing norms derived from prior PRC contract regulations. Thus, chapter 1 outlines the basic conflict between the norms of the ECL and the pre-existing norms with which the ECL competes for legitimacy. Chapter 2 offers the doctrinal perspectives of the central political and legal communities.[37] Thus, chapter 2 examines the prospects for recognition by economic actors of the doctrine underlying the ECL. Chapters 3 and 4 contain analysis of the operational reality of contract practice, based on reports of 131 cases drawn from Chinese newspapers and legal journals.[38] Chapter 3 focuses on contract formation, and the extent to which doctrinal provisions on the role of contracts and the supervision of contracts are realized in practice. Chapter 4 contains analysis of the operation of dispute resolution, assessing the extent of consistency between doctrine and practice regarding the role of contract law and the methods and institutions for dispute resolution. The conclusion summarizes the analyses presented throughout the book, and offers conclusions as to the prospect for the ECL acquiring legitimacy and fostering the growth of autonomous contract rights.

The approach taken in this study is predicated on the assumption that the effectiveness of law in China depends on whether the subjects of the law extend to it practical as well as abstract legitimacy. It assesses the potential of the ECL to acquire such legitimacy and thus to become a basis for expanded contract autonomy in China. It is hoped that it may be of some assistance to future studies concerning the potential for law to create conditions for expanded autonomy in other spheres of Chinese life.

CHAPTER 1

The Conflict of Norms

The ECL and Prior Contract Regulations

The ECL was enacted in December 1981 as part of ongoing efforts to implement the Third Plenum economic reform policies by displacing pre-existing collectivist norms.[1] The law was aimed primarily at fostering increased autonomy for economic transactions, while retaining for the state a modicum of supervisory control under the aegis of the state planning system. Although the ECL was consistent with prior contract regulations in that it was imposed in furtherance of the regime's economic policy, the law encouraged transactional autonomy to an extent not previously seen. As imposed law, however, the ECL faces the challenge to acquire legitimacy through the conscious assessment of the economic actors who are its subjects. This entails conflict with pre-existing norms.

The challenge that pre-existing norms pose for the ECL can be assessed through review of the ECL's major provisions by reference to prior Chinese contract regulations. The content and operation of these pre-existing regulations provide a normative standard with which the new law competes for legitimacy. While reaffirming certain principles and components of prior contract regulations, the ECL contained changes of emphasis that downplayed collectivist norms. In addition, the new law revised various features of prior contract regulations so as to support contract autonomy as a complement to economic reform.

Pre-Existing PRC Contract Regulations

Between 1950 and 1965, the Chinese government enacted nearly twenty sets of regulations concerning economic contracts.[2] During the 1950s, contract activity was governed primarily by the Provisional Methods for Signing Contracts by Institutions, State Enterprises and Collectives (1950),[3] together with the Central People's Government Trade Ministry Decision Concerning the Careful Signing and Strict

Fulfillment of Contracts (1950).[4] Contract activity during the early 1960s was governed mainly by the 1962 Central Committee and State Council Circular Concerning the Strict Enforcement of Basic Construction Procedures and the Strict Fulfillment of Economic Contracts,[5] together with the 1963 State Economic Commission's Provisional Regulations Concerning the Basic Provisions in Contracts for Ordering Factory and Mining Goods.[6]

These early regulations were comparable to the ECL for several reasons. First, these regulations and the efforts to implement them faced the same challenges of legitimation that later confronted the ECL. Attitudinal and practical obstacles to legitimation made enforcement of these contract regulations problematic. Second, the regulations of 1950 and 1962–63 represented the use of formal rules to complement economic policies enacted in response to the economic dislocation caused by the upheavals of the war of liberation and later by the disaster of the Great Leap Forward. Similarly, the ECL complements economic policies formulated in response to the disruption brought on by the Cultural Revolution and its aftermath. The 1950 and 1962–63 regulations also addressed a broad range of economic contracts, similarly with the ECL.[7] Finally, these early contract regulations are perceived by Chinese legal officials as the main antecedents to the ECL.[8] Accordingly, the PRC's past experience with contract regulations is examined best through focus on the 1950 and 1962–63 regulations.

The 1950 Regulations

Origins. The first contract regulations enacted by the PRC, the Provisional Methods (September 1950) and the Trade Ministry Decision on Careful Signing and Strict Enforcement (October 1950) were intended to facilitate state control over local economic activity.[9] The regulations recognized the role of contracts as the basis for economic interaction but subjected them to the approval and supervision of state institutions. The 1950 regulations complemented the regime's preexisting policy priority of state intervention in economic activity that was aimed at reorganizing agricultural production and national construction in the aftermath of liberation and land reform.[10]

Thus, the regime sought to integrate the individual peasant economy with the national economy through contracts formed by supply and marketing cooperatives that acted as the conduit between the agricultural mutual aid teams and the state enterprises.[11] However, these attempts at the establishment of a contract system met with limited success. The peasantry, habituated by centuries of individual petit capitalism, were reluctant to embrace the role of the state in arranging their affairs. As one commentator noted, "Part of the masses don't understand the role of signing contracts . . . some of the masses think that the signing of procurement contracts by cooperatives represents the state making deals with the common people so as to bring benefits to the cooperative by profiting at the expense of the common people."[12] The masses' reluctance to embrace the role of contracts was criticized as evidence of a one-sided attitude that ignored the interests of the state.[13] This reflected a basic attitude of agricultural producers that favored individualism and autonomy over collectivism and state intervention, and exemplified the conflict between proposed and preexisting norms for economic activity.

In addition, there existed shortcomings in the handling of contracts by officials. The cadres charged with signing production amd marketing contracts with peasants were not careful in drawing up contracts and took the attitude "whether or not a contract is signed doesn't matter."[14] This resulted in contract clauses being overly vague. The problems of "blindly signing contracts and signing big contracts" (*mang mu ding hetong, ding da hetong*) were common.[15] The problem of "big contracts" referred to the signing of contracts without conducting adequate investigation of both the needs of the market and the capabilities of the contracting parties.[16] Moreover, enforcement problems emerged as cadres took the attitude that "enforcement and nonenforcement don't matter" (*zhixing bu zhixing mei you guanxi*).[17] When combined with attitudinal obstacles raised by the peasantry, these political obstacles exacerbated the difficulties that the regime faced in implementing its new contract system.

Regulatory Response. The 1950 regulations provided specific rules intended to resolve many of the problems hampering the establishment of contracts as an extension of state control over local economic activity. Article 1 of the Provisional Methods described the regulations as directed at "promoting normal business relations among organizations, state enterprises, and cooperatives. . . . ," thus clarifying that the contracts foreseen under these regulations were to form linkages between state enterprises and the remnants of private industry remaining after liberation.[18] In the agricultural sector, the Provisional Methods provided rules for economic transactions among the mutual aid teams, the state enterprises, and the supply and marketing cooperatives.

The 1950 regulations attempted to impose regularity and consistency on contract practice through a framework by which contracts were to be approved and supervised. Article 9 of the Provisional Methods required that higher level organizations be notified of the signing of contracts.[19] Article 9 also provided that all contracts be recorded directly with the leadership of the finance committee and a copy filed for reference with the financial offices on the same level as that of the contracting parties.

The 1950 regulations were also intended to strengthen the state's control over planning and accounting. The preface to the Trade Ministry Decision on Careful Signing and Strict Enforcement of Contracts noted that contracts were one of the basic forms for ensuring mutual economic planning and for carrying out economic accounting.[20] Article 13 of the Trade Ministry Decision also gave to business offices under the ministry responsibility for ensuring the careful signing and strict implementation of all contracts signed with these business offices.

These requirements restricted the discretion of inexperienced local cadres by requiring that contractual relations at the local level be supervised by offices under the authority of central ministries. Contracts signed by agricultural enterprises, for instance, would be under the supervision of an office of the Agriculture Ministry,[21] while contracts signed by the supply and marketing cooperatives were supervised by offices under the Trade Ministry.[22] By requiring parties to notify superior level organizations when contracts were signed, the 1950 regulations enabled the state ministries to have control over all contracts signed by subordinate offices and thus strengthened central control over local economic activity.[23]

In addition to establishing the supervisory role of offices under the state ministries, the 1950 regulations sought to ensure central control over the financial accounting of local enterprises. The Trade Ministry Decision's reference to contracts as a basic method of carrying out accounting, together with the requirement in Article 9 of the provisional methods that copies of contracts be filed with the local finance committees, gave to these committees an additional source of information by which to assess the financial health of the enterprises under their jurisdiction. Records of contracts supplemented the accounting information already submitted to the local finance committees by subordinate enterprises. Since the local finance committees were organizationally subordinate to the State Finance Committee, the filing of contracts with the local committees strengthened further the state's ability to control economic activity at the local level.

Provisions for naming guarantors in economic contracts served further to extend central control over local contract activity. Article 6 of the Provisional Methods required that higher level organizations play the role of guarantor for contracts involving the national construction plan.[24] Such guarantors were charged with supervising fulfillment, and bore responsibility in the event of breach. Thus, contracts between county-level organizations were required to have a prefecture-level organization serve as a guarantor, while contracts between prefecture-level organizations required that a provincial-level organization serve as guarantor.[25] Such supervision not only ensured more fully the fulfillment of contracts but also ensured greater central control.

Complementing the organizational framework established by the 1950 regulations to promote the supervision of contractual interactions, a three-tiered hierarchy was set up for resolving contract disputes. The first step in the dispute resolution process, mentioned obliquely in Article 10 of the Provisional Methods and more directly in Article 4 of the Trade Ministry Decision, involved mutual consultation and investigation by the business offices of the disputing parties.[26] If no resolution was forthcoming, either of the parties could appeal to the district finance committee or to the prefecture committee if the parties were located in different districts.[27] The third level of dispute resolution involved the people's courts, which could be called upon to resolve a dispute if the aforementioned administrative measures were ineffective.[28]

Thus, the 1950s regulations offer the first example of the PRC government's efforts to implement economic policy through contract regulations. The regulations established organizational frameworks for supervising contract formation and enforcement and for resolving disputes. Such measures to control contract practices were intended to promote central control over economic activity and to reduce the operational discretion of the local economic officials.

Contract Performance During the 1950s

Despite the enactment of the 1950s regulations, however, problems remained regarding the contract system. Many of the problems that the 1950 regulations had been designed to remedy continued unabated. Lack of concreteness and clarity remained a problem in contract provisions,[29] as did the cavalier approach that both cadres and masses took to the signing and supervision of contracts.[30] The problem of "blind contracts" continued as contract management officials sometimes failed to investigate adequately the conditions underlying contracts, resulting in contracts that failed to take into account changes in agricultural markets.[31]

New problems also emerged regarding the management of the contract system. Cadres responsible for signing contracts with agricultural producers sometimes acted arbitrarily to reduce the prices paid to peasants for their goods.[32] This highhandedness on the part of contract management officials was termed a "capitalist management attitude" and was criticized as a failure to carry out the policy of serving both the needs of producing peasants as well as the interests of the state.[33] The mechanical implementation of the 1950 regulations, on the other hand, resulted in contracts taking too long to sign and in the overcomplexity of contract provisions.[34]

Problems also arose in the settlement of disputes. The penalties for breach imposed through the administrative mediation process were sometimes substantially less than those required by regulation, resulting in the aggrieved party doubting further the effectiveness and enforceability of contracts.[35] Despite the 1950 provisional methods allowing a party to seek redress from the courts if administrative mediation proved unsatisfactory, in practice the courts rarely handled such disputes.[36] Consequently, administrative inequalities continued to distort the resolution of disputes as pressure on subordinates inhibited the strict enforcement of contracts.

Despite these difficulties, however, the 1950 regulations were generally effective in establishing state-supervised contracts as a basis for economic transactions. The regulations facilitated the extension of central control over local economic activity, despite continued difficulties in achieving consistency of doctrine and practice of the regulations and the policies they expressed.

Early 1960s Regulations

By 1962, the regime faced a second economic crisis brought on by the Great Leap Forward and by the natural disasters that followed. As a result, economic policies were adopted that sought to rekindle individual initiative and spur productivity. As it had in 1950, the regime again used contract regulations as a complement to economic policy in the attempt to rebuild the economy. In the industrial sector, the Seventy Articles on Industry, adopted in 1961, approved broader use of contracts.[37] In the agricultural sector, the Sixty Articles on Commune Management were issued in 1962 in an effort to stimulate agricultural production.[38] These policy statements laid the groundwork for subsequent regulations on contracts.

In contrast to the 1950s regulations by which the regime sought to promote central control over local economic activity, in 1962–63 the regime wanted to encourage greater autonomy of economic activity by promoting the enforcement of contracts. The extension of central control over the economy had reached its height during the Great Leap Forward when the government attempted to exercise control over virtually all economic transactions.[39] The policies of state control, although not fully effective, served ironically to exacerbate the problems of contract enforcement. The cost of nonperformance of contracts was perceived correctly as accruing to the state rather than to individual enterprises, and thus enterprises had little incentive to insist on contract performance.

The difficulties were severe in discarding these collectivist attitudes and practices. As the *People's Daily* pointed out, "Some people think that economic contracts already have no significance and no function under the conditions where the socialist economy is based on common ownership of the materials of production and where everything is produced and managed under the unified state plan."[40] Natural disasters in 1960 and 1961 also helped to undermine contract performance. For example, officials in a supply and market cooperative in Fenyang County in Shanxi stopped altogether the supervision of contracts after a variety of natural disasters had hit the area.[41]

In response to the problems of enforcing contracts, the Central Committee and the State Council issued in December 1962 a Circular Concerning the Strict Enforcement of Basic Construction Procedures and the Strict Fulfillment of Economic Contracts (hereafter, the 1962 Circular).[42] Some months later, there followed the State Economic Committee's Provisional Regulations Concerning the Basic Provisions in Contracts for the Ordering of Factory and Mining Goods (hereafter, the Ordering Contracts Regulations).[43] Whereas, with the exception of references to the national construction plan, the 1950 regulations had focused primarily on the supply and marketing of agricultural products, the 1962 Circular and the Ordering Contracts Regulations that followed were directed at industrial and commercial contracts.[44]

The regime's concern with contract enforcement was borne out both by the title and contents of the Central Committee/State Council 1962 Circular and by the detailed provisions regarding responsibilities for nonfulfillment contained in the Ordering Contracts Regulations.[45] The regulations addressed separately the responsibilities to be borne by the supplier or the customer in the event of nonfulfillment. These responsibilities were differentiated according to the nature of the breach. Thus, for example, the supplier bore liability for penalties for untimely delivery or deficiencies in quality of materials, while failure to accept delivery or last-minute changes in required specifications rendered the customer liable for penalties.[46]

These detailed discussions of responsibilities for nonfulfillment contrasted with the provisions of the 1950 regulations that had merely emphasized the need for consultation to prevent nonfulfillment and the obligation of the party in breach to compensate the losses of the aggrieved party. The use of penalty payments in the Ordering Contracts Regulations also contrasted with the prior practice of using specific performance as the primary remedy for nonfulfillment.[47] By formally asserting the role of punitive damages, the Ordering Contracts Regulations underscored the enforceability of contracts.

The Ordering Contracts Regulations also established a hierarchy of regulatory authority governing specific contract clauses.[48] Article 5 required clauses pertaining to the technical standards of contracted goods to follow state, regional, and enterprise regulations, and finally, regulations worked out through consultation by the parties. Regarding calculations of the quantity of contracted goods, Article 6 required contract clauses to follow state regulations, regulations enacted by the State Council Management offices, and regulations worked out through consultation between the parties. Such references to hierarchies of authority attempted to correct uncertainties as to the applicability of relevant regulations, and also to provide the contract with substantive terms and conditions where the parties had not done so. Omissions and ambiguities in substantive contract clauses had previously hampered determinations as to both the existence of and the responsibility for breaches of contract.[49] By specifying the regulations to be followed in interpreting contract clauses, the Ordering Contract Regulations were intended to ensure that contractual obligations were fixed more clearly, thus making contracts themselves more easily enforceable.

Renewed attention to the enforcement of agricultural supply and marketing contracts was also evident in the early 1960s, as the provisions of the 1950 regulations were applied in the commune system.[50] The production brigade had replaced the Mutual Aid Team in signing contracts with the state's supply and marketing cooperatives. These contracts were, in turn, supervised by the commune committee. Additionally, the supply and marketing cooperatives signed subsidiary contracts with the production teams.[51] Both the cooperatives and the communes had established contract management offices while the production brigades and production teams within the commune each had small groups for contract investigation.[52] This structure was supplemented by the role of the party secretaries of the cooperatives, communes, and brigades who were charged with giving additional supervision to contract enforcement.[53]

Continuing Obstacles to Enforcement of Contract Rights

Despite emphasis on contract enforcement in the 1962–63 regulations pertaining to industrial contracts and the revitalization of supervision over agricultural contracts, problems remained. The system of state ownership continued to hamper the enforcement of contracts. Enterprise budgets were fixed and were generally unaffected by the nonfulfillment of contracts. Enterprise managers bore little responsibility for losses caused by nonperformance of contracts, since such losses were generally made up by the state, either through an adjustment of the aggrieved party's planned production quota or by directly absorbing the deficit suffered by the aggrieved party.[54] The ambivalence of the entity to which performance was due led, in turn, to attitudes by the obligor that the strict fulfillment of contracts was unimportant (*wu suo wei de*).[55] Thus, the organizational environment in which economic actors operated emphasized collective responsibility rather than autonomy and hence undermined the recognition of contract rights.

In addition, the enforcement of contracts was made difficult by the dispute resolution system. Administrative mediation of a dispute was carried out first by the management offices and secondly by the various financial committees. Article 36 of the 1963 Ordering Contracts Regulations referred to contract disputes indirectly by alluding to instances where "one party doesn't agree to a change or cancellation of the contract." Such disputes were to be resolved by higher level management offices with the approval of various economic committees or other designated departments.[56] The 1962 Circular required the various economic committees to arbitrate (*zhong cai*) contract disputes. Clearly, however, arbitration was not to be undertaken unless mediation by management offices failed to resolve the dispute.[57]

The absence of a dispute resolution process independent of the economic management system resulted in disputes being resolved based on the collective interests of the system rather than on the autonomous interests of individual enterprises. The emphasis on collective over individual interests was heightened, according to several informants, by the parties to a dispute often being subordinate to the same management office (*zhu guan ju*).[58] Thus the management office's concern was with the totality of the enterprises under its control rather than with the interests of individual enterprises. Strict enforcement of contract rights was perceived by economic managers as less important than maintenance of good relations among all related units within the economic system. Enterprises were also concerned with avoiding conflict with higher level organizations, thus avoiding requests that higher level management offices resolve disputes, since this might result in criticism being leveled at the officials making the request.[59] As a result, disputes over the fulfillment of contracts were played down. This emphasis on collective interest and de-emphasis on the autonomous rights of aggrieved parties hampered further the strict enforcement of contracts.

The use of specific enforcement as the primary remedy for breach posed an additional obstacle to contract enforcement.[60] Despite the provisions for economic penalties contained in the 1963 Ordering Contracts Regulations, such penalties were seldom used. When compensation was used as a remedy, it took the form of a negotiated reduction in payment.[61] For instance, in cases of late delivery, the remedy for nonfulfillment usually took the form of an apology and a promise to deliver as soon as possible. An informant who worked in a commercial office in Guangzhou pointed out that problems involving time of delivery were so common that enterprises often took expected delays in delivery into account in their own planning.[62] Where the quality of the delivered goods was substandard, the aggrieved party faced the Hobson's choice of accepting the defective goods or waiting for the party in breach to attempt to produce conforming goods. Thus, as described by an informant who worked in the management office of a machinery factory in Guangdong, if the ordering party refused to accept substandard goods, they would be sent to another unit. However, since such nonacceptance resulted in the ordering party being unable to fulfill on time its production plan, the substandard goods were usually accepted.[63] In neither case would the party in breach be required to pay punitive or compensatory damages. The use of specific performance reflected the view that the costs of nonperformance were not borne independently by the aggrieved party, but by the collective system. Specific performance also denied the autonomy of the contract relationship, as the right of one party to receive performance depended on the ability of the other party to perform, rather than on the terms of the contract.

Thus, despite the emphasis on enforcement embodied in the 1962–63 regulations, the system of state ownership, the lack of an independent system for dispute resolution, and the emphasis on specific performance reflected the primacy of the norm of collectivism over that of autonomy. The dominance of the collective ethic in contract activity reinforced the role of *guanxi* (personal relationships), the traditional Chinese basis for commerce, in conducting economic activity.[64] As economic transactions became continually and unavoidably dominated by unpredictable external factors such as state policies, the political interests of management offices, and the ability of other economic actors to perform, economic actors came to rely on personal relationships to provide predictability and stability.

Yet reliance on personal relationships was itself an external influence on contract practice that undermined the autonomy of the contract relationship in favor of the collective interests of those in the *guanxi* network. Contract practice came to depend on the *guanxi* between enterprise managers rather than on contract terms. In an economic environment in which shortages were commonplace, *guanxi* was the method by which enterprises acquired dependable supplies of scarce commodities. Thus, goods produced under contract between two enterprises might be shipped instead to a third enterprise with whom officials in the producing enterprise had good relations. This problem was compounded when the third party to whom contracted goods were shipped had good relations with officials responsible for mediating a dispute between the contracting parties.[65] The dominance of *guanxi* in economic relationships indicated that these relationships remained subject to external influences, even though these derived from personal ties rather than from the political or economic environment. The influence of such external factors reflected the dominance of collective norms that obtained prior to enactment of the ECL.

Thus, prior to the enactment of the ECL, the practice of contracts in China had been characterized by the primacy of collectivist norms and the denial of autonomy in contract relations. Continued state ownership of economic enterprises deprived economic actors of autonomy in their economic transactions, leaving little incentive to perform or enforce contract obligations. Dispute resolution remained essentially consensual and was carried out by organizations not fully independent from the parties themselves. The use of specific performance denied the impact of nonperformance on the aggrieved party as an autonomous entity, making performance dependent on the circumstances of the parties rather than the terms of the contract. The role of *guanxi* was but another example of the external collective influences undermining the autonomy of contracts. Although the ECL synthesized many of the provisions of pre-existing contract regulations, the new law was enacted in large part to challenge the collective norms that had obtained previously and that were viewed as contributing to economic rigidity and stagnation.[66]

The ECL as a Restatement of Prior Contract Principles

The ECL reaffirmed certain of the principles contained in prior regulations. In the past, contract activity had been subject to a variety of circulars, notices, decisions, and directives in addition to formal regulations.[67] The ECL combined into one unified statute a number of provisions from these prior regulations.

Regulation of Contract Terms

Consistently with prior regulations, the ECL emphasized uniformity in the content of contracts and reflected the concern expressed in prior regulations that the contracts contain certain required clauses. For instance, Article 12 of the ECL carries forward certain provisions of the 1963 Ordering Contracts Regulations requiring that economic contracts contain clauses specifying the purpose of the contract; the quality and quantity of goods provided, the price or payment for such goods, the time, place, and manner of delivery, and the responsibilities for failure to fulfill. The 1950 Central People's Government Trade Ministry Decision Concerning the Careful Signing and Strict Fulfillment of Contracts contained similar requirements to the effect that contracts should stipulate quantity, quality, time of delivery, installation, price, and time of payment.[68]

The ECL also carried forward provisions of prior regulations that guided the content of contract clauses by reference to other parallel rules. For example, Article 17, concerning purchase and sale contracts, established a hierarchy of applicable regulations to be followed regarding the quality, quantity, and prices of goods. This approach had been contained in the 1963 Ordering Contracts Regulations that established a hierarchy of regulations to be followed in setting the quality, quantity, and prices of contracted goods.[69]

The Role of the State Plan

One of the basic principles contained in prior contract regulations and expressed in the ECL involved the role of the state plan. The purposes of the ECL were set out in Article 1 and included ensuring the fulfillment of the state plan.[70] The principle of the primacy of the state plan can be traced back to the 1950 Provisional Methods for Signing Contracts by Organizations, State Enterprises, and Cooperatives, which had the avowed purpose of preventing oppressive contracts that "affected the implementation of the state plan."[71] The importance of state planning had also been evident in the State Economic Commission's Provisional Regulations Concerning the Basic Provisions in Contracts for Ordering Factory and Mining Goods, which were intended in part to ensure "conscientious implementation and all-round fulfillment of the state plan."[72]

The ECL's provisions concerning performance of state plan contracts were consistent with provisions of previous contract regulations, and indicated that the state plan remained the dominant force in economic activity in China. However, the ECL also promoted aspects of contract relationships that had not been evident previously. The role of the state plan was listed as but one of several objectives of the ECL, including protection of the rights of the parties and increasing economic efficiency.[73] Thus, even as it restated the state planning principles of prior contract regulations, the ECL did so in ways that suggested new alternatives to the collective planning ethic.

The Role of the "Legal Person"

In an effort to ensure supervision over contract activity, the ECL expressed in Article 2 the principle that the legal person (or its legal representative) was the only proper party to an economic contract. A common feature in European civil law, the concept of the legal person as used in contract regulations in the PRC can be traced back to the 1950 Provisional Methods that stated "the signing of a contract or charter must take the legal person as the object and its manager as the representative and cannot take an individual as the object."[74]

Although the ECL itself did not provide a definition of "legal person," the definition associated with the ECL was that a legal person must have an independent budget, independent cost accounting, and the right to possess capital.[75] The legal person, then, is one that not only has the authority to commit finances to a contract but also has the capacity to be held financially accountable in the event of nonfulfillment.[76] This contrasted with the definition of legal person as simply a registered enterprise under the Provisional Methods.[77] Although both definitions restricted the range of economic units participating in contracts, the purposes of the two definitions differed. The 1950s approach was intended to ensure that only those enterprises registered with the state, and thus subject to state control, could enter into meaningful economic activity. The focus of the legal person for purposes of the ECL, on the other hand, encompassed a broader range of parties, permitting units (or individuals) who had the requisite financial capacity to perform their obligations and to provide remedies in the event of a failure to perform, to execute contracts.

The focus on the independent financial status of the contracting parties represented a recognition of the autonomy of the contract relationship, which autonomy could not be effective unless the parties were sufficiently independent financially. In addition, the broader definition of legal person suggested that the capacity to form contracts and to receive the protection of contract law could be extended to any enterprise that possessed independent budgeting. Thus, even as the ECL carried forward the principles of prior contract regulations relating to the role of the legal person, the new law added broader recognition for autonomy and diversity in contract transactions.

Although the ECL's provisions reflected the influence of prior contract regulations, this influence was muted by the influence of new economic policies favoring autonomy and diversity in economic activity. Thus while the ECL's provisions on the content of contracts reflected certain of the collectivist priorities that had obtained in the past, new approaches to the role of state planning and the legal person indicated that the ECL would be supportive of broader autonomy and diversity of contract activity.

The ECL's Reformist Provisions

The role of the ECL in supporting autonomy and diversity was evident in the provisions that departed from the norms of prior contract regulations. These new provisions were tied directly to reforms in economic policy that gave greater emphasis to the role of market forces, profits, and material incentives.[78] Individual enterprises were given greater autonomy in economic activities, both in relation to the fulfillment of the state plan and the conduct of nonplan activities. The purpose of these policies was to give economic enterprises greater incentives to increase production and efficiency.[79] With the increased responsibility for profit and loss lay increased need for, and the potential for increased acceptance of, the autonomy of contracts. The remedial function of the ECL represented an attempt to provide the means by which this interest can be realized.

Rights of Contracting Parties

The ECL departed significantly from the principles of prior regulations in asserting the need to "protect the legal rights of the parties."[80] Prior regulations did not mention the rights of the parties and subjected the parties' interests to needs of the state plan.[81] Certainly the rights of individual enterprises were circumscribed by the caveat that economic contracts could not contravene state policies, the state plan, state interests, or the common interests of society.[82] Nonetheless, the ECL's recognition of the parties' rights suggested recognition of the autonomy of the parties, in contrast to emphasis given in prior regulations to collective interests.[83]

Monetary Remedies for Nonperformance

In a further departure from prior regulations, the ECL's provisions for monetary remedies in the event of nonperformance emphasized accountability of the contracting parties. The role of economic compensation for nonperformance of contracts, particularly through the use of liquidated damages clauses, contrasted to the prior reliance solely on specific performance as a remedy for breach. While the ECL still required the party in breach to perform the contract even after paying damages for previous nonperformance, the ECL treated specific performance as a given to be supplemented by economic remedies intended to compensate the aggrieved party.[84]

The use of monetary remedies in the event of nonperformance ensured that an economic cost was imposed in cases of breach of contract.[85] Indeed, the ECL did not limit the remedy to the amount of damages specified in the contract, but permitted further compensation if necessary to make good the aggrieved party's loss.[86] These provisions, combined with the rule requiring damages to be taken from operating funds rather than treated as an expense (which might be made up from state budgets)[87] strengthened the potential for true accountability for nonperformance of contracts. The use of such monetary remedies also indicated that the parties were given greater responsibility for the cost of nonperformance of contracts, a key element in building the autonomy of the contract relationship.

In emphasizing the use of liquidated damages clauses,[88] the ECL avoided the problems of rigidity posed by the penalty requirements of the 1963 Ordering Contracts Regulations, which had unrealistically calculated the penalties for nonperformance regardless of the actual circumstances of the transaction.[89] The ECL also avoided the problems of vagueness posed by the 1950 regulations, which permitted the contracting parties undue discretion in determining remedies.[90] Instead, the ECL granted the parties autonomy to calculate the cost of nonperformance themselves, thus strengthening the autonomy of their relationship, while expressing the basic principles of compensation for losses.

The liquidated damages clause also strengthened the importance of the contract as independent evidence in the resolution of disputes.[91] Previously, the contract served merely as evidence of the existence of an agreement, but was of little use in determining the remedy for nonperformance.[92] Often, the difficulty in calculating compensation had contributed to the reliance on specific performance as the only remedy upon which the parties could agree.[93] With contracts encouraged under the ECL to contain liquidated damages clauses, however, the remedy for nonperformance could be determined by dispute resolution bodies based on the terms of the transaction itself. This contributed to the autonomy of the transaction by shielding the calculation of remedies from external factors.

Compulsory Dispute Resolution

The ECL also contained provisions supporting the use of compulsory dispute resolution with regard to contracts. While continued emphasis was placed on the use of mediation, the ECL granted contracting parties the right to take their disputes directly to court.[94] This emphasis was reiterated in the Supreme People's Court's Opinion Concerning Several Questions Related to All-Round Implementation of the Economic Contract Law.[95] Aimed in large part at providing a forum for the resolution of contract cases, establishment of the economic chambers of the people's courts was begun in 1979.[96] The economic chambers were empowered to hear contract cases of first instance, and also to handle appeals from contract arbitration under a 1979 Joint Circular Concerning Several Issues on Managing Economic Contracts.[97]

Arbitration of contract disputes was also strongly encouraged, thus permitting resort to semicompulsory resolution in which submission of the dispute was voluntary but compliance with the arbitration decision was compulsory.[98] By permitting disputants the opportunity to bypass the consensual mediation process, the ECL marked a departure from previous dispute resolution practices.[99]

The ECL's provisions for direct adjudication of contract disputes and its support for arbitration indicated increased acknowledgment of the need for compulsory dispute settlement by disinterested parties. Support for arbitration and adjudication of contract disputes strengthened the potential for the dispute resolution process, and also the contract rights at issue, to be free from external influences. This contributed further to the autonomy of the rights and obligations conferred under contracts and, accordingly, strengthened the autonomy of the contract relationship.

The ECL's provisions recognizing the rights of contracting parties, promoting the use of monetary remedies for nonperformance, and encouraging compulsory dispute settlement all represent departures from prior norms. They were an effort to strengthen contract autonomy in the face of pre-existing collectivist norms that favored the needs of state planning over the rights of contracting parties, relied on specific performance as the only remedy in cases of breach of contract, and emphasized consensual resolution of contract disputes. Thus, the ECL serves as a basis for implementing the economic reform policies of the Third Plenum by providing a mechanism for contracting parties to assert autonomous contract rights and obtain the incentives permitted under these policies.

Doctrinal and Operational Consistency in Implementation of the ECL

The tension between the norm of autonomy represented by the ECL and the pre-existing norms of collectivism are reflected in doctrinal discussions and in the operation of the ECL. The resolution of this tension depends to a large extent on the extent to which obstacles to effective implementation of the ECL's norms are overcome. These obstacles relate mainly to contradictions in the ECL's expression of conceptual issues on the role of contracts and contract law, technical issues concerning the prerequisites for contract formation, and administrative issues relating to contract activity and dispute resolution.

Conceptual Issues

The ECL's recognition of the rights of the contracting parties suggests that economic actors are possessed of autonomous rights, while the ECL's nod to the importance of the state plan and economic order suggests that these rights are circumscribed by state policies. These contradictions in the purposes of the ECL are tied to conceptual views as to the proper role of contracts and contract law in China.

Attitudes about the role of contracts are unavoidably tied to the relationship between contracts and the state plan. One alternative in resolving this question holds that all contracts be based on the state plan.[100] A directly contrasting view is that contracts should form the basis for state planning because they reflect the actual supply and demand relationships at the local level.[101] A middle ground suggests that some contracts should be based solely on the state plan while others might be signed independently.[102]

These varying positions on the role of contracts also entail attitudes as to the role of contract law as an instrument of policy enforcement or as a mechanism to enforce the rights of the contracting parties. Emphasis on the subjugation of contracts to the needs of state planning suggests that the imperative of contract law is to promote such subjugation, thus elevating implementation of policy above enforcement of contract rights as the purpose of contract law. On the other hand, emphasis on the autonomy of contracts from the state plan suggests that the role of contract law is to protect such autonomy by recognizing and enforcing the rights of contracting parties.

The resolution of these conceptual issues has consequences for the conflict between the norms of autonomy and collectivism. Thus, conclusions as to the proper relationship between contracts and the state plan imply the limits of permissible autonomy in contract activity. Conclusions as to the relationship between contract law and state policy indicate the extent to which collectivist norms will be permitted to dictate the recognition and enforcement of the contract rights of economic actors. The very centrality that the concepts of the role of contracts and contract law bear to the conflict between autonomy and collectivism suggests imposing obstacles to consistent doctrinal and operational application of these concepts. Nonetheless, such consistency will be essential not only to the ability of economic actors to identify and assimilate the norms embodied in the ECL, but also to the confidence of economic actors that the ECL's norms will be reliable bases for economic transactions.

Administrative Issues

The major questions relating to the administration of contracts concern the supervision of contract activity and the handling of dispute resolution. Consistent implementation of the ECL's provisions on these matters must overcome a number of doctrinal and operational problems.

Supervision of Contract Formation. The ECL established a framework for supervising the formation of contracts in part to remedy the ambiguities of the ECL's provisions on contract formation.[103] This framework included the alternative processes of certification (*jianzheng*) and notarization (*gongzheng*), both of which entail external supervision by institutions that are organizationally unrelated to the contracting parties. Certification is intended mainly to verify the legal capacity of the parties to fulfill their contractual obligations, and to resolve questions involving the interpretaton of contractual obligations.[104] Notarization is intended also to verify the legality of contracts.[105]

However, the relationship between these two methods and the circumstances for application of each of them was not resolved in the ECL. Indeed, in his speech explaining the ECL to the fourth session of the Fifth National People's Congress, Gu Ming noted initially that disagreement existed regarding the role of certification.[106] Some officials believed that all contracts should be subject to certification by higher-level authorities, others felt that certification was unnecessary altogether, while still others thought that the issue of certification should be handled on a case-by-case basis.[107]

The uncertainty regarding certification placed on the notarization process a greater burden to harmonize the wishes of the contracting parties with the requirements of the ECL. The role of notarization of contracts was recognized following the enactment in 1982 of the Provisional Regulations for Notaries.[108] Notarization served a similar function as certification in assuring the legality and enforceability of contracts.[109] Notarization also was intended to verify the legal status of the parties so as to prevent disputes,[110] and to serve an evidentiary function by recording the contents of contracts.[111]

Uncertainty over the respective roles of certification and notarization pose potential problems for their effectiveness as mechanisms for external supervision of contracts. Neither of these processes is required for contracts to be effective. This may lead to continued reliance on internal supervision by various organizationally related management offices and in turn to the continued influence of external relationships on the recognition of contract rights. In addition, the uncertainties regarding the use of certification and notarization may make it more difficult for contracting parties to clarify contract terms. While many of these questions may be resolved by the legal advisers retained by various enterprises, the still incomplete institutional framework for contract supervision may result in continued problems of vagueness in contracts and in an increase in disputes.

Economic Chambers of the People's Courts. A further administrative question concerns the economic chambers of the people's courts. It remains unclear whether the establishment of these institutions will succeed in overcoming the Chinese cultural ambivalence to the use of law in the resolution of disputes. Moreover, a shortage of trained lawyers has prevented the economic chambers from being staffed adequately to serve as the major source of dispute resolution.[112] Moreover, the economic chambers are the forum in which the state brings cases involving economic crimes, which puts further demands on the court's time.[113] To limit their case loads, the economic chambers adopted the practice of referring the majority of economic disputes back to administrative mediation.[114] Despite the provisions for direct submission of contract disputes to the courts, litigants were encouraged to consider arbitration as an alternative.[115]

Thus, the availability of adjudication in dispute resolution remains a question. The ECL's emphasis on arbitration reflected commitment to at least semiconsensual dispute resolution. But the uncertainty of the role of the people's courts in enforcing contract rights poses a challenge to consistent application of the principles of the ECL emphasizing adjudication of contract disputes.

These issues related to supervision of contract formation and adjudication of contract disputes pose obstacles to the uniform administration of contract practice. The treatment of these issues both doctrinally and operationally is a crucial factor in the process of recognition and legitimation of the ECL.

Technical Issues of Contract Formation

The prerequisites for contract formation are critical indicators of when transactional agreements are granted contract status and receive the protections of contract law. The ECL's provisions related to the formation of contracts contain a number of ambiguities that may possibly hamper consistency of doctrine and practice.

Agreement on Terms and Conditions. Article 9 of the ECL states that a contract is formed when the parties have reached agreement on the major articles. Presumably the "major articles" are those such as price, quality, time of performance, and remedies that are required under Article 12 to be included in economic contracts.[116] However, this is not clearly specified. What constitutes agreement is also uncertain. Moreover, if agreement on the major articles is sufficient to form a contract, the issue remains whether disagreement on other provisions bars formation.[117]

Consideration. The question of consideration is also a source of potential problems.[118] Article 5 of the ECL states that contracts must be based on the principle of "exchanges of equal value" (*deng jia you chang*). However, the ECL lacks any details of the standards by which value is calculated. While fixed prices may apply to goods produced and distributed according to the state plan, the ECL contemplated increased use of contracts outside the state plan for which there would be no state pricing structure.[119] Also, as a result of reformist economic policies placing greater emphasis on market forces as the basis for pricing, the value of goods and services might vary in response to market changes, and the equality of the exchange of value contemplated in the contract might be eroded, casting doubt on its enforceability.

Contract Form. A third question related to contract formation concerns the required form of contracts. Article 3 of the ECL states that all contracts except those that are settled immediately must be in written form. The emphasis on written contracts reflects an attempt to resolve some of the aforementioned interpretive questions and to provide an evidentiary basis for the resolution of disputes.[120] The reference to contracts that are settled immediately pertains to spontaneous purchase and sale transactions for which a written contract is unnecessary.[121] The requirement that contracts be in writing, however, may deny contract protections to many transactions. Moreover, the provision that telegrams and letters between the parties may constitute part of a contract raises the issue of the circumstances under which such telegrams and letters may form a contract where other "major articles" are absent, or are permitted to amend a contract.[122]

Ambiguities in the ECL's provisions relating to the formation of economic contracts pose challenges to consistent administration of contracts. The resolution of such ambiguities will depend on conceptual uniformity in perceptions of the proper role of contracts and contract law. These issues require consistent resolution in doctrine and practice in order to build abstract and practical legitimacy for the ECL itself, a task made more difficult due to the resilience of pre-existing norms favoring informal agreements as the basis for economic transactions.

The ECL contains a number of provisions related to the formation and administration of contracts that require uniform resolution if the ECL is to be effective. Such uniformity is essential to the ability of economic actors to recognize the norms expressed in the ECL. Issues related to conceptual views as to the role of contracts and contract law must be resolved consistently for economic actors to identify the respective limits of autonomy and collectivism in contract transactions. The administration of contracts through supervision and dispute resolution must be handled uniformly if the rights of economic actors embodied in contracts are to be recognized and enforced effectively. Consistent handling of ambiguities about the formation of contracts is required for economic actors to determine when transactional agreements will be accorded contract status and the protections of contract law. The ECL's capacity to achieve legitimacy will depend on the extent to which issues related to the underlying conceptual question of the role of contracts and contract law and to contract administration and contract formation are resolved consistently in such as way as to permit recognition of the ECL's norms by economic actors.

Summary

The ECL presents a challenge to the collectivist norms that dominated prior Chinese contract practice. These collectivist norms were initially imposed by the new regime following the Chinese revolution as a way to strengthen central control over the economy, and continued as a result of the state's ongoing intrusion into economic activity. As an adjunct to the economic reform policies of the Third Plenum, the ECL embodied a range of new norms favoring autonomy in contract activity. Where the ECL restated provisions from prior regulations, it did so in a way that downplayed the collectivist norms that had obtained previously. In addition, the ECL contained provisions that specifically departed from past regulatory norms in an effort to promote contract autonomy.

The ability of the ECL to become an effective regulator of contract activity in China depends on whether the norms of autonomy expressed in the legislation can achieve legitimacy and supplant pre-existing collective norms. For this to occur, the economic actors who are the subjects of the law must recognize in the ECL's norms values that are preferable to those of pre-existing norms. This process requires consistency in the doctrine and practice of the new norms expressed in the ECL. The absence of doctrinal and operational consistency will undermine legitimacy as economic actors perceive that the law has insufficient support from the political leadership to ensure reliability and predictability in its application.

Consistency of doctrine and practice faces obstacles born of ambiguities in the ECL's provisions on the role of contracts and contract law, the institutions and methods for administration of contracts, and the prerequisites for formation of contracts. These obstacles are heightened by the resiliency of pre-existing collectivist norms. The potential for the ECL to acquire legitimacy may be determined by the extent these obstacles are overcome. The doctrinal viewpoints of the communities charged with interpreting and applying the ECL, as well as the operational record of contract practice, offer useful evidence as to whether the concepts of contracts and contract law and the questions of formation and administration of contracts will be resolved with sufficient consistency to permit economic actors to recognize the norms of the ECL and grant it practical as well as abstract legitimacy.

CHAPTER 2

Doctrinal Norms

The Central Political Leadership and the Central Legal Community

The challenges to legitimacy of the ECL borne of conceptual conflicts and the resulting ambiguities in the ECL's provisions for formation and administration of contracts represent barriers to the recognition by economic actors of the norms expressed in the ECL. Doctrinal interpretations of the ECL represent an important vehicle for communicating the norms of the ECL to economic actors and thus overcoming these barriers to recognition.

The extent to which economic actors recognize the new norms of autonomy expressed in the ECL depends on consistency in the expression of doctrinal norms. Such consistency is hindered in part by the conflict between the ECL's norms of autonomy and pre-existing collectivist norms. Accordingly, doctrinal consistency regarding the ECL's norms is best examined by focusing on the conceptual and administrative issues where this conflict is most acute. As discussed in chapter 1, these issues are (1) the role of contracts and contract law and (2) the institutions and methods for administration of contracts, which may be divided into the subsets of contract supervision and dispute resolution. Focusing on these issues is useful to determine the effect of pre-existing norms on ECL doctrine, and also to assess the capacity of the ECL's norms to supplant pre-existing norms.

Doctrinal interpretations of the ECL reflect policy preferences of government officials charged with interpreting and applying the law. The views of the central political leadership and legal communities, the two groups most directly involved in formulating and expressing viewpoints in the doctrine of the ECL, form the doctrinal underpinnings for the law.[1] These views are expressed in the daily newspapers, in broadcast speeches and reports, and in regulatory pronouncements relating to contracts.

Examination of the doctrinal views of the central political and legal communities can facilitate conclusions as to the level of doctrinal consistency related to the core issues of the ECL. Conclusions as to doctrinal consistency in turn suggest the potential for recognition by economic actors of the ECL's new norms, a precursor to legitimation of these norms.

The Role of Contracts and Contract Law

Attitudes of the Central Political Leadership

Contracts Outside the State Plan. The central political leadership has consistently viewed the role of contracts primarily as an adjunct of economic policy. This implies reliance on the norm of collectivism in viewing contracts as subject to the dictates of state policy rather than the objectives of individual economic actors. Nonetheless, following the Third Plenum of the Eleventh Central Committee, the doctrinal views of the central political leadership began to suggest that contracts might play a valid role outside the collective imperatives of the plan.

Following the Third Plenum, doctrinal discussions among the central political leadership on the role of contracts centered on whether contract relationships should derive primarily from the requirements of state planning or from market forces. Shortly after the Third Plenum, the theoretical journal of the Chinese Communist party (CCP) suggested that contracts might replace plan-mandated allocations as the basis for economic relations between enterprises.[2] Contracts even were suggested as forming the basis for the formulation of the state plan itself.[3]

Ultimately a policy compromise was reached between those who advocated greater reliance on market forces and those who urged more doctrinaire views on the primacy of central planning as the determinant for economic transactions.[4] This compromise involved bifurcation of the state plan into the "mandatory plan" (*zhiling jihua*), which imposed fixed quotas and fairly rigid directives on the source of inputs, and the "guiding plan" (*zhidao jihua*), which offered suggested production targets, but required enterprises to buy production inputs from the local market.[5] This formalized the emerging role of nonplan transactions, and created the potential for expanded use of contracts in such transactions.

During the economic retrenchment of 1979 and 1980, broad acceptance within the central leadership emerged for the proposition that contracts should be used to regulate transactions outside the state plan.[6] Thus, contracts could be used to free the allocation of goods and services from the restrictions of hard-pressed state financing. Even in heavy industry, where plan directives still held sway, contracts were presented as enabling producing enterprises to account for market realities in the production and supply of goods to the state.[7] Thus, the collectivist views on the role of contracts in the Chinese economy had given way to recognition by the central political leadership that contracts should be permitted to allocate goods and services outside the strictures of state planning.

Increased Diversity of Transactions. Following the Third Plenum, the central political leadership expressed support for the use of contracts in an increased variety of economic transactions. Prior to the enactment of the ECL, contracts began to play an important role in the state's agricultural procurement process. The use of contracts in connection with agricultural production evolved toward the use of production responsibility contracts. These reflected increased recognition of peasants as individual producers, first under the *bao chan dao hu* (household responsibility for production), then under *bao gan dao hu* (household responsibility for assigned tasks as an individual accounting unit), and finally under long term contracts for the use of land.[8] The autonomy granted peasants in managing their production plots under production responsibility contracts went a step further than the "three guarantees and one reward" system of the early 1960s, under which peasants guaranteed output, time, and costs and received a bonus if production exceeded the quota.[9] This increased recognition of peasant producers as economic actors reflected the increased devolution of contract authority away from collectivist agricultural production organizations. In addition, agricultural production contracts strengthened the autonomy of peasant producers by granting them greater independence to make production management decisions.

Contracts were emphasized in the context of commercial transactions as an important if not the primary mechanism for economic transactions.[10] This reflected an effort to insulate commerical purchase and sale transactions from the strictures of the state plan. This separation was attainable in commerce as in agriculture in part because commercial transactions often did not involve other enterprises beyond the contracting parties. Thus, the consequences of contract failures in commercial purchase and sale transactions could be limited more easily to the contract parties. In addition, commercial transactions did not have direct side effects in the heavily regulated areas of energy, raw materials, and labor that might compromise the state's regulatory authority in these areas. These aspects of commercial transactions implied a degree of insulation of commercial units from other economic units, and thus justified extending to commercial units greater transactional autonomy.

In industry, the use of contracts was recognized, although the extent of contract autonomy in transactions between enterprises at various stages of the production process lagged, coming into play just prior to promulgation of the ECL in 1981.[11] A major reason for this was that contract autonomy entailed management autonomy, a characteristic relatively easy to achieve in the context of agricultural production by individuals or small groups and in relatively simple sales transactions, but more difficult in larger and more complex industrial enterprises.[12] In addition, the interrelationships between industrial enterprises and other economic units meant that the consequences of failures of contract performance could not be limited to the contracting parties themselves. Also, industrial enterprises were inextricably tied to the areas of energy, raw materials, and labor where the imperative of state regulation was deemed incompatible with full managerial autonomy.

Thus, the central political leadership expressed support for increased diversity in the use of contracts, although such support varied depending on the sector of the economy involved. Agricultural contracts were seen as an integral component of the agricultural reforms, and thus were given great emphasis. In commerce, contracts were emphasized as efficient mechanisms for distributing commodities without disrupting other planned sectors of the economy. In industry, the state plan remained the primary basis for allocation of goods and services, thus restricting the role of autonomous contracts.

Contract Law and Policy Enforcement. The views of the central political leadership on the role of contract law focused primarily on the ECL as an instrument of enforcement of the policies of economic reform.[13] The law was intended to delineate both the permissible extent of the use of contracts, and the relationship between contracts and state planning, as well as to make clear that contracts were an accepted instrument for economic transactions only so long as their use did not conflict with the state's policy objectives.[14] To this end, the ECL represented an important instrument to lend uniformity to the framework of varied ministerial regulations that had governed contract activity previously. Thus, the primary emphasis of the central political leadership was on the role of the ECL as an instrument for ensuring continued state control over economic transactions undertaken in a policy environment of increased decentralization.

Despite this emphasis on the ECL as an instrument of control, the central leadership also recognized that the law provided a source of limited private economic rights. The ECL itself stated that its purposes included the protection of the rights and interests of contracting parties.[15] It was presented as a basis for resisting demands by state officials that the terms of contracts be changed as conditions warranted.[16] In addition, the ECL was presented as a basis for the economic rights of individual parties to contracts even where the state was not involved.[17]

Thus there were three primary functions of the ECL in the view of the central political leadership. First was the law's role in ensuring fulfillment of state policies. In pursuit of this, the law lent uniformity to the multitude of contract transactions being undertaken pursuant to the post-Third Plenum economic reforms by its provision of general principles from which specific contract regulations were to proceed. Second, the law also promoted continued state supervision over contract activity through its requirement that virtually all economic transactions take the form of written contracts, thus facilitating examination and supervision by higher levels. Third, the law protected the interests of the parties by requiring that contracting parties be treated equally, regardless of their position in various administrative hierarchies. The success of the ECL in supporting autonomy for economic actors will depend ultimately on the ability of the law to fulfill this third function.

In sum, the doctrinal pronouncements from the central political leadership reflected the view that contracts should be used in an increasing diversity of transactions outside the strictures of state planning. Contract law was viewed primarily as an instrument of policy enforcement, although the policy of the moment supported recognition and enforcement of contract rights. Relative consistency in these doctrinal views strengthens the potential for identification and recognition by economic actors. The doctrinal attitudes of the central political leadership on the role of contracts and contract law laid a foundation for the possible emergence of autonomous contact rights by presenting opportunities for economic actors to utilize the ECL to justify autonomy from the state in certain spheres of economic activity.

Attitudes of the Legal Community

The doctrinal views of the central legal community about contracts and contract law in China differed in important respects from those of the central political leadership. Significant diversity also existed within the community itself. These differences reflected varying doctrinal and policy priorities of various legal scholars and the legal organizations in whose journals they published.

Doctrinal Discussions on Contracts. Prior to enactment of the ECL, the Beijing legal community shared the preoccupation of the political leadership concerning the relationship of contracts to the state plan. However, the legal community was not unified on how this relationship should be handled.

Prior to enactment of the ECL, legal scholars from the Chinese Academy of Social Sciences (CASS) and related organizations publishing in *Legal Studies Research* (*Faxue yanjiu*) and elsewhere suggested that economic contracts might replace the state plan as the mechanism for allocating goods and services.[18] A more restrictive view that contracts should be viewed as a mechanism for implementing plan objectives was asserted by the Beijing Law Society journal, *Legal Studies Magazine*,[19] and by the Chinese Communist party legal committee's publication, *Chinese Legal System Gazette*.[20]

Following enactment of the ECL, differences within the Beijing legal community regarding the role of contracts continued. CASS's journal, *Legal Studies Research*, expressed more strongly the view that contracts could be used outside the strictures of state planning and that contracting parties should be permitted broader independence to form contract relationships.[21] This view was reiterated in discussions of the need for broader autonomy in the agricultural contract responsibility system.[22]

Both the Law Society and the party's legal commission continued to emphasize a restrictive view of the role of contracts following enactment of the ECL. The Law Society journal focused on the role of contracts in ensuring fulfillment of the state plan,[23] extending this approach to the role of contract law as well by asserting that contract law belonged to a category of "socialist public law" aimed at ensuring enforcement of socialist economic policy with its emphasis on central planning.[24] The party's legal journal also gave primacy to the role of contracts as instruments of state planning.[25]

The dichotomy of views regarding the relationship of contracts to the plan reflected differences between CASS on the one hand, and the Law Society and the CCP's legal commission on the other, with regard to the proper degree of autonomy that should be accorded contract activity. Emphasis on the primacy of the state plan suggested priority should be retained for collective norms in economic transactions, whereas support for autonomy was evident in positions whose emphasis was on market factors in determining the characteristics of specific transactions.

Doctrinal Views on Contract Law. Doctrinal conflict on the role of contracts was also evident in the views on the role of contract law. Prior to the enactment of the ECL, the Beijing legal community's views on the role of contract law reflected the tensions in the community's views on the use of contracts in market-based transactions and in the state planning process. As applied to contract law, this tension showed a dichotomy between the horizontal and vertical dynamic of contract law, which in turn relates to the norms of collectivism and autonomy. Emphasis on law as a mechanism for enforcing vertical relationships suggests support for the primacy of the collective and for the use of law to ensure subordination of economic activity to the directives of higher levels in the administrative bureaucracy. On the other hand, emphasis on law as protecting the horizontal relationships suggests support for the autonomy of economic actors in positions of legal equality unrelated to their positions in the administrative hierarchy.

CASS emphasized that contract law should focus on the horizontal relations between entities at relatively equal levels in the socioeconomic hierarchy, independent of the vertical relationships between economic actors and the state.[26] This approach was consistent with the emphasis on contracts as mechanisms for increasingly autonomous transactions outside the purview of the plan. The academy also emphasized the importance of the ECL in protecting the autonomy of contracting parties. Initially, the CASS position conceded the importance of contract law as an aspect of economic law designed to further the state's policy goals in the economic sphere.[27] Gradually, however, there emerged a budding consensus that despite its policy implications, contract law contained civil law characteristics and thus was aimed to an important degree in protecting activities (including economic transactions) outside the realm of state control.[28]

In contrast, the Law Society and the CCP's legal establishment focused instead on the vertical, hierarchical aspects of contract law as a means of enforcing state policies.[29] These organizations also focused on the role of contract law as an instrument of the state's management of economic activity pursuant to policy priorities.[30] These positions were consistent with these organizations' collectivist views on contracts in the Chinese economy.

The conflicts that emerged between the views of the legal scholars in CASS and their counterparts in the Law Society and the party apparatus regarding contract law generally paralleled doctrinal differences on the role of contracts in the economy.[31] Disagreements over these issues reflected policy differences within the legal community regarding the norms of autonomy and collectivism.

Doctrinal discussion concerning the role of contracts and contract law in China reflected conflict between the norms of autonomy and community. Discussions that subjugated the role of contracts to the needs of state planning suggested that contract transactions should be subjected to external factors imposed based on the relationship of the parties to the economic administrative system rather than on the relationship of the parties to each other. Discussions that encouraged contract terms to be dictated by the circumstances of the transaction suggested that contracting parties be granted autonomy from the collective requirements of state planning priorities. Doctrinal discussions on the role of contract law reflected similar conflicts with regard to whether law should protect the priorities of the collective by enforcing state policy or rather protect the autonomous rights of the contract parties.

In addressing the role of contracts and contract law, the general orientation of the central political leadership and of the more establishment-oriented sector of the Beijing legal community, namely the Law Society and the party legal commission, was in favor of the norm of collectivism, whereas CASS generally tended toward the norm of autonomy. Doctrinal differences among these communities represented a potential obstacle to the ability of economic actors to identify the doctrine of the ECL. The relative unity of the political leadership with certain segments of the legal community suggested that the collectivist norm remained strong, but subject to the dissenting views CASS. These doctrinal disparities encouraged economic actors to continue to rely on pre-existing norms favoring collectivist approaches to the role of contracts and contract law.

However, reliance by economic actors on the protections of the ECL likely depends on more than simply the doctrinal resolution of abstract issues concerning the role of contracts and contract law. The aspects of ECL doctrine related to the formation and administration of contracts are likely to receive more focus from economic actors. While these certainly are affected by doctrinal principles on the role of contracts and contract law, they may possibly assume independent significance in encouraging economic actors to rely on the ECL's norms of autonomy. Nonetheless, the absence of doctrinal unity regarding the norm of autonomy in the role of contracts and contract law is a factor hampering full acceptance of this new alternative to the norm of collectivism.

Contract Formation and Performance

Supervision over contract formation and performance unavoidably entails diminution of the autonomy of the contracting parties. However, this is a matter of degree, as the selection of methods and institutions for contract supervision reflect different views on the acceptable level of autonomy in the contract transaction. Supervision by organizations unrelated to the contract parties focuses on the terms of the transaction rather than the relationships of the parties, and thus tends to emphasize the autonomy of the contract transaction. Alternatively, supervision by entities with organizational ties to the contracting parties implies that the contract relationship is subject to the collective interests of the organizations to which the contracting parties belong. Thus, doctrinal views concerning supervision of contracts reflected preferences for autonomy and collectivism, depending on whether emphasis was placed on external or internal supervision.

Doctrinal Views of the Political Leadership on Contract Supervision

As indicated in the reports and editorials accompanying passage of the ECL, the methods and institutions for supervision of contract activity were important doctrinal issues. The central political leadership's views on this issue were expressed mainly through regulations, and centered on the selection of supervisory institutions as well as supervisory methods.

Conventional Internal Supervision. Prior to the Third Plenum of the Eleventh CCP Central Committee in December 1978, the conventional practice of supervising economic transactions in the PRC entailed the management offices (*zhuguan bumen*) of various ministries and commissions overseeing the transactions of subordinate enterprises. This method of supervision represented a classic example of internal supervision by units organizationally tied to the contracting parties. Thus, management offices in the Ministry of Commerce supervised the transactions of lower level offices within the ministry, management offices of the State Economic Commission supervised the work of lower level departments, and so forth.[32]

However, overlapping jurisdictions between and among management offices within ministerial organizations and those of various state commissions created duplication and inconsistency of regulatory interpretation. Construction contracts, for example, were subject to supervision by departments of the State Capital Construction Commission.[33] The management offices of state ministries whose subordinate enterprises were concluding contracts continued to exercise supervision over these activities.[34]

Following the Third Plenum, an effort was made to institute independent external supervision through the banking system. The 1979 Construction Contract Regulations provided that the various construction banks were to supervise the fulfillment of contracts through their control over credit and finances and by issuing performance bonuses and penalties upon the completion of contracts.[35] The banks were empowered by the 1979 Joint Circular on contract management to "supervise the situation of performance of economic contracts by enterprises through the management of credit and accounting."[36] This authorization was reiterated in Article 52 of the ECL. However, due to their specialized nature, banks were not ideally suited for supervision of all types of contracts. While bank control over credit was useful in ensuring that contract payment provisions were performed, other details of performance remained outside the banks' purview.

Prior to the enactment of the ECL, the methods of supervision over the formation and fulfillment of contracts involved initial approval and ongoing inspection by the management offices under whose authority the contracting parties operated. Such methods of supervision remained essentially internal, in that they were exercised by offices and departments with existing relationships to the contracting parties. These existing relationships made objective enforcement of contract regulations difficult, and also undermined the autonomy of the parties and their transactions from external influences. The difficulties of internal supervisory mechanisms effectively policing the formation and performance of contracts had been evident during the 1950s and 1960s. Nonetheless, the resilience of these methods of supervision was evident in that the ECL itself acknowledged the role of such internal supervision.[37]

The SAIC as an Interagency Organ for Contract Management and the Issue of Certification. The State Administration for Industry and Commerce (SAIC) was revitalized after the Third Plenum, and had potential to serve as an instrument for external supervision of contracts. A major method for the SAIC's supervision of contract activity was certification (*jianzheng*). However, uncertainties regarding the role of certification limited the power of SAIC to act effectively as an institution for external supervision over contract activity.

In early 1979, the SAIC was given responsibility for supervision over the formation and performance of contracts, particularly in the context of state planning.[38] In May 1980, SAIC offices were given supervisory authority over certain industrial contracts, as well as over contracts between commercial departments and the departments of industry, transportation, construction, materials, and agriculture.[39] These types of partially industrial and partially commercial transactions previously had been subject to supervision by the State Economic Commission.[40] The new distribution of supervisory authority provided that industrial contracts between different bureaucracies were supervised by the various economic committees while commercial contracts were subject to supervision by the SAIC. Thus, the SAIC acted as an interagency organ charged with ensuring that agreements between units from different bureaucracies were properly formed and carried out.

The supervisory role of the SAIC bureaucracy grew as the diversity of contracts expanded beyond the confines of the state plan. Thus, the State Council's 1980 Regulations on Promoting Economic Cooperation empowered SAIC offices to approve the formation of contracts concluded by enterprises outside their established "cooperative arrangements."[41] In June 1981, the State Council approved a report issued by the central SAIC office promoting their supervision over a vast array of production and sale contracts in both urban and rural areas.[42] SAIC's supervisory role was codified in Article 51 of the ECL.

Following passage of the ECL, the role of the SAIC continued to be emphasized in carrying out supervision and investigation.[43] Indeed the official explanation of the role of contract management under the ECL was provided by the director of the SAIC central office in an interview on the eve of the law taking effect in June 1982.[44] The SAIC's supervisory role was reconfirmed by the 1984 regulations on agricultural and industrial purchase and sale contracts,[45] and in the 1985 regulations on certification.[46]

Thus, the central political leadership espoused the supervision of contracts by the SAIC offices. The SAIC system was organizationally separate from the contracting parties, and thus exhibited certain aspects of an institution for external supervision. However, the SAIC departments also exercised ongoing administrative supervison over a variety of activities by economic entities in such areas as company registration and licensing, enforcement of regulations, and dispute settlement. Thus, the SAIC offices had extensive relationships with the entities under their jurisdiction that went beyond contract supervision.

While SAIC supervision over contract activities could not be said to be fully external, the emphasis by the central political leadership on the role of the SAIC system in supervising contract activity represented initial recognition of the need for supervision by institutions that were organizationally separate from the contracting parties. As an alternative to supervision by enterprise and ministerial management offices whose relationships to the contracing parties was more direct, the SAIC system represented the beginnings of a fully independent supervisory system. As such, it also encouraged autonomy for contract transactions by making supervision of such transactions a more or less objective exercise carried out by external entities.

Although the SAIC was empowered to exercise general supervisory authority over contracts, a major aspect of this authority entailed the supervision over contract formation. The SAIC supervised formation of contracts mainly through certification (*jianzheng*) of the contents of the contract and of the capacity of the parties to ensure legality and enforceability of contracts.[47] Although the role of certification had been noted prior to the Third Plenum of the Eleventh CCP Central Committee, uncertainties were evident as to how and when certification of contracts should be required.[48] The question of certification was raised again in the 1979 Joint Circular on contract management, but a definitive ruling was specifically avoided.[49] Although there were those who advocated a larger role for certification,[50] a SAIC report of June 22, 1981, also stopped short of requiring the use of certification.[51] Regulations issued in 1981 on negotiated purchase and sale of agricultural byproducts provided for the certification of contracts by SAIC offices but only "when necessary," also stopping short of a universal certification requirement.[52] Thus, prior to enactment of the ECL, the central political leadership was not prepared to insist on certification as a method of supervision of contracts.

The ECL itself contained no specific mention of certification, thus lending more ambiguity to the issue. In introducing the ECL to the National People's Congress, Gu Ming explained this by noting the existence of disagreement on the question and concluding that the best approach was to wait until specific regulations could be issued.[53] When the Provisional Regulations on the Certification of Economic Contracts were finally issued in September 1985, they underscored that certification was to remain a voluntary method of contract supervision.[54]

The inability to reach a consensus among the central political leadership requiring certification of contracts indicated continued difficulties in displacing the pre-existing practices of internal supervision. This suggested that the influence of the contract management bureaucracy within the economic administrative system remained strong enough to oppose efforts to augment or displace their supervisory authority over contract activity. Thus, despite support for the increased role of the SAIC, the political leadership was ultimately unable to reach consensus to the effect that external methods should replace internal methods for contract supervision.

Revitalization of the Notary System. Notarial offices were viewed by the central political community as an alternative to the SAIC in the supervision of contracts. During the summer of 1980, a national notarization work conference was held in Beijing under the auspices of the Ministry of Justice at which support was given to the role of contract notarization and the establishment of notarization offices down to the county level.[55] Prior to the conference, the view was suggested that notaries should take an active role in policing and enforcing contracts.[56] Although these views were not accepted ultimately, they reflected the importance attached to contract supervision by notary offices even prior to enactment of the ECL.

After passage of the ECL, the importance of notarization in supervising contract activities continued to be emphasized. In April 1982, shortly before the ECL went into effect, the State Council issued The PRC's Provisional Regulations on Notarization that listed contract notarization first among the tasks undertaken by notary offices.[57] Similarly with certification, however, notarization was to be exercised only upon request by the contracting parties. The regulations empowered the notarial organizations with wide investigative authority, including the right to demand additional documents and materials from the units whose activities were subject to notarization. However, the regulations stopped short of conferring on the notaries specific enforcement powers.

The main focus of contract notarization has centered on ensuring the genuineness and legality of contracts.[58] Notarization has been exercised in connection with forestry contracts,[59] as well as construction contracts, purchase and sale contracts, and agricultural responsibility and specialization contracts.[60] Not only have the notaries been active in the preperformance stage, but they have been active in supervising contract performance.[61]

Thus, prior to and following enactment of the ECL, the central political leadership attached significance to notaries as an institution for external supervision. While this raised the prospect of organizational conflict with the SAIC system, the prospects for greater autonomy of contracts was strengthened by the addition of yet another potential source of external supervision. Indeed, as they are under supervision of the Ministry of Justice and have no other supervisory roles with regard to economic enterprises, the notaries are arguably more independent of the contracting parties than the SAIC offices, and thus better able to exercise external supervision.

The central political leadership's efforts to revitalize the SAIC system for supervising contract formation, and the increased emphasis on certification and notarization of contracts created a basis for expanded reliance on external institutions and methods for contract management. This augered well for increased autonomy of contracts by enabling supervision to be carried out by units with no direct organizational links to the contracting parties. However, uncertainty as to the respective roles of certification and notarization have potential to undermine doctrinal and operational consistency.

Attitudes of the Central Legal Community

Discussions within the central legal community on the issue of supervision over contract activity focused mainly on supervisory methods, although this had direct implications for organizational preferences. Certification was referred to as an administrative method of supervision whereas notarization represented a legal method.[62] The matter of contention was whether external supervision should be carried out by administrative or by judicial organs.

Prior to enactment of the ECL, the Academy of Social Sciences noted the need to strengthen administrative supervision over the contract formation process in part through reliance on the banks.[63] This view included support for the role of certification in: (1) ensuring implementation of party and state policies and curtailing illegal economic activity; (2) strengthening the legal conceptions of the contracting parties; and (3) affecting beneficially the rate of contract fulfillment.[64] These early views espousing administrative supervision reflected an appreciation that no judicial alternative existed, as the notaries had not yet been fully established. Thus, administrative supervision by the SAIC and the banks represented the only alternative to internal supervision.

Following enactment of the ECL, however, the Academy of Social Sciences began to urge even greater autonomy in contract relations, questioning whether certification of contracts was necessary in all cases.[65] The absence of strict rules for certification was seen as permitting enterprises more leeway to mobilize productivity by forming contracts unfettered by bureaucratic procedural requirements. Urging that practical experience be summarized further before the enactment of specific regulations, *Legal Studies Research* took the position that certification should not be required in nonplan commodity contracts. This was particularly significant since the nonplan contracts were those outside the normal bureaucratic relationships, and thus arguably more in need of supervision. Plan contracts, on the other hand, were formed within a well-established process of bureaucratic regulations, thus arguably rendering certification superfluous

Although *Legal Studies Research* was reluctant initially to urge compulsory use of notarization, even after promulgation in 1982 of the notary regulations, these reservations were ultimately put aside.[66] CASS began urging notarization first for agricultural production contracts,[67] and later for all contracts as *Legal Studies Research* began to support notarization as the preferred method of contract supervision.[68]

Notarization was described by *Legal Studies Research* as a legal method that could establish contract documents as admissible evidence in the event of a dispute, in juxtaposition to certification, which was described as an administrative method not resulting in admissible evidence.[69] The academy's support for notarization over certification was motivated at least in part by institutional and organizational priorities. Notarization represented a legal method exercised by judicial organs over which the legal community generally and the CASS Legal Research Institute specifically had significant influence. Certification by the SAIC, on the other hand was seen as an intrusion by administrative organs over which the legal community had little influence.

Support for the role of the notaries also indicated that CASS supported further decentralization of the contract management system.[70] This suggested additional support for contract autonomy, as local notary offices enjoyed broad discretion in supervising contract activity. By clarifying the legal responsibilities and lending legal force to contract terms, the localized notarization of contracts reduced the need for further administrative involvement in contract relations, thus strengthening their autonomy.

The Law Society was reluctant to promote alternatives to the conventional role of enterprise management offices in supervising contracts. Although *Legal Studies Magazine* supported the role of certification, it was not to be the limited province of the SAIC departments, but was also to be carried out by enterprise management offices, capital and goods exchange committees, banks, and commune offices.[71] In its discussions of the ECL, the Law Society continued to support management and planning department offices for the supervision of contract activity to ensure that contracts were formulated and carried out in accord with the state plan.[72] This support for internal supervision of contracts by offices with existing organizational ties to the contrasting parties stood in marked contrast to the CASS view that external supervision was preferable.[73]

However, following enactment of the ECL, new support for the role of notarization became evident. *Legal Studies Magazine* discussed notarization as a legal method of contract supervision that was superior to administrative supervision (i.e., certification) in ensuring contract performance, preventing disputes, improving enterprise management, and preventing the use of contracts for illegal activity.[74] In contrast to the CASS position, however, the Law Society suggested that notarization should ensure the vertical collectivist aspects of contract practice rather than horizontal autonomous features.[75] Thus, although the Law Society gradually came to support external supervision of contracts by judicial organizations, the timing and content of this support revealed significant differences from the positions enunciated by CASS.

The CCP Legal Affairs Committee's legal journal, *Chinese Legal System Gazette,* conceded that certification was a useful mechanism for ensuring the performance of contracts by verifying the capacity and intent of the parties and ensuring mutual understanding of the content of the contract.[76] However, the *Gazette* also carried a wealth of articles on notarization prior to the enactment of the ECL, expressing support for this newly emerging method of contract supervision.[77] The *Gazette* continued to publish consistently and favorably on notarization work both prior to and following enactment of the ECL.[78]

Following enactment of the ECL, the *Gazette* continued to support the role of notarization as the preferred method of supervision over contract formation. From the time of its September 1980 report on the national meeting on notarization work through mid-1984, the *Gazette* reported on notarization on an average of twice per month, a rate that far exceeded the reporting on certification.[79] While each of these and other reports on notarization were short, their sheer number and the appearance of many of them on the front page of the *Gazette* indicated the journal's support for notarization as an important method of contract supervision.

The CCP legal affairs bureaucracy's support for notarization reflected a preference for external judicial supervision over contracts over administrative supervision by SAIC. This indicated an affinity for legal as opposed to administrative supervision of contracts, thus sharing the preferences of the Academy of Social Sciences. Support for notarization also indicated confidence that party policies could be enforced through the notarial system more easily than through ministerial or SAIC systems of contract supervision.

Although differences were evident regarding the supervisory role of existing management offices, the Beijing legal community expressed a fairly unified doctrinal position in favor of notarization as the primary external method of contract supervision. This reflected in part the ability of the Ministry of Justice to promote the role of its notary offices over the SAIC bureaucracy. The unified emphasis accorded notarization also reflected the institutional and organizational priorities of the Beijing legal community to resist the granting of supervisory authority to administrative entities not subject to its influence.

The support for notarization of contracts strengthened the potential for autonomy in contract relations. By virtue of their organizational independence from the contracting parties, the notaries were in a better position to exercise disinterested supervision than were the SAIC offices with existing ties to the contracting parties. SAIC supervision of contracts would unavoidably be affected by relationships derived from general supervisory authority of the SAIC offices over economic actors. Supervision by the notaries could be better insulated from such factors, since the notaries did not exercise other types of supervision over the contracting parties. Thus, while the reasons for the legal community's support of notarization may have been grounded in organizational politics, the results increased the potential for greater objectivity in the supervision of contracts, and thus greater autonomy of contracts from external influences.

The doctrinal views of the central political and legal communities evinced recognition of the importance of external supervision of contracts as a replacement for the internal supervision that had obtained previously. The emphasis on the SAIC system, while not espousing mandatory certification of contracts, indicated that even the quasi-external supervisory role of the SAIC was preferable to that of the enterprise management offices. The priority given to notarization indicated further support for external supervision by legal institutions operating independently of the parties.

However, the absence of consensus regarding the methods to be used for contract supervision remained a problem. Debate over the respective roles of notarization and certification reflected the influence on doctrine of the bureaucratic conflict between the SAIC and the Ministry of Justice. Doctrinal consistency regarding external supervision was undermined by uncertainty over the overlapping spheres of authority of the SAIC and the notaries. Thus, despite the potential benefits to contract autonomy derived from the increased role for SAIC and notarial supervision over contract formation, the competition between these entities represented an obstacle to doctrinal consistency.

Nonetheless, the support for and expansion of notarization reinforced the recognition of contract autonomy by positing the contract relationship as independent of the administrative system to which the parties belonged. External supervision by notaries would help ensure that the supervision over formation of contracts focused on the objective terms of the transaction rather than on the external relationships of the parties. Although these factors do not completely free the contracting parties from the constraints of their respective bureaucratic superiors, they lay the conceptual groundwork for recognition of autonomous contract rights.

Sanctions for Nonperformance and Dispute Settlement

Enforcement of contracts is a subset of contract administration, and is essential to reliance on contracts as mechanisms for economic transactions. Enforcement involves the closely related issues of dispute settlement methods and sanctions for nonperformance. The methods and institutions for dispute settlement involve processes that validate and enforce the contract relationship. The sanctions imposed for nonperformance represent an inducement to contract performance when other inducements are unavailing. They also reveal conceptual attitudes regarding the cost of nonperformance as expressed in the measure of remedies. The character of dispute settlement and the nature of sanctions are central to the issue of whether the ECL can effectively promote contract autonomy.

Attitudes of the Central Political Leadership

The Emergence of Economic Remedies. The most pronounced feature of the doctrine expressed by the central political leadership on sanctions for nonperformance of contracts has been the emphasis on economic penalties. Contract practice during the pre-Third Plenum period was characterized by an emphasis on specific performance as the main sanction for performance of contract.[80] This entailed the issuing of administrative orders that the party in breach should cure any defects in performance. While these orders might possibly have resulted in fulfillment of the contract at issue, and hence the plan requirements on which the contract was based, they accomplished little else. Losses to the aggrieved party were not compensated nor was any real cost imposed on the party in breach.

As the use of contracts was encouraged following the Third Plenum, the need for sanctions for nonperformance also increased. In view of the need to ensure fulfillment of contracts tied to plan quotas, and in light of economic policies that began to hold enterprises responsible for their own profits and losses, the principle of compensation was central. The 1979 Joint Circular on contract management made clear that compensation for losses was required in addition to liquidated damages paid the aggrieved party.[81] The 1980 SAIC regulations on commercial contracts with industry and agriculture calculated fines, for breach of contract measured by a proportion of the value of the contracted goods subject to the breach.[82] If such fines did not fully make up the losses caused by nonperformance, additional compensation was required.[83] In addition, the regulations provided that fines and compensation not be added to the breaching enterprise's cost of production but rather be paid out of profits.[84]

The doctrine of economic sanctions, particularly in connection with compensation of losses, depended in part on careful assessment of the causes of nonperformance. The central political leadership recognized that if sanctions were going to be imposed, the party responsible for nonperformance had to be identified accurately. Thus, there emerged the doctrine of subjective analysis of fault, which held that liability should be imposed on the person actually responsible for nonperformance.[85] Thus, where the nonperformance was caused by higher level departments or by third parties, the contracting party in breach did not necessarily bear liability. However, if the party in breach did not take measures to avoid nonperformance even where caused by third parties, liability might still attach. Thus, the effort was made to establish doctrinal principles for establishing liability to complement principles on economic sanctions for nonperformance.

The ECL also formalized the principle that compensation was required whenever the predetermined penalty payment for nonperformance was insufficient to make good any actual losses.[86] When combined with the penalty payment, compensation could not exceed incurred losses. The penalty payments themselves, however, were considered punitive and were required even where no losses were sustained. In addition, the law required that the contract continue to be carried out even after the payment of fines and compensation for failure to comply strictly with contract provisions. This indicated the central leadership's view that the imperatives of economic planning still required actual, even if imperfect, performance of contracts.

Thus, the central leadership's views on sanctions for nonperformance emphasized the role of compensation as well as fines, a reflection of the greater responsibility for profits and losses imposed on enterprises by the leadership economic policies. The emphasis on economic sanctions also ensured that parties to economic transactions had a tangible stake in performance of contracts. This enabled contracts to be viewed as independent of the administrative organizations that had dominated economic conduct and decision making previously. The emphasis on economic sanctions also underscored the rights of the parties to contracts to receive performance or the equivalent value.

Dispute Settlement: The Emergence of Compulsory Resolution. Following the Third Plenum, the government also placed increased emphasis on compulsory dispute resolution, rather than on the traditional method of consensual mediation.[87] Under mediation, the parties to a dispute were brought together under the auspices of a third party in a position of administrative superiority and a voluntary settlement was reached. In contract disputes, mediation remained a suggested method of settlement following the Third Plenum. Thus, the 1979 Joint Circular provided in Article 6 that in the event of a dispute, either contracting party could apply for mediation.[88] This provision was substantially retained in Article 48 of the ECL, which allowed either party to request mediation from the state-designated management organs.[89] These organs included the ministerial management offices, the various economic committees and the SAIC offices.

Inasmuch as mediation was essentially a voluntary undertaking by the contracting parties, its utility as a dispute settlement tool was greatly diluted by the post-Third Plenum economic reforms. Enterprise officials charged with greater responsibility for profits and losses under the reforms were not likely to concede voluntarily to liability in a dispute where such concession would result in the payment of unrecoverable fines and compensation. So, too, officials were reluctant simply to accept losses due to nonperformance of contracts when such losses would not be made good by state financial allocations. Although Chinese traditional social norms favor the amicable resolution of disputes and militate against the emergence of a litigious ethic among enterprise managers, the imposition of economic responsibility on enterprises nonetheless created an incentive for greater reliance on compulsory dispute settlement methods. Consequently, while mediation remained an option, the more compulsory methods of arbitration and adjudication became increasingly prominent as the Third Plenum economic reforms began to take effect.

Arbitration is similar to mediation in its procedural simplicity and informality.[90] In addition, as with mediation, submission to arbitration is voluntary. An important distinction, however, is that compliance with arbitration decisions is compulsory, unlike mediation. The courts can be called upon to enforce arbitration decisions where necessary.

Following the Third Plenum, the central political leadership stressed arbitration for the settling of industrial contract disputes. The April 1979 regulations governing construction contracts provided for arbitration of disputes where the parties could not reach a voluntary settlement.[91] These regulations provided that arbitration would be carried out independently by institutions such as the economic committees at various levels that were either superior to or separate from the disputing parties. The arbitration function of the management offices and economic committees was again emphasized in Article 9 of the regulations on 1979 plan contracts.[92]

Arbitration received renewed emphasis in the 1979 Joint Circular on contract management.[93] Article 6 of the circular combined into one the terms *mediation* and *arbitration* so as to imply that arbitration was available in dispute settlements without requiring prior attempts at mediation. Article 6 provided that if the disputants failed to reach a settlement through consultation, "either party may apply for mediation-arbitration to the various economic committees (or corresponding organs) or to the SAIC offices in the county, town, or district of the large and midsized city where the opposing party is located."[94]

The circular's reference to arbitration by both economic committees and SAIC offices suggested that the SAIC system had not yet been established fully and thus the economic committees remained a necessary institutional resource for dispute settlement. In contrast to their uncertain role in the supervision of contracts, the SAIC offices were given clear authority to arbitrate contract disputes under the 1980 Provisional Methods for Arbitration Procedures by SAIC Offices.[95]

The SAIC regulations evinced a concern with at least the appearance of objectivity and fairness in the results of arbitration decisions. The success of arbitration as a means of dispute resolution was seen as dependent on the perception by contract disputants that arbitration was sufficiently fair and reliable to be preferred over the more personal methods that had obtained in the past. If contract performance was to be ensured, contract enforcement and the imposition of sanctions for breach by dispute settlement organs had to be perceived by the parties as fair and rational. Otherwise, enterprise officials would hesitate to use the dispute settlement organs to enforce contracts and indeed contracts themselves would fall to disuse. Moreover, if arbitration decisions were perceived as arbitrary, coordinated enforcement by other institutions such as the banks would be difficult to achieve. In a political environment dominated by personal relationships, enforcement institutions would be reluctant in any case to carry out the decision of an unrelated institution against a close individual or enterprise, the more so if the decision were seen as unfair and irrational.

The inclusion in the ECL of arbitration as a preferred method of dispute settlement expanded the scope of arbitration beyond the context of procurement contracts envisioned in the 1980 SAIC arbitration regulations. The law retained the provisions for written decisions and for appeal to the courts, while discarding the "two levels of arbitration" method of contract dispute settlement that had been incorporated in the SAIC regulations, but later criticized as unwieldy.[96] Thus, binding arbitration became available for the settlement of disputes relating to all ten of the contracts specified in Article 8 of the ECL as well as to the agricultural responsibility system of contracts discussed in Article 54.

A regulatory framework for arbitration of contract disputes was enacted in mid-1983 under the PRC Regulations for Arbitration of Economic Contracts.[97] The regulations expanded greatly the powers of the SAIC bureaucracy by explicitly authorizing the SAIC offices to set up economic contract arbitration committees as the sole source for mediation and arbitration.[98] The authority of the SAIC arbitration committees included power to seize and hold property of the parties pending a decision, "in order to avoid causing relatively serious financial losses," although such seizure was generally limited to the property within the scope of the arbitration.[99]

Although problems remained with the procedures and with the substantive criteria for arbitration of contract disputes,[100] arbitration increasingly came to be a preferred method of dispute settlement. The enactment of the PRC arbitration regulations expressed the views of the central political leadership that arbitration represented a preferred method for resolution of contract disputes, which had swelled in number from 1982 to 1987 to more than 100,000 arbitrated contract disputes involving amounts of 14 billion yuan (US $3.7 billion).[101]

While it was not as heavily emphasized as either mediation or arbitration in the central leadership's view on contract dispute settlement, the role of court adjudication began to take on greater significance as contracts themselves became more widely used. The use of the courts in the enforcement of contracts began to be discussed shortly after the close of the Third Plenum.[102]

Initially, the role of the courts was limited to hearing appeals from arbitral decisions. The 1979 Joint Circular on contract management made clear that the role of the people's courts was to be limited to this appellate role.[103] The 1980 Tentative Opinion Concerning Methods for Accepting Cases By the Economic Chambers of the People's Courts issued by the Economic Chamber of the Supreme People's Court emphasized that the courts were not to be used as tribunals of first resort, but rather were to serve primarily as avenues for appeal of arbitration decisions.[104] The types of contracts that the supreme court viewed as appropriate for adjudicative dispute settlement also were limited generally to those involving large state projects or technical matters.[105] In addition, contract disputes involving different provinces, counties, or communes were not be be handled by the courts.[106] Thus, initially, both the functions of the courts in resolving contract disputes and the types of contracts subject to adjudicative dispute settlement were sharply limited.

The limitations on the role of the courts was due primarily to the court system being not yet fully re-established following its dismantling during the Cultural Revolution. Prior to enactment of the ECL, the central political leadership began to emphasize the need to establish a system of economic chambers within the people's courts to handle contract disputes.[107] By the end of 1980 more than one thousand such chambers had been set up in all twenty-nine of China's higher-level (provincial) people's courts.[108] While the economic chambers were slow initially to actually adjudicate disputes,[109] following enactment of the ECL, the activity of the economic chambers increased substantially.[110] In April 1984, the first national meeting on economic trials emphasized the importance of court adjudication of contract disputes.[111] During 1986, the economic chambers of the people's courts throughout China handled some 322,000 cases, of which more than 90 percent involved economic contract disputes.[112]

The central view on dispute settlement extended the dominant role to arbitration by SAIC offices, although adjudication by the economic chambers of the people's courts received increased emphasis. Whether in support of arbitration or adjudication, the central political leadership expressed clearly its support for compulsory methods that could lend certainty to dispute settlement. When combined with the emphasis on economic sanctions for nonperformance, the central political leadership's support for compulsory dispute settlement expressed broader recognition of the rights of contracting parties, even as such rights were becoming free from bureaucratic restraints.

The Attitudes of the Legal Community

Sanctions for Nonperformance. The Chinese Academy of Social Sciences supported very early on the use of such economic sanctions as penalty payments and compensation for nonperformance on contracts.[113] In a nod to the underlying principles of the responsibility system, CASS urged that compensation for losses caused by nonperformance could not be included as part of the cost of production in the budget of the enterprise in breach but rather must be paid out of capital accounts or from profit. This principle was later incorporated into the ECL.[114]

Following enactment of the ECL, CASS continued to emphasize the importance of economic sanctions as inducements to performance.[115] The academy drew a direct connection between the use of economic sanctions and increased reliability of contracts, while agreeing with the position taken by the central political leadership in supporting the doctrine of subjective assessment of fault.[116] *Legal Studies Research* also supported the use of preperformance guarantees to ensure contract performance.[117] These included liquidated damage clauses, deposits of funds with the obligee, the use of third parties to guarantee performance, the establishment of liens on the property of the obligor, and the use of mortgages. Even where the academy discussed the role of specific performance as a remedy for breach of contract, it was as a complement to, not a substitute for economic remedies.[118] Thus, CASS's position on remedies for nonperformance of contracts centered on the role of economic sanctions, indicating a move away from the administrative sanctioning practices of the past.

The Law Society was noticeably more reticent to support the use of economic remedies. Mention was made, albeit indirectly, of the need for economic compensation in cases of nonperformance.[119] However, the society also gave prominence to the use of administrative and criminal sanctions in the context of punishing the use of contracts for criminal purposes.[120] The Law Society's reluctance to support strongly the use of economic remedies revealed a generally conservative view in favor of internal methods of contract administration. Such methods would obviate the need for economic remedies in cases of nonperformance, as the administrative sanctions provided by internal supervision would be sufficient to chastise the party in breach. Moreover, providing the other party with economic remedies would be contradictory to the collective ethic of the economic bureaucracy.

The CCP Legal Affairs Committee's support for economic sanctions was expressed in part through the reprinting in *Chinese Legal System Gazette* of excerpts from a book on contracts by two scholars, Bai Youzhong and Li Zhuguo.[121] By devoting two issues to this question, the *Gazette* indicated its view of the importance of this issue. The responsibility for breach of contract was discussed as going beyond merely the compulsory performance of the contract and included the payment of penalty payments and the payment of compensation for losses incurred as a result of the breach. The *Gazette's* legal adviser column also revealed the party legal committee's support for economic sanctions.[122] Of the sixteen instances where the *Gazette* responded to an inquiry concerning contracts, the issue of remedies for nonperformance came up in six cases. Of these the compensation of losses stemming from nonperformance was recommended in five instances and in the other case the remedy was not specified. This indicated further the *Gazette's* favorable view as to the rights of the aggrieved party to damages under the contract.

With the implied exception of the Law Society, the Beijing legal community's views on sanctions for nonperformance echoed the political leadership's support for the enforceability and independence of contracts. By emphasizing economic inducements to performance, the Beijing legal community sought to lend monetary value to contract rights, and revealed a conceptual view of contracts as autonomous nonbureaucratic relationships. Thus, the community urged the use of a universal standard for sanctioning nonperformance, rather than a parochial standard of contract enforcement subject to collective priorities of bureaucratic organizations, as was the case with administrative sanctions and specific performance.

Dispute Resolution. Prior to enactment of the ECL, the Academy of Social Sciences drew an explicit connection between establishing formal institutions for dispute settlement and the reliability on contracts as a mechanism for economic transactions.[123] Noting that in the past arbitration tribunals were not fully established and judicial organs did not handle contract disputes, *Legal Studies Research* addressed the need to establish and perfect these institutions while avoiding assertions as to the preferability of either.

Following the enactment of the ECL, CASS expressed support for judicial mediation of contract disputes.[124] CASS's support for judicial mediation, however, did not imply support for consensual dispute resolution. Once the case was before the court, the voluntariness that characterized administrative mediation was largely eliminated since the court's authority to enter a compulsory decision, in the event mediation failed, strongly encouraged compliance with a mediated alternative. Thus, by conditioning support for mediation on its being carried out by the courts during the course of formal dispute resolution, CASS indicated its view that this traditional method of dispute resolution should be made more compulsory. The courts also were better able to offer disinterested dispute resolution than were the organizationally related management organs.

In addition, CASS suggested that contract disputes be resolved through either binding arbitration or direct court litigation, indicating support for introducing an element of finality to the resolution process.[125] Following enactment of the Contract Arbitration Regulations in 1983, CASS reiterated its support for resolution of contract disputes through SAIC arbitration.[126] Thus, through discussions in *Legal Studies Research,* CASS indicated its support for compulsory dispute resolution, and for the increased role of the courts.

Prior to enactment of the ECL, the Law Society confined its discussions of dispute resolution to the presentation of specific guidelines for handling contract disputes, and indicated a marked preference for arbitration. While acknowledging the need to establish judicial organs for handling contract disputes, the Law Society cautioned that most contract disputes should be handled through arbitration and that only a very few should go to litigation.[127]

Following the enactment of the ECL, *Legal Studies Magazine* continued to concentrate on the selection of institutions for resolving contract disputes and, consistently with the CASS view, supported the role of the courts. Judicial mediation was emphasized through references to contract disputes that had been successfully resolved through judicial mediation.[128] Support for the role of the courts was also evident in publication of specific guidelines for judicial resolution of contract disputes.[129] Adjudication of contract disputes was also viewed as a complement to judicial mediation and arbitration.[130] Thus, the Law Society's support for judicial handling of contract disputes revealed fairly strong consensus with CASS regarding the importance of compulsory dispute settlement.

The CCP Legal Committee journal, *Chinese Legal System Gazette*, was largely silent on the issue of contract dispute settlement prior to the enactment of the ECL, indicating continued uncertainty as to the respective role of the courts and the arbitration organs. Following the enactment of the ECL, however, the *Gazette* gradually began to acknowledge the role of SAIC arbitration.[131] After the PRC Contract Arbitration Regulations were enacted in August 1983, the *Gazette* reported that the SAIC offices were the sole source of arbitration and contended that disputes should be taken to court only as a last resort.[132] The *Gazette's* reporting on arbitration continued with the publication of commentaries by national and local SAIC officials on its role.[133]

The *Gazette* also gave attention to the role of judicial dispute resolution, first by publishing formal guidelines for the work of the economic chambers of the people's courts that included discussion of contract dispute resolution.[134] The *Gazette* gave prominence to a report by Ren Jianxin, associate justice of the Supreme Court (later chief justice) calling explicitly for the use of court resolution of contract disputes.[135] The *Gazette's* reporting on the resolution of actual contract cases also reflected a predisposition in favor of judicial settlement. Of the twenty-four cases reported by the *Gazette* following the enactment of the ECL, fourteen were resolved by the courts, either through mediation or formal adjudication. By contrast, in only four of the cases was final resolution carried out through the SAIC offices.[136]

Thus, the *Gazette* expressed a preference for compulsory resolution of contract disputes. The *Gazette's* emphasis on the role of SAIC arbitration was more extensive than that provided by other legal journals. Nonetheless, regarding the conflict between the norms of consensual and compulsory dispute resolution, the *Gazette* expressed doctrinal views of the CCP legal bureaucracy that were generally consistent with the positions of the other components of the central legal community.

The doctrinal discussions of the central legal community concerning the institutions and methods for resolving contract disputes indicated that, as with its discussion of certification and notarization, the legal community was prone to assert its own organizational interests. Thus, even though the role of formal adjudication of disputes was not emphasized heavily, there was uniform support for the role of the courts in overseeing mediation and arbitration of disputes. This reflected the influence of the Supreme Court's Opinions on this issue, which downplayed formal adjudication while encouraging a role for the courts in other methods of dispute resolution.[137] Judicial dispute resolution, whether through the methods of mediation, arbitration, or adjudication, provided a basis for legal specialists to replace administrative officials who had dominated previously. Furthermore, by emphasizing the role of compulsory dispute settlement, the Beijing legal community expressed the view that effective reliance on contracts required processes and institutions that would ensure that disputes over performance would be settled finally. When combined with the emphasis on economic remedies, the legal community's emphasis on compulsory dispute resolution evinced further support for contract autonomy.

As opposed to the differing viewpoints that characterized discussions on the role on contracts and contract law, and to a lesser extent on the issue of supervision of contracts, the issues of sanctions and dispute settlement showed marked uniformity of viewpoint. This convergence of views between the central political and legal communities on the issues of economic sanctions for nonperformance of contracts and the use of compulsory dispute settlement provided a strong foundation for the autonomy of contracts.

Summary

Because the ECL is an imposed law, its legitimacy depends on a conscious assessment by the economic actors who are the subjects of the law that the ECL's norms of autonomy are preferable to the collectivist norms that went before. Economic actors must be able to identify the norms of autonomy expressed in the ECL, before that assessment can begin.

The ECL's norms of autonomy were expressed through provisions espousing the rights of contracting parties; providing external mechanisms for the supervision of contracts; and supporting the use of compulsory dispute resolution and monetary remedies. However, the statutory provisions contain ambiguities derived from the compromises endemic to legislation of policy-driven law. The resolution of these ambiguities occurs in part through doctrinal discussion articulating the law's norms. The doctrinal bases for the ECL provide an important focus of this process of assessment by which economic actors recognize and legitimate the norms expressed in the ECL.

The doctrinal discussions on the issues at the core of the ECL's new norms revealed important differences of viewpoint between the central political and legal communities, as well as within these communities. Significant doctrinal differences emerged regarding the role of contracts and contract law. Differences as to the proper role of contracts emerged that derived from differing policy preferences in favor of market- or plan-oriented economic decision making. Differences on the role of contract law emerged reflecting different ideas on the role of law as an instrument of policy or a protector of rights. Thus, these conflicts of viewpoint potentially may undermine the ability of contracts to foster autonomous economic transactions based on enforceable rights under the protection of contract law.

In the context of their impact on the process by which economic actors recognize norms that they value in the doctrine of the ECL, doctrinal disagreements provide both the opportunity and the challenge for the legitimacy of the ECL. Differences of opinion possibly lead to refinements and improvements in legal doctrine, and thus enable law to be a more effective mechanism for ordering economic and social relationships. Thus, to the extent that doctrinal differences and their resolution lend credibility to the lawmaking process, these are a force supporting the ECL's ability to garner abstract legitimacy.[138]

However, doctrinal inconsistencies pose a more severe challenge to the ability of the ECL to acquire practical legitimacy. Regardless of the abstract virtues of doctrinal diversity, the perception of economic actors likely will be that the law being imposed has uncertain support from the political leadership and hence the potential for unreliability. Doctrinal differences cause Chinese economic actors, already skeptical of the utility of law, to doubt further the practical effectiveness of the ECL's new norms in lending predictability to economic relationships. Although they tended to relate to conceptual rather than operational issues, doctrinal differences on the role of contracts and contract law have an important effect on capacity of the ECL to acquire practical legitimacy.

On the other hand, the areas where the political and legal communities reached broad conformity of doctrine hold promise for potential legitimacy of the ECL. The relative uniformity of support by the central political and legal communities for external supervision over contract formation, primarily by notarial offices but also by the SAIC system, may lend confidence in the autonomy of contracts. Relatively uniform support for economic sanctions and compulsory dispute resolution may strengthen confidence in the enforceability of autonomous contract rights.

The potential for the ECL to acquire practical legitimacy will require more than consistency of doctrine on the administration of contracts. While doctrinal consistency is an important indicator of the potential for economic actors to recognize valued norms of autonomy in the ECL, such recognition also depends on the operational record regarding contract practice. Throughout the process by which economic actors make the conscious assessments that are required for practical legitimacy of imposed law, the operation of the doctrine in practice is an important center of focus. Accordingly, examination of the practical circumstances regarding the formation of contracts and the resolution of contract disputes is an important component of the inquiry into the legitimation of the ECL. These issues are addressed in the following two chapters.

CHAPTER 3

Operational Aspects of Contract Formation and Recognition of Contract Autonomy

The operational record of contract practice in China offers an important point of comparison with the doctrinal viewpoints on the ECL examined previously.[1] The extent to which operational characteristics of the ECL are consistent with doctrinal views is an essential determinant of the law's capacity to acquire practical legitimacy.[2]

This chapter examines the extent of consistency between doctrine and practice regarding the conceptual issue of the functions of contracts and the administrative issues of institutions and methods of contract supervision. The doctrinal views of the central political and legal communities on the role of contracts in China, although not fully uniform, indicated support for broader diversity in the use of contracts for agricultural, commercial, and ultimately industrial transactions. The case data on contract formation indicate the operational impact of these doctrinal viewpoints. In addition, the diversity of transactions in which contracts are used indicates the breadth of contract autonomy.

The autonomy of contract rights is indicated by a variety of factors such as the types of transactions in which contracts are used, the negotiating authority of the contracting parties, the contract terms and conditions, and the degree to which contract transactions are insulated from external factors. Such autonomy in the context of contract formation is indicated also by the character of contract supervision. The case data on contract formation offer insights as to whether the doctrinal viewpoints expressed by the political and legal communities were carried out in practice.

Pre-Economic Contract Law Cases

Of the 131 cases reported[3], 81 were formed before the ECL went into effect. Of these, 15 involved agriculture, 66 involved various industrial and commercial transactions. The reports reveal a varied mix of supports for and obstacles to the recognition of contract autonomy.

Agricultural Contracts

The two main types of agricultural contracts that were the focus of case reporting during the pre-ECL period were production responsibility contracts (PRCs) and agricultural procurement contracts (APCs). Of the fifteen case reports on pre-ECL agricultural contracts, eleven involved production responsibility contracts while four concerned agricultural procurement contracts.

Under production responsibility contracts, individual peasants or households contracted to manage plots of land and to turn over a certain proportion of production to the production team or brigade, retaining the remainder for their own consumption or to sell on the free market.[4] The responsibility contracts often extended beyond simply growing of food products to the production of agricultural byproducts and the management of sideline industries. Under the agricultural procurement contracts, the contract was formed generally between a local government procurement office and multiperson production units, although individual peasants occasionally became parties to these types of contracts as well. The agricultural procurement contracts usually called for the delivery of certain amounts of agricultural product to the local state procurement office.

Supports for Recognition of Contract Autonomy. The recognition of contract autonomy was evident in a variety of aspects of the contract formation process. The use of competitive bidding to determine who would be awarded the right to participate in production responsibility contracts reinforced the autonomy of agricultural producers, since their responsibility for performing the bid was coupled with management autonomy necessary for such performance. The use of contracts to formalize agricultural procurement transactions between government entities and private producers indicated that producers enjoyed some measure of autonomy from the state, supported by rights conferred under contract. The diversity of transactions subject to contracts demonstrated the scope of activities that peasant producers could engage in and acquire measured autonomy.

The use of competitive bidding was evident in a number of the agricultural contracts reported. In four of the reported cases of pre-ECL production responsibility contracts, the peasant awarded the contract had submitted a bid for contract (case nos. 6, 8, 9, and 10). The use of bids to determine which peasants would be awarded production contracts underscored the autonomy of producers to calculate independently the cost of production as a basis for the bid, and to perform the contract at the bid price. In addition, the juxtaposition of the producer's right to remuneration with the state's right to receive the product at the bid price indicated that the relationship between the producer and the state was based on reciprocal obligations, not on administrative dictates. This reciprocity suggested an increased recognition of the autonomy of the producer.

The use of contracts to formalize the reciprocal obligations between producers and the state reinforced the nascent autonomy of the producers. The crucial aspect of the agricultural procurement contracts was the formal expression of the state's obligation to pay certain pre-agreed amounts in exchange for the delivery of specified products, suggesting formal recognition of producers' rights to receive payment in exchange for production. Agricultural procurement contracts generally involved initial outlays by the state of such production supports as fertilizer, feed, and cash to the producers. These subsidies permitted procurement entities to exercise significant economic as well as political dominance over the producers. Indeed, as was the pattern prior to the implementation of the Third Plenum reforms, the obligation of producers to deliver fixed quantities of product to the procurement entity could simply have been ordered under the state plan without a contract. The use of contracts to express the terms of state procurement transactions suggested that the state was beginning to recognize the autonomous contract rights of producers.

The scope of this recognition was evident in the diversity of transactions subject to contracts. Even prior to enactment of the ECL, this diversity was significant. The production responsibility contracts covered responsibility for management of fruit orchards (case nos. 2, 6, 9, 10);[5] management of a reed pond (case no. 5); operation of an automobile (case no. 3); operation of a fireworks factory (case no. 1); the management of a store selling pork (case no. 7); and management of a variety of agricultural sideline activities, including a tea garden and tea processing factory (case no. 8). The pre-ECL agricultural procurement contracts reported also extended to a variety of activities, including contracted production for state procurement of chickens (case nos. 11,

12) and nonstaple crops (case nos. 13, 14). This diversity was an important complement to the factors supporting contract autonomy.

Obstacles to Contract Autonomy. Although the case reporting on pre-ECL contracts in agriculture suggested several factors that provided possible support for increased recognition of contract autonomy, significant obstacles to such recognition were also evident. A major problem lay in the continued dominance of state planning, which undermined the autonomy of the parties to negotiate the terms of agricultural production contracts. The vast majority of agricultural production contracts involved state plan quotas, which suggested that the contracts remained instruments for recording production duties rather than genuine sources of rights. This meant also that the rights and obligations of agricultural producers were subject to policy determinations external to the contract transaction. Thus, while the use of contracts to replace administrative orders as the instrument for implementation of the state plan suggested some recognition of contract autonomy, the dominance of the plan itself continued to be an obstacle to such autonomy.

The short duration of production responsibility contracts also indicated that the contract autonomy of agricultural producers was limited. Most agricultural contracts were limited to a single year, during which the contracting peasant had little practical management discretion regarding production. This suggested that the peasants were still restrained in their autonomy and discretion to manage the contract property.

The absence of external supervision over production responsibility contracts suggested further limits to contract autonomy. Only two of the contracts reported went through certification, while none of the contracts was notarized. This suggests that prior to the implementation of the ECL, supervision over the contract process took the form of internal supervision by administrative units with organizational ties to the parties. This increased the likelihood that contracts were subject to external influences unrelated to the terms of the contract transaction itself. The absence of external supervision reflected lack of recognition for the autonomy of the parties, while the effect of external influences diluted the autonomy of the contract transaction.

In sum, the pre-ECL agricultural contracts reported revealed several characteristics that suggested the potential for broader recognition of contract autonomy. Various aspects of contract practice, including use of competitive bidding, the formal expression of reciprocity of obligations between of state organs and agricultural producers, and greater diversity of transactions subject to contracts, indicated increased recognition of the autonomy of economic actors. Nonetheless, significant obstacles remained. The short duration of contracts limited the effects of the contract autonomy that did exist. Moreover, continued reliance on collectivist practices emphasizing the primacy of state planning and the role of internal administrative supervision remained important obstacles to autonomy. These obstacles revealed the effect of preexisting collectivist norms that the ECL was intended to reform.

Industrial and Commercial Contracts

Of the eighty-one contracts reported as being formed prior to enactment of the ECL, sixty-six concerned industrial or commercial transactions. The circumstances of formation of these contracts revealed a variety of supports for and obstacles to contract autonomy.

Supports For Contract Autonomy. The characteristics of the formation of industrial and commercial contracts prior to the ECL reflected various supports for the recognition of contract autonomy. The increased role of direct negotiations, the use of interregional contracts, and the expanded diversity of contract transactions indicated that contracts were coming to be recognized as autonomous bases for enforceable rights.

Direct contract negotiations between producers and suppliers had potentially great significance for the autonomy of parties to industrial and commercial contract transactions. In the sixty-six contracts reported, administrative units intervened at the formation stage in only six, indicating that the contracting parties enjoyed a certain degree of negotiating autonomy. Although contracting parties may well have selected each other as a result of their subordination to common organizational hierarchies, the increased ability of the parties to negotiate contract terms directly was a departure from past practice, by which the supply of goods and equipment was undertaken through the intervention of state planning organs.[6] Such direct relations had characterized agricultural contracts between producers and collectives or procurement entities, although these relationships had involved parties at unequal positions in the administrative hierarchy. In industrial and commercial contracts, however, the emergence of contracts directly negotiated between the parties at relatively equal levels in the hierarchy reflected expansion in the autonomy of economic actors to negotiate and form contracts. This suggested increased recognition of autonomous contract rights as well, since direct negotiations between the parties allowed contract rights and obligations to be based on the transaction at issue rather than on external relationships and other factors.

The expanding scope of contracting autonomy was also evident in the prominence of interregional transactions. Of the forty-six pre-ECL industrial commercial contracts where the location of the parties was specified, twenty-one (46%) involved parties from different regions.[7] In one case, for example, a group of thirty tractors was supplied under contract by a Henan agricultural machinery factory to a production materials service company in Shaanxi (case no. 60). Since tractors were items subject to state planned distribution it was necessary for approval of the transaction by the planning departments in both provinces but evidently that did not prevent their shipment across provincial boundaries. Interregional transactions between the centrally administered cities and units in the outlying provinces were also evident. In one case a Beijing crafts factory purchased under a contract cloisonne rough casts from a porcelain factory in Handan city, Hebei (case no. 62). Conversely, the municipalities served as the source for finished goods sent to enterprises in the surrounding provinces. For example, in one report, a Shanghai instruments factory contracted to supply specialized metering equipment to an outside factory (case no. 34), while in another a Shanghai textile factory supplied blankets under contract to a department store outside the area (case no. 35).

The growth of interprovincial contract relations also suggested that contracts with distant producers were used to satisfy demands for industrial equipment and materials of local enterprises. For example, an asbestos factory in Harbin entered into a contract with a commune asbestos factory in Zhejiang for the purchase of asbestos thread (case no. 77). That the Harbin factory had to obtain its raw materials from distant Zhejiang suggests that the materials were unavailable closer to home. Similarly, an automobile repair facility in Jilin acquired camshafts from Wuhan, suggesting an inability to acquire them locally despite the close proximity of a major automotive manufacturing complex in Changchun (case no. 51). One contract for the manufacture of insulation baseboards for a low tension switching plant in Jilin was undertaken in 1977 by an urban production brigade in neighboring Liaoning (case no. 82). In another instance, a brigade factory in Zhejiang undertook several manufacturing contracts to make signs for four different industrial enterprises located as far away as Heilongjiang, illustrating again the role of interregional contracts to supplement local supplies (case no. 96). Such use of interregional contracts suggests that contract transactions were coming to be founded on the objectives and requirements of contracting parties, rather than requirements external to the contract relationship, further broadening contract autonomy.

As with the use of contracts in agriculture production, a major complement to recognition of contract autonomy in industrial and commercial contracts prior to the ECL was the diversity of transactions that were subject to contracts. The goods subject to the forty-seven purchase and sale contracts reported varied to such extent that only three types were duplicated. These were contracts for the supply of bulldozers (case nos. 59, 70), brickmaking machines (case nos. 33, 42), and tractors (case nos. 41, 60). Several reports did not specify the goods subject to the contract (see, e.g., case no. 81), Otherwise, the purchase and sales contracts whose goods were reported covered transactions in such goods as reed mats (case no. 53), bricks (case no. 50), tea (case no. 37), wine jugs (case no. 39), wine yeast (case no. 80), cloisonne casts (case no. 62), and a wide variety of machinery and equipment including trucks (case no. 72), derricks (case no. 55), automobile camshafts (case no. 51), transformers (case no. 52), meters (case no. 34), and boilers (case no. 61). Contracts also were signed for transactions involving overhauling of equipment (case nos. 84 and 93), printing (case no. 47), and as instruments for terminating previously agreed transactions (case no. 46). In addition, a variety of manufacturing contracts were formed in connection with the production of such products as glass (case no. 44), prefabricated building materials (case nos. 82, 85, 86, 89, and 94), and machinery (case nos. 87, 90, and 91).

In addition to such product diversity in contract transactions, the variety of contracting parties indicated further the scope of recognition for contract autonomy. The most common relationship was between different factories: in one case, an electric stove factory in Changchun signed a contract with a transformer factory for the purchase of transformers (case no. 52). Other contract relationships involved contracts between factories and retail stores, such as where a glass factory in Shanghai agreed under contract to supply thermos bottles to a retail shop (case no. 32). Also prevalent were supply contracts between factories and specialized companies (case no. 56) and between various specialized companies (case no. 60). Contracts were also formed between factories and a wide variety of agricultural enterprises including farms (e.g., case no. 75), brigades (e.g., case no. 82), and communes (case no. 53). Factories also signed contracts with schools (case nos. 40 and 68), street committees (case no. 31), material bureaus (case no. 65), and mines (case no. 48). Thus, the contract autonomy supported by direct negotiations and arm's-length transactions was evident over an increasingly diverse array of economic activities between an increasing variety of economic actors.

Obstacles to the Recognition of Contract Autonomy. There were also obstacles to contract autonomy in industrial and commerical transactions. As with agricultural contracts, many of these obstacles derived from the resilience of pre-existing collectivist norms involving dominance by state planning bureaucracies, methods of payment, and the absence of external supervision and ratification of contracts.

The dominance of state approval for economic contracts prior to the ECL represented a significant obstacle to the recognition of contract autonomy. In each of the three construction contracts reported (case nos. 45, 83, and 95), higher level approval was a prominent aspect of the transaction. In one case involving a contract for the construction of a dormitory for a factory in Henan, construction was begun on the site but the factory refused to make its scheduled progress payments on grounds that the contract had not received approval from higher level authorities (case no. 83). In another, a contract for the construction of housing for factory personnel in Jilin was approved and sent down from higher levels but the party responsible for the actual construction fell so far behind schedule that the factory demanded that the contract be given to another building company (case no. 45). That these contracts were not fulfilled reflected not only a lack of coordination between the higher level approval organs and the unit responsible for performance, but also that the bureaucratic command and approval process was given higher priority than the issue of the contracting parties' rights to receive performance.

The dominance of the administrative bureaucracy in contract activity was also evident in that, in fourteen of the cases involving pre-ECL industrial and commercial contracts, the reason for nonperformance involved some type of administrative intervention, including changes in the state plan, repudiation of contracts formed without requisite approval, and nullificaton due to regulatory violations (case nos. 34, 39, 53, 58, 71, 72, 74, 77, 79, 80, 83, 87, 90, and 92).

Thus, the requirement that higher level approvals be obtained to ensure the validity of contracts tended to diminish the negotiating and management autonomy of the contracting parties. Also, the prevalence of higher level approval meant that the obligations and rights of the parties to the transactions stemmed not from the agreement itself, but rather from the involvement and approval of the approval organs.

Another feature of pre-ECL industrial and commercial contracts was the provision for payment prior to performance. While this was not the rule, it obtained in fifteen of forty-seven purchase and sale contracts (case nos. 31, 32, 40, 42, 48, 50, 52, 61, 63, 65, 70, 75, 76, 85, and 86). Prepayment contracts were used both for complex manufactured equipment and for simple products. Thus a contract for the purchase of a horizontal quick-loading boiler called for payment before delivery (case no. 61) as did a contract for the supply of bricks (case no. 50). Prepayment of the contract price was also a characteristic of the pre-ECL construction contracts reported (case nos. 45, 83, and 95).

The use of prepayments undermined contract autonomy in several ways. First, the purchaser's willingness to make these prepayments was founded on the contracts being generally formed pursuant to planning directives such that the purchaser would be reimbursed through administrative planning channels for the prepaid contract price and any losses caused by nonperformance of the supplier. This further undermined contract autonomy since the protection of the purchaser was founded not in the contract but in the purchaser's relationship to the administrative planning authorities.

In addition, the use of preperformance payments suggests that in many instances the producer had neither the operating capital to produce the goods specified in the contract nor the supply inventory from which to make delivery. Thus, the producer/supplier was not in an autonomous position regarding contract performance, but depended on receiving funds to perform its contract obligations. Prepayments allocated most of the risk to the purchaser and reflected the attitude of producer/suppliers that the performance by the purchaser in making payment could not be assured based on rights embodied in the contract.

Supply contracts formed prior to the implementation of the ECL generally were not subject to formal ratification by entities organizationally separate from the parties. Of the sixty-seven industrial and commercial contracts reported, only two (case nos. 31 and 74) were reported as undergoing certification by supervisory contract management agencies, while only one (case no. 95) was notarized.

The bulk of the case reports did not address supervision at all, suggesting that the pre-existing practices of internal supervision remained in effect. Three of the pre-ECL industrial and commercial contracts were reported specifically (case nos. 32, 50, and 52) as subject to internal approval by management offices related organizationally to the parties. Under the conventional state planning system, contracts were subject to internal supervision and approval by the planning offices superior to the contracting enterprise and usually by the management bureau under which the particular contracting entity was operating (see e.g., case no. 25). This internal supervision, however, merely underscored the lack of independence and autonomy of the contracting parties, and did not indicate that the parties to the contracts had rights derived from the contracts themselves. Had the newly emergent external methods of supervision been applied to the contracts reported, this almost certainly would have been noted.

Thus, prior to enactment of the ECL the record regarding formation of commercial and industrial contracts revealed a number of obstacles to contract autonomy that undermined the supports for contract autonomy derived from direct negotiations, interregional contracting, and transactional diversity. These included continued administrative intervention, use of preperformance payments, and the absence of external supervision, and represented the effect of pre-existing collectivist norms on contract practice.

Following the Third Plenum and prior to the enactment of the ECL, the circumstances relating to the formation of contracts revealed a mixture of supports for and obstacles to the recognition of contract autonomy. The supports for such recognition varied, depending on the types of contracts at issue. In agriculture, the use of competitive bidding and the formalizing of reciprocal obligations between the state and the producers suggested increased recognition of the autonomy of economic actors. In industry and commerce, contract autonomy was supported by the use of direct negotiations and the prevalence of interregional transactions. Transactional diversity in all three sectors indicated the extension of contract autonomy to a broad variety of economic transactions.

However, obstacles to contract autonomy remained. In agriculture, these included the continued dominance of state planning, limited duration of contracts, and the general absence of external supervision. In industrial and commercial contracts, the obstacles were the dominance of bureaucratic approval authority, reliance on preperformance payments, and the absence of external supervision. Each of these obstacles derived mainly from the resilience of pre-existing collectivist norms expressed in bureaucratic management policies. It was the reform of these collectivist norms that was the focus of many of the principles of the ECL.

Post-Economic Contract Law Cases

The enactment of the ECL was intended in part to provide a legal basis for reforming the collectivist norms that had dominated contract activity previously. As indicated by the case reports on contract formation prior to enactment of the ECL, the norms of autonomy fostered by the Third Plenum reform policies were already in evidence, although the pre-existing collectivist norms remained strong. The case reporting on contract formation following enactment of the ECL provides data on operation in practice of the norms of autonomy expressed in the ECL's doctrine. Consistency of the operational record with the doctrinal views explored previously indicates the potential for the ECL's provisions regarding contract formation to acquire practical legitimacy.

Of the fifty case reports involving contracts formed after the ECL went into effect, fifteen concerned agricultural production or small-scale projects undertaken pursuant to the rural responsibility system, and thirty-five concerned industrial and commercial contracts. The circumstances of the formation of these contracts reflected the continued tension between supports for and obstacles to recognition of contract autonomy.

Agricultural Contracts

Of the fifteen agricultural contracts reported, three were agricultural procurement contracts, one entailed the leasing of water rights, while the remainder were signed pursuant to the production responsibility system.

Supports for Contract Autonomy. The use of contracts to express reciprocal obligations between the state and agricultural producers remained an important indicator of the expanding autonomy of rural economic actors, as did the use of competitive bidding. In addition, the duration of contracts began to be extended, indicating further expansion of autonomy for economic actors. In the nine cases where the duration was specified, multiyear contracts up to five years were used in five instances (case nos. 17, 20, 24, 26, and 27). This contrasted with the predominance of single-year contracts formed prior to the ECL and indicated that the ECL was being implemented in concert with the CCP Central Committee's 1981 directive on medium- and long-term responsibility contracts in agriculture.[8] The extension of contract duration meant that agricultural producers had broader management authority. Thus the peasantry was gradually achieving more autonomy to establish crop mixes and planting plans and, in general, to manage the contract property. In sideline industries, extended contract duration again meant greater management powers over rural enterprises.

The diversity of activities made subject to contract continued to expand. Contracts signed with peasant producers under the agricultural responsibility system extended increasingly beyond mere agricultural production. Indeed, contracts for other rural activities were discussed more often than those involving conventional agricultural production. Responsibility contracts reported included contracts for operation of an orchard (case no. 26); pig raising (case no. 16), chicken raising (case no. 25); unspecified production (case no. 18), and various sideline activities such as operation of mills (case nos. 20, 21, and 27); operation of brick kilns (case nos. 23 and 24); hotel management (case no. 17) and food-processing operations (case no. 28).

This diversity following the enactment of the ECL extended to procurement contracts as well. Of the three procurement contracts reported, one concerned production of oranges (case no. 19), one involved the production of salted cauliflower (case no. 29), and one pertained to the supply of chickens (case no. 30). Such transactional diversity augmented the factors supporting contract autonomy in agricultural transactions.

Obstacles to Contract Autonomy. However, the expansion of contract autonomy was hampered by the continuing lack of emphasis on external supervision over contract formation. External supervision was enforced in two of the cases reported (no. 29, involving SAIC certification, and no. 24, involving notarization). Internal supervision through certification by a supervisory management office was applied in one instance (no. 20). Thus, despite the doctrinal emphasis on external supervision of contracts following the enactment of the ECL, and the proliferation of notarial offices and SAIC departments to carry out such supervision, there was little operational effect on agricultural contracts.

The difficulty of establishing a system of external supervision and ratification of contracts can be attributed, first, to the lack of doctrinal consensus on the role of external supervision generally, and particularly on the institutional format that it should take once adopted. As discussed in chapter 2, this lack of consensus reflected the impact of organizational politics as well as policy differences among the political and legal communities. Second, the expansion of newly established systems for external supervision was hindered in the rural areas of China where most of the agricultural contracts were used, because quick responses to central directives were not always possible or practical. As a result, external supervision over agricultural contracts was limited during the years following enactment of the ECL.

The expansion of factors supporting contract autonomy in connection with the formation of agricultural contracts following enactment of the ECL suggested that the ECL's provisions specifically recognizing individual agricultural producers as proper parties to contracts were having an effect on the contract formation process.[9] Thus, the norms embodied in the ECL appeared to be affecting attitudes and practices in the formation of agricultural contracts. The consistency of factors supporting contract autonomy such as competitive bidding and reciprocity of obligations are likely to motivate agricultural producers to try to rely on the ECL's provisions relating to the rights of the contracting parties and the availability of contracts for a wide variety of transactions.

On the other hand, the lack of external supervision posed a significant obstacle to the capacity of the ECL's provisions on contract formation to acquire practical legitimacy. Agricultural producers, seeing that doctrinal disunity on the issue of external supervision translated into its general absence in practice, will likely be skeptical of the extent to which contract formation can be insulated from the intrusion of political and organizational relationships. Rural economic actors are likely to conclude that the ECL's principles supporting autonomy in contract formation are not sufficiently reliable to supplant pre-existing collectivist norms favoring reliance on external relationships.

Nonetheless, doctrinal and operational consistency in supporting the use of contracts to express reciprocal obligations between the state and agricultural producers in a wide variety of transactions is likely to encourage fuller reliance on contracts. Their use is likely to expand as a replacement for informal personal ties, with the potential for rural economic actors to accept and rely on contracts as sources of contract rights independent of collective interests.

Industrial and Commercial Contracts

Of the thirty-five industrial and commercial contracts reported as being formed following the going into effect of the ECL, twenty-nine were purchase and sale contracts, and the remaining were in connection with transportation, construction, manufacturing, guarantees, and the allocation of responsibilities after dissolution of a pre-existing contract.

Supports for Contract Autonomy. Following the implementation of the ECL, the circumstances of formation of industrial and commercial contracts revealed a variety of supports for autonomy: an increasing reliance on direct negotiation and interregional contracting; the decline of reliance on preperformance payments; and the growth of transactional diversity.

Direct negotiations between the parties continued in evidence following the going into effect of the ECL as only five of the twenty-nine purchase and sale contracts reported involved third-party negotiations. The autonomy of contracts was thus strengthened as contract terms were dictated increasingly by the circumstances of the transaction rather than the priorities and preferences of outside parties. The autonomy of the contracting parties was underscored as the contractual expression of their interests and their obligations was formalized separately from the collective economic organizations to which the parties belonged.

The geographic dispersion of enterprises entering into contracts following the ECL increased slightly, as twelve of the twenty-three contracts (52%) where the location of the parties was specified involved parties from different provinces whereas prior to the ECL twenty-one of forty-six contracts (46%) involved interprovincial transactions. Thus, interregional contracts continued to be used to augment the capacity of local economies, reflecting increased autonomy of economic actors to conduct transactions outside the local economic confines. The use of contracts in interregional transactions also reflected confidence in the enforceability of contract rights and obligations, since the policing of performance of interregional transactions through the pre-existing methods of personal and organizational relationships involved greater inconvenience (and probably expense) due to the distances involved. Such confidence in contract enforceability also meant confidence in the autonomy of the contract obligations.

Expanding recognition for the autonomy of economic actors was also evident in the decline in the use of preperformance payments. Of the thirty-five industrial and commercial contracts formed after the ECL went into effect, only four called for prepayment, a significant decrease from the situation prior to the ECL, when nearly one third of comparable pre-ECL contracts called for prepayment. This decline indicated that customers were increasingly less willing to bear the risk of the producer's nonperformance. In a recognition of their own autonomy, purchasers realized that the cost of the producer's failure to perform would not be covered by the state. In addition, the decline in preperformance payments suggests that producers increasingly recognized that their protection against the risk of the customer's failure to pay lay in the enforceability of the contract. Thus, declines in preperformance payments indicated that producer/sellers and customers recognized increasingly their own autonomy to bear the benefits and costs of economic transactions, and also were willing to rely on the enforceability of contract rights and obligations as the basis for managing their commercial risks.

The recognition of contract autonomy was also evident in the increased reporting on the use of contract clauses aimed at enforcement of contract rights: arbitration and guarantee clauses that reflected an expanded presumption that contract rights and obligations were independently enforceable. Thus, in case no. 114, a contract was reported as containing an arbitration clause.[10] In case no. 108, the lessor of an automobile required the lessee to arrange for a guarantor to assure payment in the event the lessee was unable to make the payments required by the contract.[11] These clauses reflected the view that the risks and responsibility for nonperformance lay with the contracting parties, rather than with external entities that might cover the costs of nonperformance. By their use of these clauses through which contract performance and related remedies would be secured from the contracting parties, economic actors expressed increased confidence in contract autonomy.

The expansion in the supports for contract autonomy was also evident in the continued growth in transactional diversity. In addition to purchase and sale transactions, contracts were used to express terms and conditions for guarantees (case nos. 108 and 128), transportation (case no. 109), termination of joint venture (case no. 129), and manufacturing (case nos. 130 and 131). The contracts reported involved a wide range of products, including miscellaneous equipment (e.g., case nos. 100, 107, 112, 118, 119, and 130), bamboo gangplanks (case no. 110), poplar seedlings (case no. 113), calcium superphosphate (case no. 115), and food products (case nos. 116 and 121).

Economic actors also varied. Although factories continued to be the dominant economic actors entering into contracts, cases were reported of contracts formed by stores and materials outlets (case nos. 112, 114, 115, 121, 126, 128); a mine (no. 129); a printing plant (no. 99); a textile mill (no. 104); management offices (nos. 109, 110, and 113); shipping companies (nos. 109 and 111). This diversity indicated the expanding scope of contract autonomy.

In addition, individuals began to emerge as contracting parties in industrial and commercial transactions following enactment of the ECL. In one case, an individual contracted to manufacture a piece of machinery for a certain factory in Nanjing (no. 131), while in another an individual peasant contracted to put up funds to be used by a factory to manufacture an automobile, which then would be turned over to the individual (case no. 103). While contracts continued to be used predominantly in transactions between enterprises, the gradual emergence of individuals as parties to contracts was significant as an indicator of the scope of application of the economic rights being conferred under the ECL.

Thus, the formation of industrial and commercial contracts after the ECL went into effect revealed that contract practice was increasingly supportive of autonomous contract rights. Pre-existing support for contract autonomy such as direct negotiations between the parties and the use of interregional contracting expanded. In addition the discontinuation of preperformance payments suggested expanding confidence in and reliance on contract rights. The use of arbitration clauses and guarantee provisions represented further recognition of contract rights by expressing the presumption of the validity of enforcement measures. Transactional diversity continued to indicate the reach of the emerging contract autonomy.

Lack of External Supervision As an Obstacle to Contract Autonomy. The single major obstacle to autonomy in the formation of commercial and industrial contracts following enactment of the ECL was the continued absence of external supervision. In none of the industrial and commercial contracts reported as being formed following the ECL was either notarization or certification discussed. In the only case where supervision over contract formation was mentioned, the contract was subject to internal management approval. In the midst of official efforts to encourage external supervision of contracts through certification and notarization, the absence of external supervision in the case reporting is significant.

The absence of references to certification and notarization in case reporting on formation of commercial and industrial contracts can be ascribed largely to doctrinal inconsistencies concerning the role of external supervision. Such inconsistencies made it difficult to reform pre-existing practices favoring internal supervision. As a result, contract formation remained subject to the influence of personal and organizational factors unrelated to the transaction itself. The influence of these factors, which might have been diluted with expanded use of external supervision, impeded contract autonomy.

Thus, the operational record concerning formation of commercial and industrial contracts suggested that a number of significant factors were supporting increased expansion of contract autonomy, despite the continued absence of external supervision. These were continued reliance on direct negotiations and interregional contracting, the increased use of arbitration and guarantee clauses intended to put the risks of performance on the contracting parties themselves, and the decline in preperformance payments. As a result, although the absence of external supervision may cause economic actors to be unable (or unwilling) to accept totally the autonomy of the contract formation process, economic actors are likely to increase reliance on the autonomy of contracts, once formed, as a basis for asserting contract rights independent of collective interests.

Summary of Factors Affecting Recognition of Autonomous Contract Rights

The circumstances relating to contract formation as described in Chinese case reports suggest that the recognition of contract autonomy expanded following the enactment of the ECL. Economic actors gained a measure of autonomy to engage in increasingly independent transactional activity freed from external organizational controls. The changing content of contract clauses indicated that economic actors increasingly recognized this autonomy. However, as a result of doctrinal uncertainties borne of political and organizational rivalries, a continued lack of external supervision over contract formation was evident. This remained a significant obstacle to the full emergence of contract autonomy.

The operational aspects of contract activity with respect to the recognition of contract rights did not, however, represent a major departure from the doctrinal norms. The authority to enter into contracts and the autonomy to carry them out indicated that these features of contract doctrine were exercised. The absence of external supervision was not directly counter to doctrinal requirements, since the doctrine itself was uncertain as to the methods and institutions for contract supervision. Thus, the mix of supports for and obstacles to recognition of contract rights followed fairly closely the doctrinal pronouncements related to the ECL.

The general consistency between the doctrinal and the operational aspects of contract formation resulted in economic actors achieving in practice the autonomy described in doctrine. Such consistency permits the economic actors to identify the new norms of autonomy espoused under the ECL. To the extent that these new norms suit the interests of economic actors, they may recognize the value in such norms and come to rely on them in the formation and performance of contracts. The absence of external supervision need not be an obstacle to such recognition, since it is both consistent with doctrinal discussions and in harmony with traditional aspects of Chinese economic activity. Thus, even as economic actors continue to defer to external relationships in the formation of contracts, the willingness of economic actors to view the contract as an expression of enforceable rights borne of reciprocal obligations is likely to become stronger.

However, this will depend on the extent to which contract rights are enforced in dispute resolution. Although the doctrine of the ECL promotes such enforcement, the operational record must be examined to determine whether the doctrinal views are being carried out in practice. Accordingly, the operational record concerning dispute resolution is examined in chapter 4.

CHAPTER 4

Dispute Resolution and the Enforcement of Contract Rights

The operation of contract dispute resolution provides a basis for comparing doctrinal views and operational practices with regard to the role of contract law and on the institutions and processes of dispute settlement. This chapter focuses on the processes and outcomes of contract dispute resolution to explore the supports for and obstacles to contract autonomy in the enforcement of contract rights.

The factors giving rise to contract disputes reveal attitudes by contracting parties about the binding nature of contract obligations and the role of contract law in enforcing such obligations. Failures of performance may indicate that the contract relationship is perceived as secondary to personal and organizational relationships or other collective concerns. Such attitudes permit these concerns to take precedence over the obligations expressed in the contract, thus undermining contract autonomy by making contract performance dependent on factors external to the contract relationship.

The institutions and processes for dispute resolution reveal the extent to which doctrinal views on compulsory dispute resolution are carried out in practice. This has implications for the actual enforcement of autonomous contract rights. In addition, the extent to which the rules guiding dispute resolution processes are identified and explained indicate how contract law operates in practice as a basis for enforcement of contract rights. The results of dispute resolution show the ability of contract law and dispute resolution processes to enforce contract obligations.

The operational record on the origins of contract disputes and the processes and outcomes of dispute resolution offer insights as to the supports for and obstacles to the recognition and enforcement of autonomous contract rights. The consistency of these operational characteristics with the doctrinal views examined previously provide an indication of the potential for the dispute resolution provisions of the ECL to acquire practical legitimacy and thus to support the emergence of autonomous contract rights.

Pre-ECL Contracts

Agricultural Contracts

Support for Autonomous Enforcement of Contract Rights. Of the fifteeen pre-ECL agricultural contract cases reported, eleven were submitted for resolution by the courts, while four were submitted for resolution by SAIC organs. Of the cases taken to court, five were resolved through mediation, three resulted in adjudicated decisions and one was resolved through arbitration. Two of the disputes had not been resolved at the time of reporting. This pattern of reliance on the courts as institutions for dispute resolution indicated support for autonomous dispute resolution, as the courts had fewer organizational ties to the contracting parties than did the enterprise management offices and SAIC organs. Accordingly, judicial contract dispute resolution processes could be insulated better from outside influences. Thus, reliance on the courts represented a basis for expanding autonomy in the enforcement of contract rights.

Of the fifteen case reports involving pre-ECL agricultural contracts, the ECL was cited as the basis for resolution in six. This was despite each of the contracts at issue being formed prior to the law's effective date, so they technically were not subject to the ECL's rules.[1] The PRC constitution also was cited as support for enforcement of contract rights (case no. 2), and in another case, specific reference was made to Sichuan regulations on rural commerce (no. 14). Thus, in over half of the pre-ECL cases reported, the published decision contained reference to specific regulations.

Such reliance on fixed rules in the settlement of disputes worked to limit the discretion of dispute resolution bodies in reaching decisions, thus providing an important foundation for the predictability of the enforcement process. This predictability in turn supports the autonomy of the process, as regular citations to legal rules inhibit arbitrary intrusions. Tribunals bound by specific rules have less ability to tailor decisions to satisfy priorities unrelated to the contract transaction in dispute. Thus, citation to legal authority for dispute resolution decisions supported the autonomy of the dispute resolution process by focusing the enforcement of contract rights on the circumstances of the transactions in dispute rather than on external factors.

Monetary remedies consisting of compensation and/or penalties were imposed in nine of the twelve cases reported regarding pre-ECL agricultural contract disputes where a remedy was specified. In two of the cases (nos. 13 and 14) the party in breach was ordered to pay penalties in addition to compensation for losses caused by nonperformance. In every case where monetary remedies were imposed the party in breach was a state entity. Four of these cases were resolved through administrative investigation by the SAIC, which at the time was a relatively new organization, eager to establish its authority as an interagency control body in part by imposing on other government units monetary sanctions for nonperformance of contracts. Although these organizational motives may have been a factor, the case reports reveal a general willingness to impose monetary remedies for nonperformance of agricultural contracts.

The reliance on monetary remedies reflected both an emphasis on enforcement of contract obligations and a recognition of the increased autonomy of contracting parties. Enforceability was encouraged through the application of monetary penalties for nonperformance, rather than administrative sanctions or specific performance. Measurement of the cost of nonperformance in monetary terms permitted this cost to be imposed on the party in breach alone, which also indicated recognition of the autonomy of the aggrieved party, who but for the use of monetary remedies would bear alone the cost of nonperformance.

Obstacles to Enforcement of Contract Rights. A major obstacle to the recognition of contract autonomy lay in the disregard by state officials of their reciprocal obligations under agricultural production responsibility contracts. In all but two of the contract disputes involving production responsibility contracts formed prior to the enactment of the ECL, the contract was violated by the brigade or team cadre(s). The reasons for such violations were commonly ascribed to the "red eye disease" (*hong yan bing*), the problem of local cadres or other commune members who opposed the use of responsibility contracts because of jealousy over the increased private income derived. In one case where a group of six commune members had contracted to manage an orchard, the brigade party secretary canceled the contract and announced over the brigade loudspeaker that the other peasants should take over the orchard (case no. 10). In some cases the local cadres went so far as to incite peasants actually to attack the contracting peasants and drive them off the contracted land (case no. 2). Other causes for violation of responsibility contracts involved personal quarrels between contracting peasants and local cadres. In one case, a peasant contracted for responsibility over a pork shop but the contract was canceled by the head of the production team. Upon examination by the court, it was determined that the real reasons for the cancellation included the team head's disgruntlement over a private quarrel with the peasant (case no. 7). Each of these cases revealed significant opposition by local cadres to the increased autonomy granted under agricultural responsibility contracts.

In addition, local cadres nullified contracts to secure favor with persons unrelated to the transaction. In one instance (case no. 8), the local cadres unilaterally transferred the contract property from the original contractors to a second group with whom the cadres had a better personal relationship, which showed the intrusion of political factors into the contract relationship.

In some cases, contracts were unilaterally canceled due to changes in the needs of the brigade or team with which the agreement was signed. Thus, in one case (case no. 5), a peasant contracted to manage a reed pond, and the production team agreed to purchase a specific quantity of the reeds produced. The peasant was authorized to retain any proceeds from sales of reeds in excess of the amount promised to the team. Subsequently, however, the production team cadre determined that the quantity of reeds that the team had promised to buy exceeded the team's needs. Thereupon the cadre informed the producer that the reeds already produced were not needed and sought to cancel the contract. This type of circumstance indicated that local cadres did not recognize in practice the reciprocity of the obligations formalized in contracts.

Frequent failures of performance of agricultural procurement contracts revealed disregard of contract obligations by both peasant producers and state procurement entities. In contrast to the production responsibility contracts, however, violations of procurement contracts were evenly split between the producers and the procurement agencies.

For example, in case no. 11 concerning a procurement contract for the production of chickens, the procurement agency in Jiajiang County, Sichuan, where the producer was located, intervened and blocked the sale to the procurement agency in Leshan city (also in Sichuan) on grounds that the needs of Jiajiang County should be satisfied before goods could be sent to Leshan. Subsequently, the Leshan procuring agency canceled the contract without notice. In case no. 12, the Leshan procurement agency unilaterally terminated a contract with a producer in Jiajiang due to changes in the market demand for chickens. The contract termination in the second case was almost certainly a retaliatory response to the intervention in the first case, although the case reporting does not specify this. These types of circumstances where state entities intervened to block performance of procurement contracts revealed the consequences from competition for scarce resources among various procurement and supervisory organs and indicated that state cadres did not accept fully the binding nature of contract obligations.

Producers also were the cause for nonperformance of procurement contracts. For example, a contract for onion production was breached when the production brigade that had contracted to produce the goods failed to deliver to the state procurement agency as specified in the contract (case no. 13). The brigade had overfulfilled the contract, producing 1,500,000 kilos under a contract quota of 550,000 kilos but sold the entire lot to related units both inside and outside the province. The profit motive underlying the brigade's breach was clear, since it could have fulfilled its contract and still had 95,000 kilos remaining to sell elsewhere. The brigade's breach revealed the degree to which the responsibility system and its permissive rules on peasant income were stimulating peasant efforts to accumulate wealth, even to the detriment of contract performance.

The producer was also at fault in the nonperformance of a contract for procurement of tangerines (case no. 14). Here again the producer sold the contracted goods outside the province rather than delivering them to local procurement organs according to the contract. In this case the producer's breach netted it almost 20,000 yuan in profit. Both the effect of the profit motive and the expanded possibilities of interprovincial trade were evident in the events surrounding the breach of this contract.

Problems related to the use of compulsory dispute resolution presented additional obstacles to the enforcement of autonomous contract rights. Of the fifteen pre-ECL contracts where the method of dispute resolution was specified, although the majority were submitted to the courts for resolution, only four were resolved through compulsory dispute settlement processes, comprised of either adjudication or arbitration. Reliance on consensual dispute resolution adversely affected the enforceability of contracts. In one case (no. 7), the head of the production team who had unlawfully terminated a peasant's responsibility contract refused continually to accept the mediation decision of the local court and finally complied only after being prevailed upon three times and after the contract was reformed to satisfy the team head's basic complaints.

Contract enforcement was affected by uncertainty (tinged with reluctance) of court officials to use compulsory methods in resolving contract disputes. In one case where compulsory resolution was applied for, the aggrieved party had sought court action to enforce the contract but the court had refused to take the case (no. 1). In another, the court sought instructions as to whether to accept a case involving a responsibility contract (case no. 2). The circumstances surrounding these inquiries suggested reluctance to rely on compulsory dispute resolution mechanisms in the enforcement of contract rights.

In addition, courts faced obstacles in enforcing their decisions. In one case for example (no. 8), the head of a production brigade in Zhejiang terminated a contract under which a group of peasants was given responsibility for an orchard, giving the orchard to another group under a new contract. Upon being ordered by the county court to reinstate the original contract, the brigade head responded by distributing a letter criticizing the court's decision and claiming that the county committee agreed with these criticisms.

Thus, the pattern of circumstances underlying disputes over agricultural contracts revealed that despite some supporting factors, major obstacles to the recognition and enforcement of autonomous contract rights were evident. The performance of contract obligations often depended on political and economic factors external to the transaction. The problem of local cadres violating production responsibility contracts suggested that the structural inequality of the parties to these agreements provided opportunities for cadres to elevate their political dominance over the rights conferred under the contract.

On the other hand, economic motives were dominant forces in nonperformance of agricultural procurement contracts. The willingness of contracting parties to disregard contract obligations as a result of external factors indicated attitudinal obstacles to the acceptance of the binding nature of contract obligations. This in turn represented an obstacle to the autonomy of contract rights, as these became secondary to priorities external to the contract transaction. In addition, despite the increased role of the courts as institutions for dispute resolution, the continued prominence of consensual methods for resolving contract disputes represented an obstacle to enforcement of contract rights.

Pre-ECL Industrial and Commercial Contracts

Support for Autonomous Enforcement of Contract Rights. The courts were active in handling contract disputes in industry and commerce as well as those in agriculture. Of the fifty-seven case reports involving pre-ECL industrial and commercial contracts where the method of resolution was specified, the dispute was submitted for resolution to the courts in forty-five (79%). Although twenty-two of these cases involved court-sponsored mediation and negotiation, the involvement of the courts as institutions indicated support for autonomous resolution of contract disputes. The role of the courts as enforcement bodies was also evident in the context of compulsory enforcement of mediation decisions (e.g., case nos. 51 and 75). As institutions without organizational ties to the disputants, the courts provided disinterested dispute resolution to a greater degree than was possible with the enterprise management offices and SAIC organs. Thus, the use of the courts represented important support for the autonomous enforcement of contract rights.

Reliance on specific citations to legal or regulatory authority was evident in eight of the seventeen proposed solutions to disputes about which inquiries to legal advice columns were submitted. Reference was made to a variety of regulations including the 1981 Provisional Rules on Contracts For Industrial and Mining Goods (three cases); the 1979 Joint Circular on Certain Issues Concerning the Management of Contracts (two cases); the 1963 Provisional Regulations on the Basic Provisions in Ordering Contracts For Factory and Mining Goods (two cases); the 1979 Provisional Rules On Construction, Installation, and Engineering Contracts and the 1979 Opinion on Carrying Out the Contract System in Capital Construction (one case); and the 1982 Circular on Implementing the ECL (one case).[2] One proposal also made reference to various unspecified regulations of the Ministry of Transportation.

These references to specific regulations were not confined to responses to judicial inquiries, as half of them were addressed to the actual party to a dispute. In addition, specific regulatory citations were provided in twenty-two of the forty-nine reports where a final result was reached. Such efforts to inform disputants of the applicable contract rules indicated the recognition of the need for access by economic actors to the rules by which contract rights would be identified and enforced. Such explanations suggested that contract rules would be applied uniformly to economic actors on the basis of their contract transactions, rather than their external relationships. This revealed a recognition of the autonomy of economic actors, and supported increased awareness by economic actors that they were possessed of enforceable rights. This indicated further the extent to which the discretion of dispute resolution bodies was becoming limited and subjected to formalized rules for recognizing and enforcing rights.

Obstacles to Enforcement of Contract Rights. The most significant obstacle to the enforcement of contract rights lay in the attitudes of contracting parties that disregarded the binding force of the contract. The majority of pre-ECL industrial and commercial contracts were breached as a result of nonperformance or incorrect performance by the supplier of goods. Of the sixty-six pre-ECL industrial and commercial contract cases reported, eighteen were breached due to nonpayment, and eighteen involved either late delivery or nondelivery. An additional fifteen of the cases involved imperfect performance by delivery of nonconforming goods.

The failures of suppliers to perform contracts is particularly noteworthy in view of the prominence of agreements under which payment was required prior to delivery. That such contracts continued to be used despite the knowledge by customer units that producers were often unable to meet the conditions specified in contracts suggested that purchasing units were not altogether concerned with strict performance and were confident that they would not be required to bear the cost of nonperformance. This also revealed an attitude of contract parties that their contract obligations were subject to operational capabilities that might take precedence over the contract terms. These factors indicated that contracting parties did not perceive the contract relationship as autonomous, but rather as dependent on the external personal and organizational relationships through which the parties operated.

The failure of the manufacturer to deliver goods that conformed to the contract specifications was also a common problem, suggesting that the negotiation of these contracts was undertaken without ample investigation into the production capabilities of the manufacturer. The instances of nonpayment suggested both that contracts were formed without prior assurances of the customers' ability to pay the contract price, and that the concept that the contract created a binding payment obligation was not yet fully accepted.

In four cases, nonperformance resulted from changes in the local market situation that made resale of the contracted goods unprofitable for the contract purchaser. In two of these cases, the seller's delivery was not timely and the purchaser, deprived of the favorable market conditions that had existed at the contract delivery date but which later faded, was unable to resell the goods. Thus in one case, a Zhejiang company ordered air freshener (*weisheng xiang*) from a company in Dalian, Liaoning, the goods to be delivered before the spring festival (case no. 69). Delivery was not made until after the holiday and the purchasing company, unable to resell the goods, refused to pay the Dalian supplier. In a similar case, a purchase and sale contract between two Henan companies called for delivery of a tractor by September, in time for the fall harvest. (Case No. 41). However delivery was delayed until the end of December. Consequently, the purchaser, unable to resell in time for the fall harvest, refused to tender payment. In two other cases (case nos. 52, 81), the purchaser's refusal to make payment had less justification. In these cases, the purchaser simply refused to pay the contract price because the market situation had changed to the detriment of the purchaser.

Herein lay both the challenge to and the necessity for contracts as the basis for economic activity. For to the extent that they lend some measure of predictability to particular transactions, fixed contracts could be used to the advantage of economic actors who were able to forecast accurately market changes. However market-based contracts also faced the risk of serious losses arising from mistaken assumptions as to market changes. Thus, the inserting of market-based contracts into an economic tradition of state planning inexperienced with business forecasting brought with it the potential for uneven distribution of benefits. This in turn raised the issue of whether the strict enforcement of contract terms would be permitted to exacerbate these inequalities.

Government intervention was a direct contributor to nonperformance in thirteen cases. Of these, three involved direct intervention by an administrative agency, as, for instance, when the county office of the State Administration for Industry and Commerce acted to halt a shipment of reed mats that the bureau concluded were not permitted to be sold under private contract between enterprises (no. 53). A similar case involved a contract for the sale of coal and coke (case no. 74), where administrative officials refused to permit delivery on grounds that it would violate state controls on coal distribution. A contract for the sale of hospital beds was not performed when the bank of the purchasing unit refused to make payment on grounds that the sale was in violation of regulations restricting the supply and distribution of these goods (case no. 58). In yet another case (no. 79), the local government organ declared that a store that had contracted for the purchase of cigarettes was being managed illegally. Thereupon, the government organ transferred management of the store to a government-operated service company, which then refused to tender the contract price.

In addition, changes in the state plan affected contract performance. In case no. 34, a Shanghai instrument factory contracted to supply meters designed according to the specific requirements of an outside factory. Due to plan changes pursuant to the 1979–80 policy of economic readjustment, the outside factory no longer needed the meters and refused to take delivery. Reductions in operating capital caused the purchaser to fail performance of a contract for the purchase of light trucks (case no. 72), while cutbacks in raw materials allocations caused a pickled vegetables factory to refuse to take delivery as promised under a contract for the purchase of earthenware jugs (case no. 39).

Although the courts played a prominent role in resolution of disputes over commercial and industrial contracts, consensual methods of resolution remained dominant. Of the forty-five case reports in which the courts were involved, the result in twenty-two (49%) was reached through consensual methods. Of the fifty-seven cases reported where the method of resolution was specified, thirty-three (58%) were resolved through mediation or negotiation. The dominance of consensual dispute resolution permitted the personal and organizational relationships of the parties to affect the outcome, thus undermining contract autonomy. In addition, monetary remedies were seldom imposed in cases of nonperformance. Of the forty-six disputes involving pre-ECL contracts where a remedy was specified, thirty-three (72%) resulted only in orders requiring specific performance, permitting substituted or partial performance, or granting restitution. None of these remedies measured the cost of nonperformance in monetary terms, and none compensated the aggrieved party for the cost of nonperformance.

Thus, despite the increased role of judicial organs and their willingness to rely on specific contract rules, the general pattern of dispute resolution regarding pre-ECL industrial and commercial contracts revealed a number of significant obstacles to autonomous enforcement of contract rights. Disregard of contract obligations, state intervention, reliance on consensual dispute resolution and the absence of monetary remedies all represented barriers to the recognition and enforcement of autonomous contract rights.

The operational aspects of dispute resolution relating to agricultural, industrial, and commercial contracts formed prior to the enactment of the ECL revealed significant obstacles to enforcement of autonomous contract rights. Disregard of contract obligations was evident across a wide segment of economic actors, reflecting the influence of political as well as economic factors on contract performance. Government intervention was particularly a factor in nonperformance of industrial and commercial contracts. Although the use of monetary remedies was more in evidence in agricultural contracts, the absence of compulsory dispute resolution mechanisms was evident in reporting of disputes regarding both categories of contracts. Thus, despite positive factors such as the availability of the courts to oversee dispute resolution and the publication of contract rules, the obstacles to contract autonomy were more in evidence.

The obstacles to enforcement of autonomous contract rights prior to the enactment of the ECL reflected the resilience of pre-existing collectivist norms despite policy pronouncements urging stronger enforcement of contracts. The ECL was intended in part to overcome these by its emphasis on compulsory dispute settlement and penalities for nonperformance of contracts.

Post-ECL Contracts

Agricultural Contracts

Support for Autonomous Enforcement of Contract Rights. The case reports on resolution of agricultural contract disputes following enactment of the ECL reflected increased emphasis on the use of compulsory dispute resolution. Of the thirteen disputes involving post-ECL contracts, six were resolved through compulsory dispute settlement. Aside from four disputes that went directly to adjudication, one of the post-ECL contract disputes was resolved through judicial arbitration while an additional case was handled by SAIC arbitration following an attempt at mediation.

The increased reliance on the courts reflected that the economic chambers of the people's courts, established down to the county level, were replacing local citizens' mediation committees and permitted reliance on more compulsory methods. Thus, of the six disputes resolved through compulsory dispute resolution, four were brought directly to court without prior mediation efforts. Adjudication also represented an alternative to the arbitration functions of the SAIC. Whereas four of eleven disputes involving pre-ECL contracts were handled through SAIC investigation, only two of thirteen post-ECL contracts were submitted to SAIC, one for investigation (case no. 19) and one for arbitration (case no. 29).

In addition, courts were increasingly used to enforce contract obligations where other methods had proved unavailing. In one case in Henan for example (case no. 24), a production brigade cadre who had unilaterally violated a responsibility contract held by a group of peasants for the operation of a brick kiln refused to comply with the directives of the county vice-secretary and the county party committee to perform the contract without further obstruction. The issue ultimately was brought to the county court, which ordered the cadre to pay compensation and fines and to be removed from his position.

In another case (no. 27), a production responsibility contract was violated by the local party branch secretary who then transferred the contracting peasants to another unit and made public announcements to the effect that the contract was terminated. Here, court resolution was the only way the contracting peasants had any hope of relief. These cases indicate not only that the courts were becoming increasingly involved in the enforcement of agricultural responsibility contracts but also that as newly established institutions, often staffed with outsiders, the courts offered the only avenue for challenging abuses of power by entrenched local officials.

Increased reliance on adjudication in resolving contract disputes was consistent with the doctrinal views on compulsory dispute resolution. The rise in the number of agricultural contract disputes that were resolved through compulsory dispute resolution resulted in part from the increased autonomy of the peasantry and of a concomitant increase in their willingness to seek protection of those interests. As reforms in agricultural policy permitted the retention of profits and required that individuals bear responsibility for economic losses, the incentive grew to push for favorable solutions to economic disputes. The ECL's provision on direct adjudication[3] provided the means by which these interests could be realized. In addition, the use of the courts helped to insulate dispute resolution processes from external influences and so strengthened the autonomy of contract rights.

In nine of the fifteen cases involving post-ECL agricultural contracts, reference was made to specific regulations, representing a slight increase over the record regarding pre-ECL contracts. Reference was made to the ECL as a source for protection of contract rights in seven responses to inquiries involving post-ECL agricultural contracts. Such reliance on regulatory citations as authority for dispute resolution reflected a continued effort to control the dispute settlement process and thus the autonomy of processes for rights enforcement. Reliance on fixed rules also worked to bolster the authority of dispute resolution organs themselves, as their decisions gained legitimacy from the predictability brought on by reliance on fixed rules. These factors were also strengthened by their consistency with doctrinal views on the role of contract law in recognizing and enforcing contract rights.

Obstacles to Enforcement of Contract Rights. Attitudinal obstacles to the recognition of autonomous contract rights continued despite enactment of the ECL. As with contracts formed before the ECL went into effect, the majority of breaches of responsibility contracts were committed by local cadres. In one case for example (no. 20), the team leader tore up a three-year contract giving to a group of peasants responsibility for a flour mill and led other peasants to break into the mill, remove tools, and distribute the flour to other commune members. The contract had been certified by the production-brigade management committee and the contracting peasants had attempted to make remittance of the two-hundred yuan profit for the first year as required by the contract. The team head refused to accept the payment, insisting instead on canceling the contract. In another case (no. 21), a group of peasants signed a water supply contract for the operation of a mill that they had contracted to repair and operate. After four days of operation, the local management office shut off the water without warning or justification.

Cases were also reported of cadres unilaterally increasing the obligations of contracting peasants as a condition for not canceling their contracts. For example (case no. 24), a group of peasants contracted for operation of a brick kiln for three years. The contract was notarized. When the contract had still two years to run, the local cadre required the peasants to accept additional duties including increased remittance under the contract, paying the costs of digging a new well, repairing a spillway bridge, and repairing six common buildings. Acceptance of these new tasks was required for the contracting peasants to be permitted to continue working under their contract. In another case (no. 17), the local supply and marketing organ attempted to cancel in midstream a contract by which a group of peasants undertook responsibility for management of a hotel. Cadre violations of more conventional agricultural production contracts also were reported. In Shanghai, a peasant had undertaken to raise chickens under a one-year contract (case no. 25), but barely six months after signing, the brigade cadre renounced the contract and tried to transfer it to three other peasants.

These cases illustrate the continued disregard by local officials of the binding character of contract obligations.[4] In each case, attempts to cancel contracts derived from the political relationships of local cadres. This indicated that, despite official policy pronouncements and a high degree of doctrinal unity supporting enforceability of contracts, contract performance remained subject to external factors unrelated to the contract transaction. This suggested that doctrinal views on the autonomy of the contract relationship were not yet fully in practice.

Nonperformance of agricultural procurement contracts also remained a problem following enactment of the ECL, although the reasons tended to be economic rather than political. Violations of procurement contracts were tied explicitly to falling market prices for the contracted goods in each of the procurement contracts reported (case nos. 19, 29, and 30). In one case, the procurement agency that had contracted for the purchase of chickens found itself unable to sell them due to the drop in market price and simply refused to take delivery or pay the contract price (no. 30). In a case involving the procurement of salted cauliflower, (no. 29) the procuring agency demanded a reduction of the purchase because of falling market prices. The contract for tangerine procurement (case no. 19) was not performed because the grower had found it more profitable to sell the goods elsewhere than to the purchasing agent under the contract.

The prevalence of economic rather than political factors in attempts to cancel contracts reflected a greater equality among the parties. For as opposed to the responsibility contract, where the team or brigade had the power (if not the authority) to reclaim the peasants' means of production, the procurement contracts involved a situation in which the procuring agency had little control over the producers' means of production and hence nonperformance took the form of refusal to pay or to take delivery. The procuring agency's bargaining power still overshadowed that of the producing peasants, and its ability to withstand the producer's continued demands for payment suggested continued inequality between the parties to this type of contract. Yet the distribution of responsibility for nonperformance of procurement contracts reflected growing parity between producers and procuring agents.

The effect of economic factors such as price changes on agricultural procurement contracts revealed the conflict between the autonomy espoused by doctrinal support for contract enforceability and a reluctance to accept responsibility for such autonomy in the face of market-based pricing uncertainties.

Despite the involvement of the courts in resolution of contract disputes, the use of monetary remedies for contract violations declined. Of the thirteen post-ECL agricultural contract disputes reported where a final resolution was made, only six (46%) resulted in monetary remedies. This contrasted poorly with the pre-ECL contracts, where monetary remedies were awarded in 75 percent of the cases reported as resulting in final decisions. Specific performance was the primary remedy awarded in cases of contract nonperformance. Responsibility for nonperformance was not placed individually on the party in breach; rather the other party continued to share the cost. This indicated that the contracting parties were not yet viewed as fully autonomous, since the cost of nonperformance continued to be shared among them. This undermined contract enforcement as well as contract autonomy. The failure of local courts to impose monetary remedies conflicted with doctrinal views supporting their use. This inconsistency poses an obstacle to the acceptance by the peasantry of the ECL as an effective basis for asserting their private economic rights.

In the resolution of disputes involving agricultural contracts up through mid-1984 several trends were evident. First, there was continued reliance on judicial institutions. Reliance on specific contract rules including the ECL continued, as dispute settlement bodies endeavored to explain and justify the legal bases for dispute resolution decisions. These factors were fairly consistent with doctrinal views on the role of contract law and the methods to be used in dispute resolution. Such consistency strengthened the prospect for legitimation of the ECL as a basis for recognizing and enforcing contract rights.

Problems remained, however. Continued disregard of contract obligations, particularly by state officials and units, represented a serious problem to the legitimacy of the ECL as it conflicted directly with doctrinal views urging the enforcement of contracts. An emerging reluctance to impose monetary remedies for nonperformance of contracts indicated further inability to carry out doctrinal views in practice. These failures by state organs—cadres, state procurement companies, and courts—to implement doctrinal views on contract enforceability and monetary remedies posed a significant obstacle to acceptance by rural economic actors of the legitimacy of the ECL.

Industrial and Commercial Contracts

Support for Autonomous Enforcement of Contract Rights. The courts remained prominent in handling disputes concerning post-ECL industrial and commercial contracts. Of the twenty-three cases reported where the method of resolution was specified, seventeen (74%) were submitted for court action. Thirteen of these underwent adjudication (of which two settled prior to decision), while the courts used mediation to resolve four of the cases. Two additional disputes were resolved through the SAIC and in one case the SAIC office investigated and then referred the case to "judicial organs for handling." The courts thus continued to be involved as disinterested dispute resolution bodies. In addition, the courts relied increasingly on compulsory dispute settlement methods. The continued use of the courts and the increase in compulsory dispute resolution were consistent with doctrinal views and supported autonomous enforcement of contract rights.

Citation to legal authority increased in connection with legal adviser column discussions of disputes concerning post-ECL commercial and industrial contracts. In ten of the twelve responses by the legal adviser columns, reference was made to specific regulations as the basis for resolution of the dispute. In addition to references to the ECL, the regulatory citations focused on the 1981 regulations for factory and mining goods contracts, particularly Article 31, concerning responsibilities for nonperformance. Reference was also made to provisions of these regulations requiring strict adherence to contract provisions on quality and price. Of the references to the ECL, three dealt with the prohibition on unilateral change or cancellation of contracts, while one cited two different provisions of the law on the responsibilities for nonperformance. Issues concerning the processes for contract formation did arise in a few instances, but the bulk of the analysis and legal authorities presented concerned the rights of contracting parties to have their agreement enforced as written. The increased citation to legal authority indicated efforts to disseminate and popularize contract rules.

An additional factor supporting autonomy in industrial and commercial contract dispute resolution was the role of lawyers. Five of the twenty-three post-ECL contracts reported were resolved by lawyer mediation, as opposed to the use of lawyer mediation in five of thirty reported disputes involving pre-ECL contracts (see e.g., case nos. 96 and 113). Although they often assisted in consensual resolution of disputes through mediation, lawyers strengthened autonomy of contracting parties during the course of dispute resolution. By retaining lawyers to advocate their individual interests, economic actors were able to free themselves from the dominance of their organizational superiors during mediation. Lawyers represented a resource by which economic actors could assert their own interests over those of the collective, thus furthering their autonomy.

Lawyers often displayed initiative and zeal in furthering their clients' interests. In one case (no. 58), which involved a contract signed in 1979 but which dragged on without resolution until March 1983, the lawyer represented a county medical institute in Gansu in its efforts to retrieve payment for the sale of spring beds to a medical school in neighboring Shaanxi. The lawyer convinced the local office of the Ministry of Finance to issue a waiver so that the beds, originally subject to state monopoly, could be transferred and paid for under the contract. In another instance (case no. 114), the lawyer for one of the contracting parties used the time-honored method of achieving a settlement by threatening litigation against a supplier who had failed to deliver goods according to a purchase and sale contract. In yet another case (no. 130), the lawyer also used the threat of litigation to convince a purchaser to withdraw a refusal to take delivery of goods produced by the lawyer's client under a manufacturing contract.

In part the growing role of lawyer mediation was made possible by the increasingly publicized rules governing contracts. For as the parties to contracts—and particularly their legal advisers—gained more complete knowledge of the rules governing these transactions, there was less need to rely exclusively on judicial interpretations of the parties' contract rights. This provided broader avenues for economic actors to pursue their interests by seeking enforcement of these rights.

Obstacles to Enforcement of Contract Rights. The responsibility for nonperformance remained fairly equally divided between suppliers and customers party to industrial and commercial contracts after enactment of the ECL. Of the twenty-nine purchase and sale contracts reported, fifteen instances of breach involved either the refusal to accept goods or nonpayment by the customer. In seventeen cases reported, the supplier's failure to make delivery or to meet the quality requirements of the contract accounted for the breach. The relative balance of responsibility for nonperformance between producer/sellers and customers suggested that economic factors were a major cause of nonperformance. The uncertainties of market-based transactions were particularly evident in cases where the purchaser failed to tender the contract price for goods delivered because falling market prices made resale unprofitable (see e.g., case no. 97). In certain cases, the purchaser was unable to resell the goods due to falling demand (see e.g., case no. 110).

In seven cases, the validity of the contract itself was challenged. One of these involved an attempt simply to deny the validity of an oral contract (case no. 103). In another (case no. 117), a mistake was made in drafting the contract when the width of a lot of flagstones was written as fifteen meters instead of fifteen centimeters. The length of the flagstones was also stated incorrectly in square meters. These errors were seized upon by one of the parties as grounds for invalidating the agreement.

The acts of contract negotiators were themselves a source of problems with contract performance. In case no. 124, the agent was sent to purchase black oil (*hei you*) but instead of ordering the thirty kilos requested by his employer, the agent ordered one ton. The employer/purchaser denied liability on the contract on grounds that the agent had exceeded his authority and the agent ultimately bore liability for the excess he had ordered. In another case (no. 99), the validity of a contract for the sale of used equipment was challenged by the seller on the grounds that the official who had responsibility over the transaction was subsequently transferred and that the contract he had negotiated was no longer enforceable.

Thus, post-ECL industrial and commercial contracts continued to face problems of performance due to market uncertainties, attempts to deny contract obligations, agency difficulties, and other factors. Although the political factors evident in cases of nonperformance of agricultural production contracts were largely absent, the disregard for contract obligations in commercial and industrial transactions for external economic reasons indicated the extent of the challenge to put doctrinal norms of contract enforceability into operation.

State policies continued to affect performance of contracts in industry and commerce following enactment of the ECL. Changes in the state plan continued to lead directly to nonperformance of contract obligations. In one case (no. 111), a contract for the sale of ten-ton electric winches was canceled when the construction of the vessel on which the winches were to be used was canceled. In case no. 130, involving a contract for the supply of steel window frames, a change in the state plan eliminated the budgetary allocation that was to fund the purchaser's acquisition of the window frames. In both of these cases, the purchaser had no choice but to cancel the contract since the funds necessary for contract performance were reallocated.

Policy changes also had indirect effects on contract performance. In case no. 114 government import restrictions resulted indirectly in nonperformance of a contract for supply of polyester thread. The restrictions resulted in local shortages of thread, thus increasing the price that could be charged to a level well above the contract sales price. The supplier had stocks adequate to satisfy the contract requirements, but higher prices brought on by the local shortage made performance at a price agreed upon earlier less profitable. As a result, the supplier declined performance.

Although the courts continued to be heavily involved in dispute resolutions following enactment of the ECL, there was a continued reluctance to impose monetary remedies. Of the nineteen disputes over post-ECL commercial or industrial contracts where a final result was reported, fifteen resulted in either specific performance, substituted performance, or some other remedy that did nothing to compensate the aggrieved party's losses. As a result, the cost of nonperformance was not effectively shifted to the responsible party, which undermined contract enforceability and suggested lack of recognition of the autonomy of the contracting parties. Responsibility for nonperformance was not imposed on an individual autonomous basis. Moreover, the failure to relieve the aggrieved party of the cost of nonperformance also implied that such cost would be subsidized by external agencies, thus suggesting lack of recognition of the aggrieved party's autonomy as well.

In contrast to continued citations to legal authority in the legal adviser columns, such references were largely absent in reports of decisions on resolution of disputes involving industrial and commercial contracts after the ECL. Citation to legal authority was made in only six of twenty-three reports of decision. This suggested that although the courts were increasingly involved in dispute resolution, their decisions were to be tailored to the practical circumstances of the disputes before them, rather than being based strictly upon the provisions of the ECL and related regulations.

The absence of legal citations should be viewed in the context of the reluctance to implement the ECL's provisions on monetary remedies. As relatively new institutions, the courts in particular faced the challenge of ensuring compliance with their decisions,[5] which would be more problematic if they involved heavy monetary penalties. Thus, to build their authority without engendering insurmountable resistance, the courts were reluctant to impose monetary remedies in all cases. As this contradicted explicit provisions of the ECL, however, the judicial decision could be justified better without citation to specific legal authority.

Whatever the reason, the lack of citation to legal authority in reports of decisions potentially left the courts more vulnerable to outside influences, since it made judicial decisions more difficult to defend against challenges from organizations related to the disputants. Thus, the absence of citations to legal authority had the potential to undermine the authority of such decisions, and potentially undermine the autonomy and authority of the courts themselves.

The operational record concerning resolution of disputes over industrial and commercial contracts following enactment of the ECL indicated several factors supportive of contract autonomy: the continuing reliance on the courts in dispute resolution; and the increased role of lawyers as resources to advocate the autonomous interests of economic actors. However, problems remained regarding disregard of contract obligations, intrusion of state policy on contract relations, and the continued failure to provide monetary remedies in cases of breach of contract. These factors indicated that doctrinal pronouncements supporting contract autonomy were not being uniformly carried out in practice.

There were disparities in characteristics of dispute resolution between agriculture and industrial and commercial contracts following the enactment of the ECL. The disparities were evident both in the origins of disputes and in their resolution. External political factors appeared to influence performance of contracts more in agriculture than in industry or commerce. Consensual dispute settlement continued to be the norm in agricultural contracts, whereas compulsory dispute resolution was used more often in the resolution of industrial and commercial contract disputes. On the other hand, citation to legal authority was more evident in contract disputes in the agricultural sector than in disputes about industrial and commercial contracts. On balance, the prospects for enforcement of contract rights appeared stronger in the industrial and commercial sectors, even if the legal bases for such rights were not explained.

In all sectors, however, the continued reluctance to impose monetary sanctions for nonperformance meant that even where the parties were compelled to comply with the decision, the consequences of nonperformance were light. This tended to undercut the effect of the fairly uniform trend toward reliance on the courts. Although broader use of the courts represented the most consistent element of support for autonomy in decisions on contract dispute resolution, its effectiveness was undermined.

Summary of Operational Aspects of Enforcement of Contract Rights

This discussion has focused on the origins and also the processes and outcomes of dispute resolution in an effort to determine the circumstances in which the norms of the ECL with regard to enforcement of contract rights are presented for recognition by economic actors. Although the case reporting by its very nature tends to highlight instances of contract nonperformance, the circumstances of nonperformance reveal attitudes of economic actors toward contract obligations and resolution of disputes revealed the extent to which doctrinal views were carried out in practice.

The operational record suggested that contract nonperformance resulted not from inability of economic actors to perform but rather from unwillingness to perform due to the influence of external factors. There were local cadres who declined to honor agricultural production responsibility contracts for reasons tied to unrelated personal and organizational relationships. Similarly, nonperformance of agricultural procurement contracts and commercial and industrial contracts was most often due to economic factors that made performance undesirable to contracting parties. The influence of these external factors indicated that contract obligations were perceived not as centered only on the autonomous contract relationship, but rather were dependent on the external organizational and economic environment of the parties. Economic actors did not yet recognize in the doctrinal norms of the ECL an imperative requiring performance of contract obligations. This suggests that the ECL's provisions on enforceability of contracts had not achieved practical legitimacy.

The operational record indicated increased use of the courts and of compulsory methods in the resolution of contract disputes. The growth in importance of the courts as dispute settlement bodies independent of the parties suggested greater potential for the disinterested enforcement of contract rights. Increased use of compulsory dispute resolution raised the possibility that the rights embodied in contracts would be officially recognized and enforced. This combination of independent and compulsory enforcement of contracts was generally consistent with doctrinal views. Thus, the likelihood was high that these provisions would acquire practical legitimacy as economic actors came to accept and rely on judicially managed compulsory dispute resolution in the enforcement of contract rights.

However, the continued failure to provide monetary remedies diluted the effect of changes in the dispute resolution system. The disparity between doctrinal support for monetary remedies, and their absence in practice is likely to undermine the practical legitimacy of ECL provisions and discourage economic actors from seeking compensatory damages. This will permit the cost of nonperformance to continue to be distributed in a collectivist way, rather than imposed on the party responsible. Thus, although contract autonomy will be strengthened in certain respects by changes in dispute resolution processes, the absence of monetary remedies represents a continuing obstacle to the full recognition of autonomous contract rights.

Conclusion

This study has focused on the doctrine and practice of the ECL to determine the law's potential to acquire legitimacy. The ECL represents an example of the use of imposed law to support economic policy. In an effort to further the reform policies of the Third Plenum of the 11th CCP Central Committee, the ECL contained a number of provisions supporting autonomy in contract activity. These included provisions supporting the rights of contracting parties; expanded use of contracts; external supervision of contract formation; judicially managed compulsory dispute resolution, and use of monetary remedies for nonperformance. These norms of autonomy were intended to displace collectivist norms that had characterized contract doctrine and practice in China previously. In view of the resilience of these preexisting norms, the effectiveness of the ECL requires more than the extensive expressions of support it received from the government.

As an imposed law, the ECL faces special problems of legitimation. To be effective, it must acquire both abstract and practical legitimacy, as economic actors identify the norms that the law espouses, accept them conceptually, and rely on them in practice. Weber's expositions on political-legal rationality indicate that the legitimacy of law depends on perception. Such perception may be conceptualized by reference to Unger's term *recognition,* as the subjects of law recognize in the law valued norms that come to be accepted and relied upon in behavior.

Thus, the legitimacy of the ECL depends on the ability of the economic actors who are subjects of the law to recognize through perception the norms of autonomy espoused in the law. This requires that economic actors first identify these norms as they are expressed in the doctrine and operation of the ECL. Accordingly, this study has explored whether the doctrine and practice of the ECL exhibit sufficient consistency to permit economic actors to recognize and legitimate the ECL's norms of autonomy.

Consistency in doctrinal pronouncements is an important prerequisite for abstract as well as practical legitimacy. Although doctrinal diversity may lend abstract legitimacy to the lawmaking process (a critical attribute of Weber's rational-legal typology), it is more likely to undermine practical legitimacy as it calls into question the certainty and reliability of doctrinal norms. Doctrinal consistency, on the other hand, permits economic actors to identify the norms espoused by the law, and then to recognize in such norms values that they support. Doctrinal consistency also supports legitimacy as it imbues economic actors with confidence that doctrinal norms have uniform governmental support and therefore are reliable.

Consistency in the operation of doctrine is an important prerequisite for practical legitimacy, as economic actors must be confident that the abstract rules will be enforced in practice. Thus, the analysis of the operation of the ECL enables conclusions to be drawn as to which aspects of ECL doctrine are enforced in practice consistently enough to acquire practical legitimacy. Examination of the operational aspects of the ECL also permits conclusions as to whether economic actors will perceive and recognize in the operation of the law the valued norms set forth in legal doctrine.

Pre-Existing Norms with Which the ECL Competes for Acceptance

The process by which the ECL gains legitimacy must be viewed in the context of the pre-existing norms with which the ECL competes for acceptance. In chapter 1, it was observed that prior contract regulations and practice contributed to a norm of collectivism. During the post-revolution rebuilding period, the state used contract rules to assert control over the economy and to dilute the autonomy of remnant private interests. During the late 1950s, the regime's economic policies transformed contract transactions into a collective exercise in administrative resource allocation. The use of contract regulations to further state policy indicated that the role of contract law was to promote the state's collective interests over the autonomous interests of economic actors. Thus, in the conceptual area of the role of contracts and contract law, pre-existing norms strongly favored collectivism over autonomy.

The pre-existing norms relating to the administrative issues of contract supervision and dispute resolution also indicated the primacy of the norm of collectivism. The emphasis on internal supervision meant that reliance by personal and organizational relationships external to the contract remained an important feature of contract administration. This permitted collective interests to take priority over the individual interests of economic actors.

The dominance of internal methods of contract supervision was complemented by the prevalence of dispute settlement institutions that were organizationally related to the contracting parties. This underscored the influence of external relationships on the enforcement of contract rights, as management organs charged with dispute settlement often emphasized orderly relations among the parties under their jurisdiction rather than the contract rights of disputing parties. In addition, reliance on consensual methods of dispute resolution reflected the primacy of collective compromise over enforcement of autonomous contract rights. Little use was made of economic remedies for breach of contract, thus assuring collective sharing of costs for nonperformance.

Thus, prior to enactment of the ECL, contract activity was characterized by subservience of contracts and contract law to state policy, reliance on internal methods of contract supervision, and use of internal consensual dispute resolution mechanisms that resulted in nonmonetary remedies. These factors reflected a norm of collectivism in contract practice such that personal and organizational relationships took precedence over contract terms in economic transactions. The ECL represented an effort to modify and, to some extent, displace the pre-existing norm of collectivism.

The Abstract Legitimacy of the Doctrinal Components of the ECL

The capacity of the ECL's norms of autonomy to acquire abstract legitimacy depends on the interplay between consistency and diversity in current doctrinal pronouncements as to conceptual issues of the role of contracts and contract law, and the administrative issues related to contract supervision and dispute resolution. The doctrinal pronouncements of the central political and legal communities indicated varying degrees of consistency and diversity with regard to these issues.

The Doctrinal Standard of the Central Political Leadership

The doctrinal pronouncements of the central political leadership revealed that the respective roles of contracts and contract law continued to be seen as inseparable from economic policy. Support for the role of contracts in industry, commerce, and agriculture proceeded directly from economic policy decisions. Thus, support for contracts in agriculture emerged following decisions implementing various forms of production responsibility systems. The same pattern was followed in industry. Indeed, support for nonplan contracts in industry lagged behind the spread of agricultural contracts because the industrial responsibility system was established several years after the initial decisions were taken to promote agricultural responsibility systems.

The policy basis for contract doctrine brought with it problems, however, as competing views concerning the role of contracts emerged from proponents of differing economic policy goals. Thus, debate over the role of individual peasants as agricultural producers and concerning the extent of state planning in industry affected doctrinal pronouncements. The role of contract law also was tied closely to economic policy, with the result that it too was presented generally as an instrument for policy enforcement.

That the doctrinal pronouncements from the central political leadership focused on the economic policy foundation for contracts and contract law need not in itself represent a threat to the legitimacy of the ECL, for that legitimacy does not depend on the law being independent of transitory policy goals, but rather on whether the doctrine is perceived as having unified government support. This unity was evident in doctrinal views of the central political community on the role of contracts and contract law.

Doctrinal discussion of supervision over contract activity reflected organizational politics as various positions taken on the relative merits of certification and notarization were attributable to the struggle for supervisory authority over contract activity. The politicization of doctrinal debate on contract supervision may detract from the legitimacy of resulting doctrinal positions. On the other hand, increased support for a doctrine of external supervision as a substitute for internal methods that had obtained in the past provided a basis for broader recognition of contract autonomy for economic actors. To the extent that this opens possibilities for economic activity that are welcomed by economic actors, the emphasis on external supervision may add to the practical legitimacy of the ECL.

The doctrinal views of the central political leadership on the issues of dispute resolution were generally consistent in emphasizing the role of compulsory resolution of disputes and the use of monetary remedies for nonperformance of contracts. Compulsory dispute resolution permitted economic actors to enforce autonomous contract rights more effectively than under the consensual resolution practices of the past. The availability of SAIC arbitration and the economic chambers of the people's courts represented disinterested dispute settlement organs. From such organizational separation emerged the capacity for more recognition and enforcement of contract rights, thus diluting the impact of external relationships. Increased support for the use of monetary remedies provided a basis for relieving performing parties of the cost of nonperformance. Thus, the consistency of doctrinal views of the central political leadership on compulsory dispute resolution and monetary remedies augered well for the acquisition of legitimacy.

The Doctrinal Views of the Central Legal Community

The views of the central legal community represented an important component of ECL doctrine. These views exhibited internal diversity, as well as divergence from the views of the central political leadership. First, the specialized function of the legal community and the differentiation of its role from that of the political leadership was evident in the legal community's focus on the role of contract law instead of the role of contracts. Also, the level of diversity within the legal community was substantial with regard to the role of contract law, as certain members emphasized rights protection while others emphasized policy implementation.

On the question of the methods and institutions for contract supervision, the views of the legal communities were nearly uniform in support of external notarial supervision as opposed to either internal supervision through management office supervision, or certification by the SAIC system. In view of the consistency with which they were espoused, the doctrinal pronouncements of the legal communities may easily be perceived simply as statements in their service. Nonetheless, the doctrinal support given by the legal communities to the role of notarial supervision over contracts is likely to provide a basis for the ECL to acquire practical legitimacy to the extent that independent economic actors find external supervision preferable to pre-existing methods.

A broad consensus also emerged from the legal communities on the issue of the institutional framework for dispute settlement. General agreement emerged as to the need for compulsory dispute settlement and as to the respective roles of the courts and the SAIC arbitration bodies. While important emphasis was placed on the role of the courts, there was candid recognition that the courts still were not prepared to resolve contract disputes effectively. Such candor together with the diversity of views emerging from the legal communities likely will be perceived as the result of efforts to formulate process rules that are most appropriate to actual conditions and, thus, are likely to lend legitimacy to such views. Consequently, the role of the SAIC arbitration organs will probably gain acceptance by virtue of the support given such bodies by the legal communities. Moreover, to the extent that the legal communities were in accord with political leadership groups on the need for compulsory dispute settlement and for economic sanctions for nonperformance of contracts, these views reinforced acceptance of such doctrinal principles.

The Potential for Abstract Legitimacy and Contract Autonomy

The pronouncements of the central political leadership and legal community represent the main body of contract law doctrine that seeks to replace pre-existing norms governing contract activity. The unity of doctrinal views of the central political leadership and the central legal community on the issues of the role of contracts and contract law and the institutions and processes for dispute resolution provides a basis for abstract legitimacy. Support for current economic policies brings with it abstract legitimacy for doctrinal expressions of the role of contracts and contract law as instruments of such policies. The emphasis on external supervision of contracts also will probably support abstract legitimacy, even if the evidence of politically motivated debates over contract supervision dilute the abstract legitimacy accorded the specific methods of certification and notarization. The benefits to autonomous economic actors resulting from assertion of contract rights through compulsory dispute settlement and from the increased use of economic remedies to relieve the performing party of the cost of nonperformance will promote abstract legitimacy to these aspects of contract doctrine.

The abstract legitimacy thus accorded ECL doctrine will strengthen its effect on contract practice. Since the conceptual and administrative issues underlying the ECL were generally resolved through doctrinal views that favored autonomy, the legitimacy of the ECL's doctrinal norms can be expected to strengthen contract autonomy. The abstract legitimacy of doctrinal support for external supervision over contract activity should also promote greater autonomy and diversity in contract formation. Similarly, the abstract legitimacy accorded doctrinal support for judicially managed compulsory dispute resolution and the use of economic remedies for nonperformance of contracts will encourage in turn broader autonomy in the recognition and enforcement of contract rights. However, although the effect of doctrinal norms on contract autonomy will be strengthened by the abstract legitimacy these norms may command, reliance on the principles of the ECL in practice must derive from the practical legitimacy of the law.

The Potential for the ECL to Gain Practical Legitimacy

The legitimacy of the ECL depends on the degree to which the principles of the law become operational. The operational aspects of contract formation and dispute resolution reflect the extent to which doctrinal views on the recognition and enforcement of contract rights are realized in practice. The extent to which contract rights are recognized and enforced according to the terms of the ECL will affect the willingness of economic actors to rely on the law in protection of their interests, thus revealing the law's ability to acquire practical legitimacy.

The state's recognition of private contract rights was expressed through the ECL's doctrinal emphasis both on the use of enforceable contracts for economic transactions, and on the need to protect the rights of contracting parties. This recognition was evident in several aspects related to the practice of contract formation, such as the reciprocity of contract obligations and the transactional autonomy of contracting parties, as well as the diversity of transactions and parties subject to contracts. The recognition of contract autonomy was inhibited mainly by the continued absence of external supervision, suggesting a continued inability to overcome collective norms favoring reliance on relationships external to the contract in the recognition of contract rights. That this operational feature derived from doctrinal uncertainties borne of organizational politics suggested that the ECL's provisions on the role of external supervision face difficulties in achieving practical legitimacy. Nonetheless, the consistency of doctrine and practice regarding the role of contracts to formalize reciprocal obligations in a broad diversity of transactions indicated strong potential for practical legitimacy of the ECL's provisions on contract formation.

The enforcement of contract rights was more problematic, however, because external factors were repeatedly the cause of disregard of contract obligations. The hierarchical relationship between the parties to agricultural responsibility contracts resulted in external political factors intruding on performance of these contracts. External economic factors were also the cause of nonperformance of agricultural procurement contracts and industrial and commercial contracts, where the parties were in closer structural equality. Administrative intervention in contract performance was particularly evident, however, in industrial and commercial contracts, where changes in the state plan and state regulations, as well as direct administrative interference, hampered contract performance. The influence of these external factors on contract performance suggested that they also play a role in undermining the recognition and enforcement of autonomous contract rights.

In addition, despite the increase in compulsory dispute settlement processes, there was a continued reluctance to employ economic remedies for nonperformance. The failure to utilize economic remedies consistently in cases of breach of contract meant that the cost of nonperformance continued to be collectively shared by the contracting parties, regardless of who was responsible. This undermined the autonomy of performing as well as nonperforming parties, and also hindered effective enforcement of contract rights. The continued failure to impose economic sanctions runs counter to the provisions of the ECL and thus undermines their legitimacy.

The influence of transaction-external factors in contract performance, and the continued reluctance to impose monetary sanctions for nonperformance constitute significant obstacles to the enforcement of contract rights. Thus, although support for contract rights enforcement was evident in the increased reliance on compulsory dispute settlement processes and on fixed rules for dispute resolution, the balance of support and obstacles was such that full enforcement of contract rights cannot be assured. Thus, the utility of the ECL as a basis for enforcing contract rights will be diminished, and its practical legitimacy diluted.

These disparities between doctrinal norms and operational reality suggest that the effect of pre-existing collectivist norms remains strong. In an effort to improve consistency of contract doctrine and practice, the government has taken important steps to strengthen the effectiveness of the ECL in ensuring enforcement of contract rights. The Supreme People's Court's Opinion on Various Issues of Thorough Implementation of the Economic Contract Law (1984) emphasized the importance of economic sanctions for breach of contracts.[1] The Supreme Court's Explanation of Various Issues Concerning the Concrete Use of the Economic Contract Law in the Adjudication of Cases of Economic Contract Disputes (1987) addressed the use of economic penalties in case of nonperformance of contracts, particularly in agricultural and construction contracts.[2] These measures reflect a commitment to promote more effective enforcement of contract rights, and may provide a basis for further strengthening of the law's practical legitimacy.

Nonetheless, until disparities between doctrine and practice in the recognition and enforcement of contract rights are resolved, contract practice will reflect what might be termed "selective legitimation," as certain aspects of the ECL's doctrine are accepted and others are not. Thus, ECL doctrinal tenets regarding the use of contracts to express reciprocal obligations are likely to acquire legitimacy even as principles on external supervision do not. Doctrinal tenets on the role of the courts and compulsory dispute resolution will probably acquire practical legitimacy, even if principles on monetary remedies do not. The practical legitimacy of the ECL will not be an all-or-nothing matter, but rather will be selectively limited to those provisions of the ECL where consistency of doctrine and practice have encouraged practical legitimacy.

The selective nature of practical legitimation of the ECL will affect contract autonomy. Practical legitimacy for ECL provisions on the use of contracts likely will encourage greater transactional autonomy and diversity. On the other hand, contract autonomy will be hindered by lack of legitimacy for external supervision, permitting contracts to be supervised by units organizationally related to the contracting parties. Practical legitimacy for compulsory dispute resolution under judicial auspices should encourage broader autonomy in the recognition and enforcement of contracts, but the continued sharing of the cost of nonperformance through use of nonmonetary remedies will dilute that autonomy.

The resulting contract practice will be characterized by partial autonomy derived from selective legitimation. Economic actors will use contracts to express reciprocal obligations related to their increasingly varied transactions, but will accept certain degrees of external intrusion from personal and organizational relationships. Economic actors will realize that internal contract supervision is unavoidable as a practical matter, even as they rely on doctrinal provisions permitting use of notarization and certification of contracts. Contract parties will increasingly rely on courts and compulsory dispute resolution to assert their contract rights, but will accept use of nonmonetary remedies. This pattern of contract practice will probably continue until changes in the doctrinal and operational features of the ECL alter the pattern of legitimation of the law.

The autonomy encouraged by legitimation of certain provisions of the ECL is potentially an important precursor to expansion of autonomy in other sectors of Chinese life. Autonomy in formation of contracts may encourage autonomy in other economic activities, such as business planning and labor relations. Autonomy in the institutions and methods of dispute resolution may encourage use of these mechanisms in other kinds of disputes. Thus, the autonomy made possible in certain aspects of contract practice by the selective legitimation of the ECL may become a more extended feature of Chinese economic life.

Appendix 1a. Table of Cases

Issues Related to Contract Formation

Case No.	*Date of Formation*	*Type of Contract*	*Parties*	*Method of Supervision*
Pre-ECL Contracts Related to Agriculture				
1	1981	PR,[1] management of firecracker factory, 1 year	Production team, individual team members	Certification
2	1981	PR, management of orange orchard, duration not set	Production team, individual team members	None specified
3	Unspecified (pre-ECL)[2]	PR (oral) use of automobile, 1 year	Production team, individual team members	None specified
4	1980	PR, produce doufu, multi-year	Hubei production team, individual peasant	None specified
5	1981	PR, management of reed pond, one year	Henan farm, individual peasant	None specified
6	1981	PR, management of orchard, three years. Bid contract	Fujian brigade, individual members	SAIC Certification

Case No.	*Date of Formation*	*Type of Contract*	*Parties*	*Method of Supervision*
7	1982	PR, management of pork store, one year	Beijing production team, individual members	None specified
8	1982	PR, management of tea garden orchard, tea factory, four years. Bid contract	Zhejiang brigade, individual members	None specified
9	1982	PR, management of orchard, two years. Bid contract	Sichuan production team, individual members	None specified
10	1981	PR, management of orchard, one year. Bid contract	Qinghuangdao brigade, individual members	None specified
11	1981	AP,[3] chickens	Sichuan procurement office, specialist households	None specified
12	1981	AP, chickens	Sichuan procurement office, specialist households	None specified
13	1981	AP, onions	Shandong brigade, Shandong procurement company	None specified

Case No.	Date of Formation	Type of Contract	Parties	Method of Supervision
14	Unspecified (pre-ECL)	AP, candied tangerines	Sichuan can factory, Sichuan company	None specified
15	Unspecified (pre-ECL)	PR, establish screen factory	Liaoning commune, commune members	None specified
Post-ECL Contracts				
16	Unspecified (post-ECL)	PR, pig raising	Commune food office, key households	None specified
17	1983	PR, management of hotel, multiyear	Supply and marketing cooperative, individual peasants	None specified
18	1983	PR, unspecified products, one year	Liaoning brigade, individual members	None specified
19	Unspecified (post-ECL)	AP, oranges	Sichuan procurement office, individual households	None specified
20	1982	PR, flour mill, three years	Sichuan brigade, individual member	Internal management certification
21	1982	Lease of water rights for use in mill	Sichuan water company, individual peasants	None specified

Case No.	Date of Formation	Type of Contract	Parties	Method of Supervision
22	1981 (renewed 1982)	PR, land reclamation, single-year	Sichuan brigade, individual member	None specified
23	1982	PR, brick and tile factory, one year	Sichuan production team, individual members	None specified
24	1982	PR, bricks three years	Henan production brigade, individual members	Notarization by county notary
25	1982	PR, chickens, one year	Shanghai production brigade, individual	None specified
26	Unspecified (post-ECL)	PR, orchard, five years	Liaoning production brigade, brigade member	None specified
27	1983	PR, rice processing plant, five years	Sichuan brigade, brigade members	None specified
28	Unspecified	PR, food processing plant, duration not specified	Hebei brigade, brigade members	None specified
29	1983	AP, pickled cauliflowers	Sichuan procurement company, individual peasants	SAIC Certification
30	1983	AP, chickens	Sichuan procurement station, individual household	None specified

Case No.	*Date of Formation*	*Type of Contract*	*Parties*	*Method of Supervision*
Pre-ECL Contracts		*Contracts Related to Industry & Commerce*		
31	1978	PS,[4] plastic strips (prepayment)	Unspecified street committee office, unspecified factory	Certification
32	1978	PS, Thermoses (prepayment)	Unspecified shop, unspecified Shanghai glass factory	Internal approval
33	1979	PS, brickmaking machine	Unspecified brigade, Henan factory	None specified
34	1980	PS specialized meters. Plan contract	Shanghai meters factory, unspecified factory outside Shanghai	None specified
35	1980	PS, towels, blankets	Shanghai factory, unspecified store outside Shanghai	None specified
36	1981	PS, towels, blankets	Shanghai factory, unspecified store outside Shanghai	None specified
37	1980	PS, jasmine tea	Shaanxi warehouse Guangdong County	None specified

Case No.	Date of Formation	Type of Contract	Parties	Method of Supervision
38	1980	PS, industrial pumps	Anhui water company, Anhui machinery company	None specified
39	1980	PS, wine jugs	Two Zhejiang factories	None specified
40	1981	PS, laser equipment (prepayment)	Hebei school, Zhejiang factory	None specified
41	1981	PS, tractor	Unspecified company, unspecified factory	None specified
42	1982	PS, brickmaking machine (prepayment)	Unspecified farm, Henan factory	None specified
43	1982	PS, grain expansion machine	Henan factory, individual peasant	None specified
44	1979	Manufacture of glass	Beijing factory, unspecified brigade	None specified
45	1981	Construction (prepayment)	Unspecified tree farm, unspecified construction company	None specified
46	1981	Project termination	Two unspecified factories	None specified
47	1981	Printing	P.L.A. unit, unspecified printing plant	None specified

Case No.	Date of Formation	Type of Contract	Parties	Method of Supervision
48	1972	PS, coal (prepayment)	Hunan factory, Hunan mine	None specified
49	Unspecified (pre-ECL)	PS, electric drills	Jiangsu collective service store, Shanghai factory	None specified
50	1975	PS, bricks (prepayment)	Beijing Supply & Marketing Cooperative, Beijing brigade	Internal supervision
51	1976	PS, camshafts	Jilin tool repair facility, Wuhan auto repair factory	None specified
52	1976	PS, transformers. Plan contract (prepayment)	Changchun (Jilin) store, Jilin transformer factory	Management Bureau Supervision
53	1977	PS, reed mats. Oral contract	Hebei commune, Beijing supply & marketing cooperative	None specified
54	1978	PS, electric hoist	Beijing factory, unspecified machine building factory	None specified
55	1978	PS, derrick	Harbin factory, Shanxi warehouse	None specified

Case No.	Date of Formation	Type of Contract	Parties	Method of Supervision
56	1978	PS, diesel ship engines	Liaoning factory, Liaoning materials company	None specified
57	1979	PS, steel, metal	Guangxi machinery factory, Guangxi steel factory	None specified
58	1979	PS, beds	Shaanxi medical unit, Shaanxi hospital	None specified
59	1979	PS, bulldozer	Hunan immigration department, Hunan hydroelectric Co.	None specified
60	1979	PS, tractors	Henan machinery Company, Shaanxi materials company	None specified
61	1980	PS, boiler (prepayment)	Tianjin commune, Tianjin factory	None specified
62	1980	PS, cloisonne casts	Handan municipality (Hebei) factory, Beijing factory	None specified

Case No.	*Date of Formation*	*Type of Contract*	*Parties*	*Method of Supervision*
63	1980	PS, cement (prepayment)	Hunan cement factory, Guangdong hydroelectric bureau	None specified
64	Unspecified (pre-ECL)	PS, hypo-oxygenated zinc	Hebei chemical factory, Hunan chemical factory	None specified
65	Unspecified (pre-ECL)	PS, sheet steel (prepayment)	Liaoning repair factory, Heilongjiang materials company	None specified
66	Unspecified (pre-ECL)	PS, radiator	Liaoning unit, Liaoning factory	None specified
67	Unspecified (pre-ECL)	PS, steel	Jilin construction materials factory, Liaoning steel factory	None specified
68	Unspecified (pre-ECL)	PS, bellows material	Unspecified chemical factory, unspecified school	None specified
69	Unspecified (pre-ECL)	PS, air freshener	Zhejiang groceries company, Liaoning company	None specified
70	1980	PS, bulldozer (prepayment)	Unspecified engineering company, unspecified brick company	None specified

Case No.	*Date of Formation*	*Type of Contract*	*Parties*	*Method of Supervision*
71	1981	PS, gallium	Beijing research unit, unspecified materials company	None specified
72	1980	PS, light trucks	Harbin tool factory, unspecified supply & marketing cooperative	None specified
73	Unspecified	PS, firecrackers	Liaoning sundries company, Hunan sundries company	None specified
74	1980	PS, raw coal	Unspecified glass factory, unspecified coal company	Certification
75	1981	PS, lumber (prepayment)	Hunan management bureau, Hunan farm	None specified
76	1981	PS, flax drawing machines (prepayment)	Unspecified tool factory, unspecified flax factory	None specified
77	1981	PS, asbestos thread	Harbin asbestos factory, Zhejiang asbestos factory	None specified
78	1982	PS, unspecified	Gansu store, Gansu department store	None specified

Case No.	Date of Formation	Type of Contract	Parties	Method of Supervision
79	1982	PS, cigarettes	Unspecified factory, unspecified store	None specified
80	1982	PS, wine yeast	Guangxi factory, Yunnan factory	None specified
81	1982	PS, miscellaneous goods	Shanxi store, Shanxi sales office	None specified
82	1977	Manufacturing insulated baseboards	Jilin switching plant, Liaoning brigade	None specified
83	1979	Construction dormitory (prepayment)	Henan factory, Henan Light Industry Bureau	None specified
84	Unspecified (pre-ECL)	Renovation of metal files	Sichuan file unit, Sichuan hardware store	None specified
85	1979	Manufacturing, concrete slabs (prepayment)	Shanghai industrial company, Shanghai commune	None specified
86	Unspecified (pre-ECL)	Manufacturing, fabricated boards (prepayment)	Liaoning housing office, Liaoning rubber factory	None specified
87	Unspecified (pre-ECL)	Manufacturing, steam pot	Liaoning shop, Liaoning can factory	None specified

Case No.	*Date of Formation*	*Type of Contract*	*Parties*	*Method of Supervision*
88	Unspecified (pre-ECL)	Loan for acquisition of equipment	Liaoning scientific office, Liaoning warehouse	None specified
89	Unspecified (pre-ECL)	Manufacturing steel roof trusses	Unspecified Liaoning unit, Liaoning steel factory	None specified
90	Unspecified (pre-ECL)	Manufacturing machinery. Plan contract	Zhejiang machinery factory, Liaoning metals factory	None specified
91	Unspecified (pre-ECL)	Manufacturing, ship	Liaoning shipping office, Zhejiang ship factory	None specified
92	Unspecified (pre-ECL)	Manufacturing plastic tubs	Unspecific plastics factory, unspecified honey and sugar factory	None specified
93	Unspecified (pre-ECL)	Repair of electric mining shovel	Liaoning machinery factory, Inner Mongolia mining bureau	None specified
94	1981	Manufacturing warehouse plates	Zhejiang steel factory, Fujian cement factory	None specified

Case No.	Date of Formation	Type of Contract	Parties	Method of Supervision
95	1981	Construction clinic (prepayment)	Guizhou hospital, unspecified construction company	Notarization
96	Unspecified (pre-ECL)	Manufacture of signs (4 cases)	Zhejian sign factory, Heilongjiang enterprise offices	None specified
Post-ECL Contracts				
97	1983	PS, miscellaneous goods	Jiangsu factory, unit outside Jiangsu	None specified
98	Unspecified (post-ECL)	PS, miscellaneous goods	Two specified units	None specified
99	1983	PS, used equipment (prepayment)	Beijing factory, unspecified printing plant	None specified
100	Unspecified (post-ECL)	PS, equipment	Shanghai factory, Shaanxi factory	None specified
101	Unspecified (post-ECL)	PS, miscellaneous goods	Tianjin unit, unspecified factory	None specified
102	Unspecified	PS, miscellaneous goods	Unspecified units	None specified
103	Unspecified (post-ECL)	PS, automobile (prepayment). Oral contract	Unspecified factory individual peasant	None specified
104	Unspecified (post-ECL)	PS, mosquito netting	Unspecified textile mill, unspecified store	Internal approval

Case No.	*Date of Formation*	*Type of Contract*	*Parties*	*Method of Supervision*
105	Unspecified (post-ECL)	PS, construction goods (prepayment)	Two Jiangsu units	None specified
106	Unspecified (post-ECL)	PS, sheet steel. Plan contract	Unspecified mining company, steel factory	None specified
107	Unspecified (post-ECL)	PS, machinery	Commune members, production team	None specified
108	Unspecified (post-ECL)	Guarantee contract *re* automobile lease	Unspecified	None specified
109	Unspecified (post-ECL)	Transportation	Sichuan management office, Sichuan Shipping brigade	None specified
110	1982	PS, bamboo gangplants	Hunan management office, Hunan farm	None specified
111	Unspecified (pre-ECL)	PS, winches. Plan contract	Shanghai harbor factory, Liaoning shipping factory	None specified
112	Unspecified (post-ECL)	PS, machinery	Henan materials station, Henan factory	None specified
113	1983	PS, poplar seedlings	Gansu production team, Gansu highways office	None specified

Case No.	Date of Formation	Type of Contract	Parties	Method of Supervision
114	1983	PS, polyester thread	Jiangsu materials company, Guangdong service company	None specified (Arbitration clause)
115	1983	PS, calcium superphosphate	Anhui native produce company, Anhui supply and marketing company	None specified
116	1983	PS, milk powder (prepayment)	Beijing shop, Beijing restaurant	None specified
117	Unspecified	PS, flagstones	Heilongjiang factory, Heilongjiang farm	None specified
118	1983	PS, steel parts	Jiangxi factory, Shanghai factory	None specified
119	Unspecified (post-ECL)	PS, steel	Jiangsu factory, Shanghai factory	None specified
120	Unspecified (post-ECL)	PS, unspecified products	Manchuria factory, Tianjin factory	None specified
121	1983	PS, food products	Hebei factory, Sichuan commodity store	None specified
122	Unspecified (post-ECL)	PS, machinery drive belts	Wuhan factory, Zhejiang factory	None specified

Case No.	*Date of Formation*	*Type of Contract*	*Parties*	*Method of Supervision*
123	Unspecified (post-ECL)	PS, unspecified goods	Hebei factory, Jilin factory	None specified
124	Specified (post-ECL)	PS, oil	Unspecified unit unspecified factory	None specified
125	Unspecified (post-ECL)	PS, unspecified goods	Hubei factory, Jiangsu factory	None specified
126	Unspecified (post-ECL)	PS, synthetic yarn	Gansu materials company, Guangzhou materials company	None specified
127	Unspecified (post-ECL)	PS, bicycle parts	Unspecified factory Liaoning factory	None specified
128	Unspecified (post-ECL)	Guarantee for P.S. contract	Liaoning store, purchasing agent	None specified
129	1983	Termination of joint venture	Shandong mine, Tianjin factory	None specified
130	Unspecified (post-ECL)	Manufacturing, steel windows	Tianjin iron works, unspecified factory	None specified
131	Unspecified (post-ECL)	Manufacturing machinery	Unspecified factory, individual in Nanjing	None specified

[1]PR: Production responsibility contract

[2]Date of formation inferred from date of publication.

[3]AP: Agricultural Procurement Contract

[4]PS: Purchase and Sale Contract

Appendix 1b. Table of Cases

Issues Related to Dispute Resolution

Case No.	*Basis of Dispute*	*Method of Resolution*	*Result*	*Citation*
Pre-ECL Contracts Related to Agriculture				
1.	Failure of quota by peasants	Mediation, adjudication filed, issue of court accepting case	CM[a]: Court should accept case and resolve dispute	ECL
2.	Repudiation of contract by team cadres	Mediation; adjudication filed issue of court accepting case	CM: Court should accept and resolve dispute	P.R.C. Constitution
3.	Repudiation of contract by commune	Adjudication	CM: Mediation or adjudication to resolve dispute	ECL
4.	Failure of performance by peasant	Negotiation court mediation	Specific performance	ECL
5.	Failure of payment by form	Adjudication	Specific performance, compensation	ECL
6.	Repudiation of contract by brigade cadre	Court arbitration	Specific performance	None specified
7.	Repudiation of contract by team cadre	Court mediation	Specific performance	ECL

Case No.	Basis of Dispute	Method of Resolution	Result	Citation
8.	Repudiation of contract by brigade	Court mediation	Compensation	None specified
9.	Repudiation of contract by team	Court mediation	Compensation	None specified
10.	Repudiation of contract by brigade	Mediation, adjudication	Specific performance, penalties	ECL
11.	Repudiation of contract by local government 3rd party	SAIC investigation	Compensation	None specified
12.	Repudiation of contract by brigade	SAIC investigation	Compensation	None specified
13.	Repudiation of contract by brigade	SAIC investigation	Compensation and penalties	None specified
14.	Failure of payment by company	SAIC investigation	Compensation and penalties	[b]
15.	Repudiation of contract due to change of leadership organ	Court mediation	Compensation	None specified
Post-ECL Contracts				
16.	Failure of payment by food office	None specified	CM: Specific performance	ECL
17.	Repudiation of contract by co-op	Administrative review	CM Specific performance	ECL

Case No.	*Basis of Dispute*	*Method of Resolution*	*Result*	*Citation*
18.	Failure of performance by team members	Court mediation	Shared compensation[c]	None specified
19.	Repudiation of contract by households	SAIC investigation	Specific performance	None specified
20.	Repudiation of contract by team	Local government mediation	Compensation, penalties, specific performance (mediation decision, not enforced)	None specified
21.	Repudiation of contract by water company	Negotiation, adjudication	Compensation	ECL
22.	Repudiation of contract by brigade cadres	Local government mediation	Specific performance	PRC Constitution
23.	Repudiation of contract by brigade cadres	Negotiation, SAIC investigation, adjudication	Penalties, compensation	Rural Economic Policy, Unspecified laws
24.	Repudiation by brigade cadre	Local government mediation, adjudication	Penalties, compensation	ECL
25.	Repudiation by brigade	Local government mediation, adjudication	Specific performance	None specified
26.	Repudiation by brigade	Local government mediation	Specific performance	None specified

Case No.	Basis of Dispute	Method of Resolution	Result	Citation
27.	Repudiation by brigade cadre	Court arbitration	Penalties, compensation	ECL, CCP Doc #1 (1984)
28.	Repudiation by brigade cadres	Legal adviser, negotiation	Specific performance	ECL
29.	Refusal to take delivery by procurement company	SAIC mediation, arbitration	Partial compensation	None specified
30.	Repudiation by livestock station	Court mediation	Penalties compensation	ECL
Pre-ECL Contracts Related to Industry & Commerce				
31.	Failure of payment by office, issue of quality goods	Adjudication	CM: Shared compensation	[d, e]
32.	Failure of delivery by factory	None specified	CM: Penalty payments, in case of nonperformance. also further negotiation, mediation, arbitration or adjudication to resolve dispute	None specified
33.	Quality of goods	None specified	CM: Negotiation, arbitration, adjudication to resolve dispute	[f]

Case No.	Basis of Dispute	Method of Resolution	Result	Citation
34.	Repudiation due to change in state plan	None specified	CM: Negotiation or arbitration to resolve dispute	None specified
35.	Failure of payment by store	None specified	CM: Negotiation, arbitration, or adjudication to resolve dispute. Penalty payments in case of nonperformance.	None specified
36.	Failure of payment by store	None specified	CM: Negotiation, arbitration or adjudication to resolve dispute. Penalty payments in case of nonperformance.	None specified
37.	Quality of goods	Negotiations adjudication, appeal	CM: Lower court-imposed shared compensation. Commentator advocates payment only by party in breach.	None specified
38.	Quality of goods	None specified, issue of court's role in resolving dispute	CM: Court should examine case and resolve dispute	d, e

Case No.	Basis of Dispute	Method of Resolution	Result	Citation
39.	Repudiation due to plan change	None specified	CM: Arbitration to resolve dispute specific performance and compensation in case of nonperformance	None specified
40.	Failure of delivery by factory	Negotiations, adjudication	CM: Court mediation; compensation in case of nonperformance	None specified
41.	Failure of delivery by factory	None specified	CM: Compensation in case of nonperformance	f
42.	Quality of goods	Negotiation	CM: Compensation in case of nonperformance	None specified
43.	Quality of goods	Request for court investigation	CM: Mediation and arbitration to resolve dispute	None specified
44.	Failure of payment by factory	None specified	CM: Compensation in case of nonperformance	ECL
45.	Failure to complete construction by construction company	None specified	CM: Not specified	e, g, h

Case No.	Basis of Dispute	Method of Resolution	Result	Citation
46.	Loss of goods	Negotiation	CM: Court should resolve dispute, impose shared compensation	i
47.	Failure of delivery by plant	Consultation	CM: Negotiation, arbitration, or adjudication to resolve dispute	ECL
48.	Failure of delivery by mine	Negotiation	Unresolved	None specified
49.	Failure of payment by store	Court mediation	Substituted performance	None specified
50.	Failure of delivery by brigade	Court mediation	Restriction of purchase price	None specified
51.	Failure of payment by Wuhan factory	Negotiation, court mediation, compulsory enforcement of mediation	Penalties, substituted performance	Civil Procedure Law of the P.R.C. (Draft)
52.	Failure of payment by stove factory	Management bureau mediation, local government arbitration, adjudication	Voluntary withdrawal of suit	None specified
53.	SAIC cancellation of illegal contract	Negotiation, court mediation	Contract nullified, specific performance	Unspecified commodity regulations
54.	Quality of goods	Adjudication	Restitution (repairs)	None specified

Case No.	Basis of Dispute	Method of Resolution	Result	Citation
55.	Failure of warehouse to take delivery	Arbitration, appeal to court, appeal of court decision	Specific performance, compensation	d, e, i, j
56.	Failure of payment by materials company	Court arbitration	Cancellation of contract, restitution for goods delivered	l, m, n
57.	Failure of payment by machinery factory	Negotiation	Substituted performance	ECL, Civil Procedure Law of PRC (draft)
58.	Bank intervention for lack of contract approval	Negotiation	Specific performance	None specified
59.	Quality of goods	Negotiation, court mediation	Compensation	None specified
60.	Quality of goods	Negotiation, court mediation	Contract cancellation	Unspecified regulations on machinery specifications
61.	Failure of delivery by factory	Negotiation, adjudication	Contract cancellation, restitution of purchase price	Unspecified regulations on machinery specifications
62.	Quality of goods	Negotiation, court mediation	Shared compensation	Unspecified regulations on machinery specifications
63.	Failure of delivery by cement factory	SAIC investigation	Restitution of purchase price (not enforced)	None specified

Case No.	Basis of Dispute	Method of Resolution	Result	Citation
64.	Failure of payment	Negotiation, court mediation	Substituted performance	None specified
65.	Failure of delivery by factory	Adjudication	Cancellation of contract, restitution of purchase price with interest	None specified
66.	Failure of payment by unit	Adjudication	Substituted performance	None specified
67.	Price issue	Court-ordered negotiation	Substituted performance	None specified
68.	Repudiation by school	Adjudication	Specific performance	State Pricing Regulation Doc. #67 (1980)
69.	Issues of quality of goods, time of delivery	Negotiations, court mediation	Specific performance	Unspecified laws and regulations
70.	Quality of goods	Negotiations, court mediation	Penalties, specific performance	None specified
71.	Failure of delivery due to reallocation of goods by higher unit	Negotiations, court mediation	Compensation	None specified
72.	Failure to deliver due to administrative reorganization	Court-supervised negotiation	Shared compensation	ECL

Case No.	Basis of Dispute	Method of Resolution	Result	Citation
73.	Goods lost due to explosion	Adjudication	Shared compensation	Unspecified regulations on manufacture and sale of firecrackers
74.	Repudiation due to failure to obtain approval	Court mediation, adjudication	Penalties, compensation	Unspecified regulations on unified distribution of coal
75.	Failure of delivery management bureau	Court mediation, compulsory enforcement of mediation	Restitution of purchase price	None specified
76.	Failure of delivery by seller	SAIC arbitration	Specific performance, compensation	None specified
77.	Failure of delivery due to administrative intervention	Negotiations, court mediation	Specific performance	ECL
78.	Issues of price and quality	Lawyer mediation	Substituted performance	None specified
79.	Administrative intervention for improper management, repudiation of contract	Court mediation adjudication	Unresolved	ECL
80.	Contract invalid, in violation of government monopoly	Mediation, adjudication	Penalties, compensation	Unspecified regulations on monopolies

Case No.	Basis of Dispute	Method of Resolution	Result	Citation
81.	Refusal to deliver due to market changes	Negotiation, SAIC mediation, SAIC arbitration, adjudication	Penalties, compensation, compulsory enforcement of court judgment	ECL
82.	Failure of payment, quality issues	Arbitration by local economic committee, appeal to court, court mediation	Specific performance and payment of litigation expenses	[d]
83.	Failure of payment, issue of lack of state approval	Government mediation, adjudication	Compensation	ECL
84.	Failure to take delivery due to overstocking	Court mediation	Substituted performance, price reduction	None specified
85.	Failure of payment, issues of delivery and quality	Negotiations, court mediation	Restitution	None specified
86.	Failure of delivery by seller	Negotiations, adjudication	Specific performance	None specified
87.	Failure of payment due to lack of contract approval	Court mediation	Specific performance	None specified
88.	Failure to make loan funds available	Court mediation	Specific performance	None specified
89.	Quality of goods	Adjudication	Shared compensation	None specified

Case No.	Basis of Dispute	Method of Resolution	Result	Citation
90.	Failure of payment due to plan change	Court mediation	Compensation	None specified
91.	Quality of goods (failure of replacement part)	Adjudication	No breach of contract	Unspecified regulations on contracts and maritime laws.
92.	Failure of delivery due to change in production plan	Court mediation	Cancellation of contract	None specified
93.	Failure of payment	Negotiations, lawyer mediation	Specific performance	o
94.	Quality of goods	Negotiations, SAIC mediation	Shared compensation	ECL, [f]
95.	Failure to complete construction	Negotiations, administrative orders by planning and construction departments and notary	Compensation	None specified
96.	Failure of payment	Negotiation, adjudication, arbitration	Specific performance	None specified
Post-ECL Contracts				
97.	Failure of payment by unit	None specified	CM: Mediation, arbitration or adjudication to resolve dispute, compensation in case of non-performance	ECL

Case No.	Basis of Dispute	Method of Resolution	Result	Citation
98.	Failure of delivery by factory	None specified	CM: Mediation, arbitration or adjudication to resolve dispute	[f]
99.	Repudiation of contract by plant	Negotiation	CM: Specific performance	ECL
100.	Failure of delivery by Shanghai factory	None specified	CM: Specific performance	[f]
101.	Failure of delivery by factory	None specified	CM: Specific performance	[f]
102.	Failure of delivery by seller	None specified	CM: Compensation and penalty payments in case of nonperformance	ECL, [f]
103.	Repudiation of contract by factory	None specified	CM: Consultation to resolve dispute	ECL
104.	Repudiation due to error in contract	None specified	CM: Not specified	[f]
105.	Failure of delivery by seller	Negotiation	CM: Compensation in case of nonperformance	ECL
106.	Repudiation of contract by factory	Negotiation	CM: Negotiations, arbitration, adjudication to resolve dispute, specific performance	ECL, [f]

Case No.	Basis of Dispute	Method of Resolution	Result	Citation
			and compensation in case of non-performance	
107.	Illegality of contract	Negotiation	CM: Negotiation, arbitration, or adjudication to resolve dispute	None specified
108.	Failure of payment by lessee	Negotiation	CM: Specific performance	None specified
109.	Delay in delivery	SAIC arbitration, adjudication	Fines, detention	None specified
110.	Failure of payment, goods destroyed from improper storage	Adjudication	Specific performance, detention	None specified
111.	Cancellation of contract due to change in state plan	SAIC investigation	Compensation	None specified
112.	Failure of payment	Adjudication	Unresolved	None specified
113.	Failure of payment by highway office	Lawyer mediation	Specific performance	None specified
114.	Failure of delivery, due to market changes	Negotiation, adjudication (later withdrawn)	Voluntary performance	None specified
115.	Failure of delivery, quality of goods.	Adjudication	Unresolved	None specified

Case No.	Basis of Dispute	Method of Resolution	Result	Citation
116.	Quality of goods	Adjudication	Contract cancelled, restitution of purchase price	ECL, P
117.	Failure of payment, issue of error in contract	Adjudication	Unresolved	None specified
118.	Failure of payment	Adjudication	Compensation, penalties	None specified
119.	Failure of payment	Adjudication	Unspecified liability for non-performance	None specified
120.	Failure of payment, issue of quality of goods	Court supervised negotiation	Substituted performance	None specified
121.	Failure to take delivery goods lost due to improper storage	Negotiation, lawyer mediation	Shared compensation	ECL
122.	Failure of payment, quality issue	Adjudication	Substituted performance	None specified
123.	Failure of payment	Negotiation, lawyer mediation	Voluntary settlement	None specified
124.	Repudiation due to agent exceeding authority	Arbitration	Restitution	None specified
125.	Failure of payment	SAIC mediation	Specific performance	ECL

Case No.	Basis of Dispute	Method of Resolution	Result	Citation
126.	Quality of goods	Adjudication	No breach of contract found	Unspecified quality regulations
127.	Quality of goods	Court mediation	Substituted performance	None specified
128.	Failure of payment	Court mediation	Specific performance	Unspecified price regulations
129.	Repudiation of illegal contract	Adjudication	Contract cancelled, restitution	ECL
130.	Repudiation as result of change in plan	Adjudication (later withdrawn), lawyer mediation	Substituted performance	None specified
131.	Failure of payment	Court mediation	Specific performance	None specified

[a]"CM" refers to the Legal Commentator's recommended result (including recommended dispute resolution processes).

[b]"Sichuan Provincial Methods for Management of Collective Market Trade Between Cities and Towns." See generally, "Guowuyuan guanyu cheng zhen jiti suoyou zhi jingji ruogan zhengce wenti de zanxing guiding" (Provisional regulations of the State Council concerning several policy questions of the collective economy of the cities and towns"), Zhonghua renmin gongheguo sifa bu falu zhengce yanjiu shi (Laws and Regulations Research Office of the PRC Ministry of Justice), *Heng xiang jingji lianhe falu fa qui zhengce huibian* (Compilation of laws, statutes and regulations, and policies of horizontal economic integration) (Beijing, 1987), at 151.

[c]"Shared compensation" refers to a result where both parties to the contract share the costs and losses resulting from non-performance.

[d]"Provisional Regulations for the Basic Provisions of Contracts for the Ordering of Factory and Mining Goods (1963). See Appendix 3.

[e]"Joint Circular on Certain Issues in Managing Economic Contracts" (1979). See Appendix 3.

[f]"Provisional Regulations on Factory and Mining Goods Contracts" (1981). See Appendix 3.

[g]"Opinion of the State Capital Construction Commission Concerning Broadening the Contract System in Capital Construction" (1979). See Appendix 3.

[h]"Provisional Regulations on Construction, Installation and Engineering Contracts" (1979). See Appendix 3.

[i]"Regulations of the Ministry of Transport on Waterborne Shipment of Goods and Materials" (1979). See Appendix 3.

[j]"Reference Materials for Trying Economic Cases." Subsequently published as "Zuigao renmin fayuan jingji shenpan ting" (Economic adjudication chamber of the Supreme People's Court), *Jingji shenpan shouce* (Handbook on economic adjudication) (Beijing, 1987).

[k]"Circular Concerning Methods of Handling Machinery and Electrical Goods Ordering Contracts Following Adjustment of the State Plan" (1979). See Appendix 3.

[l]"Principles for Ensuring Repair, Exchange and Return of Agricultural Machinery." See "Jixie gongye ti gao chanpin zhiliang zhengdun qiye guanli di shi er xiang gongzuo yanshou biaozhun (shixing)" (Twelfth provisional standards for checking and acceptance of work in raising product quality and reorganizing the administration of enterprises in the machinery industry) (1978), *Zhonghua renmin gongheguo gongye qiye fa gui xuanbian* (Compilation of industrial enterprise laws and regulations of the PRC) (Beijing, 1981), at 182.

[m]Liaoning Provincial Regulations Concerning "Strengthening Administration of Standardization and Ensuring Quality of Industrial Products." See, generally, "Zhonghua renmin gongheguo biaozhunhua guanli tiaoli" (Regulations of the PRC on administration of standardization) (1979), *Zhonghua renmin gongheguo xianxing fa gui huibian* (Compilation of current laws and regulations of the PRC) (Beijing, 1987).

[n]"Regulations of the PRC on Supervising and Inspecting Products Used in Shipping." See "Zhonghua renmin gongheguo hai shang jiaotong anquan fa" (Law of the PRC on safety in maritime transport), Guojia jihua weiyuanhui tiao fa bangongshi (Office of treaties and law of the State Planning Commission), *Zhongyao jingji fa gui ziliao xuanbian* (Compilation of important economic laws and regulations) (Beijing, 1987), at 479.

[o]"Coal Ministry Regulations on Standards for Machinery Overhauls." See, "Jixie gongye ti gao chanpin zhiliang zhengdun qiye guanli di shi er xiang gongzuo yanshou biaozhun (shixing)" (Twelfth provisional standards for checking and acceptance of work in raising product quality and reorganizing the administration of enterprises in the machinery industry) (1978), *Zhonghua renmin gongheguo gongye qiye fa gui xuanbian* (Compilation of industrial enterprise laws and regulations of the PRC) (Beijing, 1981), at 182.

[p]"PRC Regulations of Food Hygiene" (1982). See *Jingji fa gui huibian* (Compilation of economic laws and regulations) (Guangzhou, n.d.), at 750.

Appendix 1c. Table of Cases

Case Citations

Case No. 1: Letter written by a member of a production team. "Gong dui si de hetong jiufen fayuan yingfou shouli" (Should the Court Accept a Contract Dispute Between Public and Private Entities), *Minzhu yu fazhi* (Democracy and the Legal System), no. 5, 1982, p. 47.

Case No. 2: Letter written by a court official. "Nongcun renmin gongshe shengchan dui yu ben dui sheyuan de hetong jiufen fayuan shifou shouli" (Does the Court Accept Contract Disputes Between This Team's Members and Rural Commune Production Teams), *Faxue zazhi* (Legal Studies Magazine), no. 1, 1981, p. 55.

Case No. 3: Letter written by an official at a high school. "Yi fang wei zao hetong shi fou goucheng wei zheng fei" (Does the Falsification of a Contract Constitute the Crime of Giving False Evidence), *Faxue zazhi* (Legal Studies Magazine), no. 4, 1983, p. 63.

Case No.4: "Yunyong falu shouduan tiaozheng caichan quanyi cujin wanshan nongye shengchan zeren zhi" (Utilize Legal Measures to Adjust Property Rights, Steadily Perfect the Agricultural Production Responsibility System), *Faxue* (Legal Studies), no. 4, 1983, p. 30.

Case No. 5: "Baohu chengbao zhe hefa quanyi de yi fen panjue" (An Adjudication Decision Which Safeguards the Lawful Rights and Interests of Contractors), *Zhongguo fazhi bao* (Chinese Legal System Gazette), June 4, 1984, p. 3.

Case No. 6: "Yi qi jingji hetong an de caijue" (Decision in An Economic Contract Case), *Jingji ribao* (Economy Daily), February 2, 1983, p. 2.

Case No. 7: "Yi qi zhuanye chengbao hetong de jiufen" (A Specialization Contract Dispute), *Jingji ribao* (Economy Daily), January 17, 1983, p. 2.

Case No. 8: "Yi jian nongye chengbao hetong jiufen an" (A Case of An Agricultural Responsibility Contract Dispute), *Zhongguo fazhi bao* (Chinese Legal System Gazette), April 18, 1984, p. 3.

Case No. 9: "Baohu zhuanye hu Zhang Youlin hefa quanyi" (Safeguard the Lawful Rights and Interests of Specialist Zhang Youlin), *Sichuan ribao* (Sichuan Daily), May 17, 1984, p. 2.

Case No. 10: "Caiding yige hetong wanjiu yi pian guoyuan" (Rule on A

Contract, Save An Orchard), *Zhongguo fazhi bao* (Chinese Legal System Gazette), April 1, 1983, p. 1.

Case No. 11: "Wu gu sihui hetong shoudao jingji zhicai" (Nullifying Contracts Without Reason Brings on Economic Sanctions), *Sichuan ribao* (Sichuan Daily), March 3, 1983, p. 2.

Case No. 12: "Wu gu sihui hetong shoudao jingji zhicai" (Nullifying Contracts Without Reason Brings on Economic Sanctions), *Sichuan ribao* (Sichuan Daily), March 3, 1983, p. 2.

Case No. 13: "Qingyuan dadui bu zhixing gou xiao hetong shoudao jingji zhicai" (Qingyuan Brigade's Non-Performance of a Purchase and Sale Contract Brings on Economic Sanctions), *Renmin ribao* (People's Daily), February 22, 1982, p. 1.

Case No. 14: "Ba xian changjiang nong gong shang fen gongsi bei fakuan" (Ba County Division of Changjian Agricultural-Industrial-Commercial Company Bears Fines), *Zhongguo caimao bao* (Chinese Finance and Trade Journal), April 17, 1982 at 1.

Case No. 15: "Shenli jingji jiufen anjian yao renshen zhixing zhengce he yi fa ban shi" (Adjudicating Economic Dispute Cases Requires Conscientiously Implementing Policy and Doing Things According to Law), *Faxue yanjiu* (Legal Studies Research), No. 4, 1982, p. 50.

Case No. 16: Letter from the Tuku School, Fangpin Commune, Huangqu County, Hubei Province. "Jingji hetong yi fang weiyue, ling yi fang shi fou yao luxing yiwu" (Where One Party Breaches an Economic Contract Is the Other Party Bound to Perform Its Obligations), *Faxue zazhi* (Legal Studies Magazine), No. 1, 1984, p. 60.

Case No. 17: Letter from a responsible person in a hotel attached to a supply and marketing co-op in Gelan on prefecture Zhangshou county, Sichuan Province. "Gao gaige, ding hetong, mo xue yegong haolong zen yang chu er fan er" (Carry Out Reform, Sign Contracts, Don't Study Lord Ye's Love of Dragons of How to Go Back on One's Word), *Zhongguo fazhi bao* (Chinese Legal System Gazette), June 13, 1984, p. 1.

Case No. 18: "Yin jia fayuan renzhen shenli bu luxing hetong an" (The Yin Jia Court Conscientiously Adjudicates a Case of Non-Performance), *Zhongguo fazhi bao* (Chinese Legal System Gazette), February 27, 1984, p. 2.

Case No. 19: "Dui nongmin weifan hetong yao yi jiao er fa" (We Need One Education Two Penalties Concerning Peasants Violating Contracts), *Zhongguo fazhi bao* (Chinese Legal System Gazette), February 27, 1984, p. 2.

Case No. 20: "Zhe zhuang sihui hetong de anjian he shi chuli" (When Should This Case of Nullification of Contract Be Handled), *Sichuan ribao* (Sichuan Daily), May 1, 1984, p. 3.

Case No. 21: "Gongya xian fayuan caijue yi qi hetong jiufen" (The Gongya County Court Arbitrates a Contract Dispute), *Sichuan ribao* (Sichuan Daily), April 10, 1984, p. 3.

Case No. 22: "Yibin xian wei yansu chuli yi qi giangzhan chengbao di shijian"

(Yibin County Committee Seriously Handled a Matter of a Seizure of Contract Land), *Sichuan ribao* (Sichuan Daily), January 26, 1983, p. 2.

Case No. 23: "Baohu zhuanye hu de hefa quanyi" (Safeguard the Lawful Rights and Interests of Specialist Households), *Zhongguo fazhi bao* (Chinese Legal System Gazette), March 14, 1984, p. 2.

Case No. 24: "Zhe qi anjian ban de hao" (This Case is Handled Well), *Zhongguo fazhi bao* (Chinese Legal System Gazette), May 16, 1984, p. 3.

Case No. 25: "Dui ganbu zhong zhi hetong chengbao hu liyi shou sun" (A Team of Cadre Cancels a Contract Midway, The Contractor's Interests Suffer Losses), *Wen hui bao* (Literary Gazette), March 21, 1984, p. 4.

Case No. 26: Reported in "Correct Unhealthy Trends to Insure the Implementation of Contracts," Liaoning Provincial Service, April 19, 1983, translated in *FBIS China Report: Agriculture,* May 16, 1983 at 27.

Case No. 27: "Fayuan caijue peichang sunshi" (The Court Decides That Losses Be Compensated), *Sichuan ribao* (Sichuan Daily), April 18, 1984, p. 3.

Case No. 28: "Zhuanye hu de rizi yue guo yue hong huo" (The Life of Specialists is Becoming Exceedingly Prosperous), *Zhongguo fazhi bao* (Chinese Legal System Gazette), March 2, 1984, p. 1.

Case No. 29: "Gongya xian caijue yi qi hetong jiufen an" (Gongya County Arbitrates a Case of a Contract Dispute), *Sichuan ribao* (Sichuan Daily), April 28, 1984, p. 1.

Case No. 30: "Zhixing jingji hetong fa, baohu zhuanye hu hefa quanyi" (Carry Out the Economic Contract Law, Safeguard the Lawful Interests of Specialist Households), *Sichuan ribao* (Sichuan Daily), April 4, 1984, p. 1.

Case No. 31: Letter written by an official in a court at an unspecified location. "Zhe jian tuo yan san nian de hetong jiufen ying ruhe caijue" (How Should We Arbitrate This Contract Dispute Which Has Dragged On for Three Years), *Faxue* (Legal Studies), No. 2, 1982, p. 50.

Case No. 32: Letter written by a person at a shop. "Dui fang bu luxing hetong, neng yaoqiu tuihuan huokuan ma" (Where the Other Party Does Not Perform a Contract, Can We Demand a Return of the Purchase Price), *Minzhu yu fazhi* (Democracy and the Legal System), No. 9, 1982, p. 46.

Case No. 33: Letter from Jinjing Brigade in Yongning county, Guangxi Province. "Dui yu zhe jia gong chang bu yanshou hetong de xingwei yinggai zen ma ban" (How Should We Handle the Actions of This Factory in Not Honoring a Contract), *Zhongguo fazhi bao* (Chinese Legal System Gazette), March 5, 1982, p. 3.

Case No. 34: Letter from a person at an unspecified factory. "Yin jingji tiaozheng er buluxing hetong yao fu jingji zeren ma" (Must Economic Liability Be Borne for Non-Performance of a Contract Due to Economic Adjustment), *Minzhu yu fazhi* (Democracy and the Legal System), No. 9, 1981, p. 47.

Case No. 35: Letter from an unspecified blankets factory. "Ju bu luxing hetong zen me ban" (How Do We Handle Absolute Non-Performance of Contract), *Minzhu yu fazhi* (Democracy and the Legal System), No. 12, 1981, p. 46.

Case No. 36: Letter from an unspecified blankets factory, "Ju bu luxing hetong zen me ban" (How Do We Handle Absolute Non-Performance of Contract), *Minzhu yu fazhi* (Democracy and the Legal System), No. 12, 1981, p. 46.

Case No. 37: Letter from a court official. "Ming zhi cha zhi di lie, qianding le hetong shi hou fanhui ru he caijue" (How Do We Arbitrate Where It is Obvious the Tea is of Substandard Quality and the Contract is Renounced After It Has Been Signed), *Faxue* (Legal Studies), No. 5, 1982, p. 50.

Case No. 38: Letter from a court official. "Dui hetong lijie bu yi, fasheng jiufen, ying ru he tiao chu" (How Should We Mediate Where a Dispute is Brought About By Inconsistent Understanding of the Contract), *Faxue* (Legal Studies), No. 3, 1982, p. 46.

Case No. 39: Letter from the Dongli Brigade of Daijing commune in Liqing county, Zhejiang Province. "Sihui hetong keyi qingqiu zhongcai ma" (Can We Seek Arbitration Where a Contract Has Been Nullified), *Faxue zazhi* (Legal Studies Magazine), No. 5, 1981, p. 58.

Case No. 40: Letter from court official. "Zhe qi 'zi bu di ze' de hetong jiufen ying ru he caijue" (How Should We Arbitrate This Contract Dispute Where Capital Doesn't Meet Responsibilities), *Faxue* (Legal Studies), No. 6, 1982, p. 51.

Case No. 41: Letter from Luoyang city, Henan Provide. "Zhe fen hetong shi fou rengran you xiao" (Is This Contract Still Valid), *Zhongguo fazhi bao* (Chinese Legal System Gazette), July 30, 1982, p. 3.

Case No. 42: Letter from Hongguang Farm, Yuanjiang county, Yunnan Province. "Ying chengdan de jingji zeren qineng lai diao" (How Can It Be That the Economic Responsibility Which Should Be Assumed is Repudiated), *Zhongguo fazhi bao* (Chinese Legal System Gazette), March 19, 1984, p. 4.

Case No. 43: Letter from an individual in Tongliang county, Sichuan Province. "Shi lai baohu wo de hefa quan yi" (Who Will Come to Protect My Lawful Rights and Interests), *Zhongguo fazhi bao* (Chinese Legal System Gazette), April 19, 1984, p. 4.

Case No. 44: Letter from Beijing. "Yin shang ji lingdao jiguan huo yewu zhuguan jiguan de guocuo, zaocheng jingji hetong bu neng luxing de, yingdang you shei chengdan zeren" (Who Should Bear Liability When Errors By Higher Level Leadership Organs or Business Management Organs Cause An Economic Contract To Be Unable to Be Performed), *Faxue zazhi* (Legal Studies Magazine), No. 1, 1984, p. 60.

Case No. 45: Letter from Chunyang tree farm under the Baihe Forestry Bureau, Jilin Province. "Zhe shifou suan wei yue xingwei" (Does This Count As Activity in Breach of Contract), *Zhongguo fazhi bao* (Chinese Legal System Gazette), December 11, 1981, p. 3.

Case No. 46: Letter from court official. "Hetong chexiao hou fasheng de jiufen ying ru he jiejue" (How Should A Dispute Brought On After Revocation of A Contract Be Resolved), *Faxue* (Legal Studies), No. 7, 1982, p. 52.

Case No. 47: Letter from a People's Liberation Army unit in an unspecified location. "Women zhe qi yin chanpin zhiliang bu fuhe guiding de hetong jiufen ru he jiejue" (How Should We Resolve This Contract Dispute Due to the Quality of Goods Not Meeting Requirements), *Zhongguo fazhi bao* (Chinese Legal System Gazette), April 23, 1984, p. 3.

Case No. 48: "Jianyi dui shedui qiye jingji hetong jiaqiang guanli jiandu" (Recommendation to Strengthen Management Supervision Over the Economic Contracts of Commune and Brigade Enterprises), *Zhongguo fazhi bao* (Chinese Legal System Gazette), August 21, 1981, p. 4.

Case No. 49: "Jige you quan jingji jiufen de anli" (Several Cases Relating to Economic Disputes), *Minzhu yu fazhi* (Democracy and the Legal System), No. 9, 1981, p. 12.

Case No. 50: "Chang qi maodun jiejue dangshi ge fang tongyi" (A Long Term Contradiction Is Resolved, Each of the Parties Is Satisfied), *Zhongguo fazhi bao* (Chinese Legal System Gazette), January 9, 1981, p. 2.

Case No. 51: "Zhixing fayuan qiang zhi zhixing falu wenshu" (Carry Out the System of Court Ordered Enforcement, Carry Out the Legal Document), *Zhongguo fazhi bao* (Chinese Legal System Gazette), February 8, 1984, p. 2.

Case No. 52: "Cong yi qi hetong jiufen kan yansu dui dai hetong de zhongyao xing" (From the Viewpoint of a Contract Dispute, Treat the Importance of Contracts Seriously), *Zhongguo fazhi bao* (Chinese Legal System Gazette), January 23, 1981, p. 2.

Case No. 53: "Chang qi maodun jiejue dangshi gefang manyi" (A Long Term Contradiction Is Resolved, Each of the Parties Is Satisfied), *Zhongguo fazhi bao* (Chinese Legal System Gazette), January 9, 1981, p. 2.

Case No. 54: Reported in *FBIS Daily Report: China,* June 26, 1980 at L. 13.

Case No. 55: Reported in *Law Annual Report of China* (1982) at 201.

Case No. 56: "Li shi wu nian gouxiao hetong jiufen de jiejue" (The Resolution of a Five Year Old Dispute Over a Purchase and Sale Contract), *Jingji ribao* (Economy Daily), March 1, 1983, p. 2.

Case No. 57: "Wu nian jiufen yi xijie ting chan qiye you fu ye" (A Five Year Dispute Is Resolved Overnight, Any Enterprise Which Stopped Production Resumes Business), *Zhongguo fazhi bao* (Chinese Legal System Gazette), June 22, 1984, p. 2.

Case No. 58: "Qingyang xian lushi jiji kaizhan jingji jiufen daili gongzuo" (The Lawyers of Qingyang County Actively Begin Representation Work in Economic Disputes), *Zhongguo fazhi bao* (Chinese Legal System Gazette), February 1, 1984, p. 2.

Case No. 59: "Yi qi maimai jiufen de tiaochu" (The Handling by Mediation of a Purchase and Sale Dispute), *Zhongguo fazhi bao* (Chinese Legal System Gazette), November 20, 1981, p. 2.

Case No. 60: "Yi fen hu tu hetong yinqi de guansi" (A Lawsuit Brought On By a Recklessly Scribbled Contract), *Sichang* (The Market), November 23, 1981, p. 2.

Case No. 61: "Wu xiao hetong bu zu wei ju" (An Ineffective Contract Is Insufficient As Evidence), *Jingji ribao* (Economy Daily), April 4, 1983, p. 2.

Case No. 62: "Yi qi wu zhiliang biaozhun de hetong jiufen shi zen yang dedao yuanman jiejue de" (How Is a Dispute Over a Contract Lacking Quality Standards to Be Satisfactorily Resolved), *Faxue zazhi* (Legal Studies Magazine), No. 2, 1982, p. 44.

Case No. 63: "Jianyi dui shedui qiye jingji hetong jiaqiang guanli jiandu" (Recommendation to Strengthen Management Supervision Over the Economic Contracts of Commune and Brigade Enterprises), *Zhongguo fazhi bao* (Chinese Legal System Gazette), August 21, 1981, p. 4.

Case No. 64: "Jingji fating zuoyong da" (The Role of the Economic Chambers Is Great), *Zhongguo fazhi bao* (Chinese Legal System Gazette), November 18, 1983, p. 2.

Case No. 65–67: "Shenli jingji jiufen anjian yao renzhen zhixing zhengce he yi fa ban shi" (Adjudicating Case of Economic Disputes Requires That We Conscientiously Implement Policy and Do Things According to Law), *Faxue zazhi* (Legal Studies Magazine), No. 4, 1982, p. 50.

Case No. 68: "Tantan dui jingji hetong jiufén anjian de shenli" (Discussion of the Adjudication of Cases of Economic Contract Disputes), *Faxue zazhi* (Legal Studies Magazine), No. 6, 1982, p. 39.

Case No. 69: "Yi qi mai mai hetong jiufen de jiejue" (The Resolution of A Purchase and Sale Contract Dispute), *Guangming ribao* (Guangming Daily), February 16, 1982, p. 3.

Case No. 70: "Yi qi tuituji mai mai jiufen an de shenli" (The Adjudication of a Case of a Bulldozer Purchase and Sale Dispute), *Minzhu yu fazhi* (Democracy and the Legal System), No. 12, 1981, p. 10.

Case No. 71: "Yong falu banfa jiejue jingji hetong zhixing zhong de jiufen" (Use Legal Methods to Resolve a Dispute in the Midst of Performance of an Economic Contract), *Guangming ribao* (Guangming Daily), September 21, 1982, p. 3.

Case No. 72: "Wu shi liang qiche de jiufen" (Dispute Over Fifty Vehicles), *Jingji ribao* (Economy Daily), January 1, 1983, p. 2.

Case No. 73: "Bu shou hetong chi guansi, hai gei duifang pei sunshi" (Not Observing Contracts Brings On a Lawsuit and Also Gives the Other Party Compensation for Losses), *Shichang* (The Market), September 14, 1981, p. 2.

Case No. 74: "Zhe qi jingji hetong shifou hefa you xiao" (Is This Economic Contract Legally Effective), *Faxue* (Legal Studies), No. 9, 1982, p. 52.

Case No. 75: "Yi xin zai jingji shenpan gongzuo shang" (Devotion in Economic Adjudication Work), *Zhongguo fazhi bao* (Chinese Legal System Gazette), April 11, 1984, p. 3.

Case No. 76: "Yi fa zhuijiu bu luxing hetong yifang de jingji zeren" (Investigate According to Law of the Economic Responsibility for Non-Performance of Contract), *Zhongguo fazhi bao* (Chinese Legal System Gazette), July 15, 1983, p. 3.

Case No. 77: "Fayuan jiejue jiufen jinqi ji shenqing" (The Court Resolves a Dispute, A Silk Banner Gives Deep Feelings), *Jingji ribao* (Economy Daily), March 19, 1983, p. 2.

Case No. 78: "Qingyang xian lushi jiji kaizhan jingji jiufen daili gongzuo" (The Lawyers of Qingyang County Actively Launch Representation Work in Economic Disputes), *Zhongguo fazhi bao* (Chinese Legal System Gazette), February 1, 1984, p. 2.

Case No. 79: "Shei shi zhe yi gouxiao hetong jiufen anjian de beigao ren" (Who Is the Defendant in This Case of a Purchase and Sale Contract Dispute), *Zhongguo fazhi bao* (Chinese Legal System Gazette), April 20, 1984, p. 3.

Case No. 80: "Qianding hetong yao hefa" (The Signing of Contracts Must Be Legal), *Jingji ribao* (Economy Daily), March 8, 1983, p. 2.

Case No. 81: "Taiyuan shi huayi shangdian shou jingji zhicai" (The Huayi Store of Taiyuan City Bears Economic Sanctions), *Zhongguo fazhi bao* (Chinese Legal System Gazette), April 4, 1984, p. 1.

Case No. 82: "Chang she jiagong hetong jiufen an" (A Case of a Processing Contract Dispute Between a Factory and a Commune), *Zhongguo fazhi bao* (Chinese Legal System Gazette), September 19, 1980.

Case No. 83: "Tamen xin zhong hai you guojia falu ma?" (Do They Still Have the State's Law in Their Hearts), *Zhongguo fazhi bao* (Chinese Legal System Gazette), February 27, 1984, p. 2.

Case No. 84: "Chongqing shi zhong ji renmin fayuan chengli" (The Chongqing Municipal Middle Level Court Is Established), *Renmin ribao* (People's Daily), July 17, 1979, p. 3.

Case No. 85: "Jige you guan jingji jiufen de anjian" (Several Cases Related to Economic Disputes), *Minzhu yu fazhi* (Democracy and the Legal System), No. 9, 1981, p. 12.

Cases No. 86–90: "Shenli jingji jiufen anjian yao renshen zhixing zhengce he yi fa ban shi" (Adjudicating Economic Dispute Cases Requires Conscientiously Implementing Policy and Doing Things According to Law), *Faxue yanjiu* (Legal Studies Research), No. 4, 1982, p. 50.

Case No. 91: "Tantan dui jingji hetong jiufen anjian de shenli" (Discussion of Adjudication of Cases Economic Contract Disputes), *Faxue zazhi* (Legal Studies Magazine), No. 6, 1982, p. 39.

Case No. 92: "Tantan dui jingji hetong jiufen anjian de shenli" (Discussion of Adjudication of Cases of Economic Contract Disputes), *Faxue zazhi* (Legal Studies Magazine), No. 6, 1982, p. 39.

Case No. 93: "Er shi wan yuan jingji jiufen jiejue le" (A 200,000 Yuan Dispute Is Resolved), *Jingji ribao* (Economy Daily), January 20, 1983, p. 2.

Case No. 94: "Yifa tiaojie jiufen gongzheng caiding hetong" (Mediate Disputes Based on Law, Impartially Arbitrate Contracts), *Zhongguo fazhi bao* (Chinese Legal System Gazette), April 22, 1983, p. 2.

Case No. 95: "Weifan jing gongzheng ji jian hetong ying ru he chuli" (How Should the Violation of a Notarized Capital Construction Control Be Handled?), *Faxue jikan* (Legal Studies Quarterly), No. 4, 1982, p. 71.

Case No. 96: "Zhong dian jiejue shedui qiye hetong jiufen" (Give Attention to Resolving Disputes Over Commune and Brigade Enterprise Contracts), *Zhongguo fazhi bao* (Chinese Legal System Gazette), April 15, 1983, p. 1.

Case No. 97: Letter from Jiangsu Province. "Zhe bi huokuan shi fou ying an hetong guiding de jiage jiesuan" (Should This Purchase Price Be Calculated According to the Price Set in the Contract), *Minzhu yu fazhi* (Democracy and the Legal System), No. 5, 1984, p. 47.

Case No. 98: Letter from Liaoning Province. "Yan qi jiaofu chanpin de ling bu jian, ying ru he jisuan wei yue jin" (How Do We Calculate Liquidated Damages for Parts Delivered), *Zhongguo fazhi bao* (Chinese Legal System Gazette), March 9, 1984, p. 3.

Case No. 99: Letter from Beijing Municipality "Chang zhang tiaozou le, ta qianding de hetong shi fou wu xiao" (Where the Factory Head is Transferred Are the Contracts He Signed Ineffective), *Minzhu yu fazhi* (Democracy and the Legal System), No. 3, 1984, p. 46.

Case No. 100: Letter from a factory in Shanghai Municipality. "Zen yang zhengque queding zhe tai shebei de jiaohuo riqi" (How Do We Determine Correctly the Delivery Date for This Equipment), *Zhongguo fazhi bao* (Democracy and the Legal System), April 16, 1984, p. 3.

Case No. 101: Letter from a unit in Tianjin Municipality. "Gong fang yan qi jiaohuo xu fang nengfou ju shou" (Where the Supplier Is Late In Delivery Can the Customer Refuse Acceptance), *Zhongguo fazhi bao* (Chinese Legal System Gazette), December 23, 1983, p. 3.

Case No. 102: Letter from unit in Hebei Province. "Yan qi jiaohuo yao fu shen me zeren" (What Responsibility Should Be Borne for Late Delivery of Goods), *Zhongguo fazhi bao* (Chinese Legal System Gazette), January 2, 1984, p. 3.

Case No. 103: Letter from an individual in unspecified location. "Zhe yi hetong guanxi shi fou cunzai, qiche chan quan gui shei" (Does This Contract Relation Exist, To Whom Is the Property Right in This Car Returned), *Zhongguo fazhi bao* (Chinese Legal System Gazette), February 24, 1984, p. 3.

Case No. 104: Letter from a store in Sichuan Province. "Hetong zhong de biwu ru he chuli" (How Is A Slip of the Pen in a Contract Handled), *Zhongguo fazhi bao* (Chinese Legal System Gazette), March 9, 1984, p. 3.

Case No. 105: Letter from a unit in Jiangsu Province. "Shei ying chengdan bu luxing hetong de zeren" (Who Should Bear the Responsibility for Non-

Performance of Contract), *Minzhu yu fazhi* (Democracy and the Legal System), No. 4, 1984, p. 48.

Case No. 106: Letter from Zhejiang Province. "Dan fangmian chexiao hetong ying ru he chuli" (How Should Unilateral Cancellation of Contract Be Handled), *Zhongguo fazhi bao* (Chinese Legal System Gazette), May 11, 1984, p. 3.

Case No. 107: Letter from Hubei Province. "Zhe fen mai mai hetong shi fou you xiao" (Is This Purchase and Sale Contract Effective), *Zhongguo fazhi bao* (Chinese Legal System Gazette), June 25, 1984, p. 3.

Case No. 108: Letter from Fanzhi county in Shaanxi Province. "Bu jing chengzu ren tongyi shou hui bing chu mai zu wu shifou hefa" (Is Repossession and Sale of Leased Materials Without the Consent of the Lessee Lawful), *Zhongguo fazhi bao* (Chinese Legal System Gazette), April 16, 1984, p. 3.

Case No. 109: "Dui nongmin weifan hetong yao yi jiao er fa" (We Need One Education, Two Penalties Regarding Peasants Breaching Contracts), *Zhongguo fazhi bao* (Chinese Legal System Gazette), February 27, 1984, p. 2.

Case No. 110: "Yi zi duan shen fu" (One Character Decides Victory and Defeat), *Zhongguo fazhi bao* (Chinese Legal System Gazette), January 11, 1984, p. 2.

Case No. 111: "Shanghai gang jichang peikuan shi er wan" (The Shanghai Harbor Machinery Factory Pays Indemnity of 120,000), *Jiefang ribao* (Liberation Daily), March 4, 1983, p. 1.

Case No. 112: "Guanyu jingji jiufen anjian you queding de tantao" (Inquiry Concerning an Economic Dispute Being Determined), *Faxue zazhi* (Legal Studies Magazine), No. 6 1983, p. 50.

Case No. 113: "Qingyang xian lushi jiji kaizhan jingji jiufen daili gongzuo" (The Lawyers of Qingyang County Actively Launch Representation Work in Economic Disputes), *Zhongguo fazhi bao* (Chinese Legal System Gazette), February 1, 1984, p. 2.

Case No. 114: "Jingji gongzuo xuyao lushi" (Economic Work Requires Lawyers), *Zhongguo fazhi bao* (Chinese Legal System Gazette), April 16, 1984, p. 2.

Case No. 115: "Chushou lie zhi linfei wenti wei he de bu dao chuli" (Why Has the Issue of a Sale of Poor Quality Phosphorous Not Been Handled), *Zhongguo fazhi bao* (Chinese Legal System Gazette), April 2, 1984, p. 1.

Case No. 116: "Yi qian dou nai fen an" (The Case of One Thousand Bags of Milk Powder), *Zhongguo fazhi bao* (Chinese Legal System Gazette), November 11, 1983, p. 2.

Case No. 117: "Dui jingji hetong yao jiaqiang guanli" (We Must Strengthen Management of Economic Contracts), *Renmin ribao* (People's Daily), June 7, 1983.

Case No. 118: "Ben shi fayuan jiji kaizhan jingji shenpan gongzuo" (This City's Courts Actively Launch Economic Adjudication Work), *Jiefang ribao* (Liberation Daily), March 10, 1984, p. 3.

Case No. 119: "Ben shi fayuan jiji kaizhan jingji shenpan gongzuo" (This City's Courts Actively Launch Economic Adjudication Work), *Jiefang ribao* (Liberation Daily), March 10, 1984, p. 3.

Case No. 120: "Jingji anjian zhong de lushi huodong" (The Activities of Lawyers in Economic Cases), *Faxue yanjiu* (Legal Studies Research), No. 2, 1983, p. 44.

Case No. 121: "Lushi bang women jiejue le jiufen" (Lawyers Helped Us Resolve a Dispute), *Zhongguo fazhi bao* (Chinese Legal System Gazette), September 30, 1983, p. 3.

Case No. 122: "Yi fa guan qi yinian lirun fan liang fan" (Managing an Enterprise According to Law, In One Year, Profits Were Quadrupled), *Zhongguo fazhi bao* (Chinese Legal System Gazette), January 20, 1984, p. 1.

Case No. 123: "Tangshan shi si shi wu jia qishiye danwei pinqing falu guwen" (Forty-five Business Units in Tangshan Hire Legal Advisors), *Zhongguo fazhi bao* (Chinese Legal System Gazette), February 1, 1984, p. 3.

Case No. 124: "Zhe fen hetong dai lai de sunhai houguo ying you shei fuze" (Who Should Bear Liability for the Harmful Results Brought On by This Contract), *Zhongguo fazhi bao* (Chinese Legal System Gazette), February 13, 1984, p. 3.

Case No. 125: "Qianjiang xian yong fa guan hetong xianshi 'fa shen' weili" (Qianjiang County's Use of Law to Manage Contracts Manifests the Power of the 'Spirit of the Law'), *Zhongguo fazhi bao* (Chinese Legal System Gazette), March 21, 1984, p. 2.

Case No. 126: "Yi xiang bi bu ke shao de zhidu" (An Indispensable System), *Zhongguo fazhi bao* (Chinese Legal System Gazette), April 4, 1984, p. 2.

Case No. 127: "Pinqing chang nian falu guwen tigao qiye jingji xiaoyi" (Hiring Legal Advisors Throughout the Year Raises the Economic Benefits of Enterprises), *Zhongguo fazhi bao* (Chinese Legal System Gazette), May 30, 1984, p. 2.

Case No. 128: "Zhe bi er kuan ying you shei chang huan" (Who Should Repay This Debt), *Zhongguo fazhi bao* (Chinese Legal System Gazette), June 22, 1984, p. 3.

Case No. 129: "Tianjin hexi qu fayuan gongkai shenli yiqi jingji jiufen an" (The Court in Tianjin's Hexi District Publicly Adjudicates a Case of an Economic Dispute), *Zhongguo fazhi bao* (Chinese Legal System Gazette), February 8, 1984, p. 2.

Case No. 130: "Jingji anjian zhong de lushi huodong" (The Activities of Lawyers in Economic Cases), *Faxue yanjiu* (Legal Studies Research), No. 2, 1983, p. 44.

Case No. 131: "Nanjing zhong ji fayuan renzhen zuo hao jingji shenpan gongzuo" (The Nanjing Middle Level Court Conscientiously Does a Good Job in Economic Adjudication Work), *Renmin ribao* (People's Daily), June 24, 1984, p. 4.

Appendix 2. Table of Interview Subjects

A. *Hong Kong Interviews.* (Interview notes on file with the author.)

1. Sex: Male
   Age: 50 years old
   Native Province: Fujian
   Relevant Employment: Worked in Secretarial office and in the foreign trade office of an oil company in Guangdong Province
   Arrived in Hong Kong in 1982

2. Sex: Male
   Age: 45 years old
   Native Province: Jiangsu
   Relevant employment: Worked in Public Security Bureaus in Nanjing and Hangzhou (1963–73); Worked in Food Processing Office in Gansu (1973–81)
   Arrived in Hong Kong in 1981

3. Sex: Male
   Age: Mid-40s
   Native City: Beijing
   Education: Beijing University Law Department, Beijing Political-Legal Institute
   Relevant Employment: Worked as investigator in higher-level people's court in Beijing
   Arrived in Hong Kong in 1978

4. Sex: Female
   Age: 55 years old
   Native Province: Guangdong
   Education: Beijing Political-Legal Institute
   Relevant Employment: Worked in Notary Office in Chongqing during 1950s
   Arrived in Hong Kong in 1978

5. Sex: Male
   Age: 45 years old
   Native Province: Guangdong
   Relevant Employment: Worked in Procuracy in Qinghai during early 1960s
   Arrived Hong Kong in 1980

6. Sex: Male
   Age: 47 years old
   Native Province: Guangdong
   Education: Economic Department of Xiamen University
   Relevant Employment: Overseas Chinese Department of State Council.
   Arrived Hong Kong in 1974

7. Sex: Male
   Age: Late 30s
   Native Province: Guangdong
   Relevant Employment: Worked in State-run Tea Market on Hainan Island from 1966–82
   Arrived Hong Kong in 1982

8. Sex: Male
   Age: 47 years old
   Native Province: Hunan
   Relevant Employment: Worked in responsible office in coal mine in Liaoning from 1959–82
   Arrived Hong Kong in 1982

9. Sex: Male
   Age: Late 50s
   Native Province: Hubei
   Education: Central China Institute of Industry
   Relevant Employment: Worked in ordering office of Central China Institute of Industry until 1973.
   Arrived Hong Kong in 1980

10. Sex: Male
   Age: 43 years old
   Native Province: Guangdong
   Education: Beijing Political-Legal Institute
   Relevant Employment: Worked in Public Security Bureaux in Xinjiang (1964–67); Worked in People's Congress of Guangdong (1967–74); Worked in management office of factory in Guangzhou (1974–80)
   Arrived Hong Kong in 1980

11. Sex: Male
    Age: 44 years old
    Native Province: Fujian
    Relevant Employment: Worked in county-level bank in Fujian (1962–78)
    Arrived Hong Kong in 1978

12. Sex: Male
    Age:
    Native Area: Overseas Chinese from Thailand
    Education: Huadong Political-Legal Institute (1 year)
    Relevant Employment: Worked in management office of machine factory in Shanghai (1962–66)
    Arrived Hong Kong in 1979

13. Sex: Male
    Age: 40 years old
    Native Province: Shaanxi
    Relevant Employment: Worked in quality management office of factory in Gansu (1973–81)
    Arrived Hong Kong in 1981

14. Sex: Male
    Age: Late 50s
    Native Area: Hong Kong
    Relevant Employment: Worked in management office of electric tool company in Nanjing for 15 years
    Arrived Hong Kong in 1981

15. Sex: Male
    Age: 58 years old
    Native City: Shanghai
    Education: Wuhan University Economics Department
    Relevant Employment: Worked in management office of Guangdong Provincial Mechanics Supply and Marketing Service Center (1972–82)
    Arrived Hong Kong in 1982

16. Sex: Male
    Age: 52 years old
    Native Province: Guangdong
    Relevant Employment: Worked in contract management office of engineering construction company in Guangdong (1973–81)
    Arrived Hong Kong in 1981

17. Sex: Male
    Age: 46 years old
    Native Province: Guangdong
    Relevant Employment: Worked in planning office of oil refining company in Guangdong (1962–82)
    Arrived Hong Kong in 1982

18. Sex: Male
    Age: 41 years old
    Native Province: Guangdong
    Relevant Employment: Worked in management office of a machinery factory in Guangdong (1970–82)
    Arrived Hong Kong in 1982

19. Sex: Male
    Age: Mid 40s
    Native Province: Sichuan
    Relevant Employment: Worked in financial office of a machinery supply and marketing department (1974–83)
    Arrived Hong Kong in 1983

20. Sex: Male
    Age: 34 years old
    Native Province: Guangdong
    Education: Kunming Industrial Institute
    Relevant Employment: Worked in management office of Yunnan Provincial engineering tools company (1976–81)
    Arrived Hong Kong in 1981

21. Sex: Male
    Age: 50 years old
    Native Province: Guangdong
    Education: Zhongshan University Engineering Department
    Relevant Employment: Worked in management office of machinery factory in Guangzhou
    Arrived Hong Kong in 1983

22. Sex: Male
    Age: 50 years old
    Native Province: Guangdong
    Relevant Employment: Worked in technical office of a supply and marketing department in Guangzhou
    Arrived Hong Kong in 1982

23. Sex: Male
Age: Late 40s
Native Province: Guangdong
Relevant Employment: Worked in the management office of a chemical factory in Zhejiang (1961–81).
Arrived Hong Kong in 1981

24. Sex: Male
Age: 41
Native Area: Overseas Chinese from Malaysia
Relevant Employment: Worked in office under Ministry of Trade in Hubei (1964–81).
Arrived Hong Kong in 1981

25. Sex: Male
Age: Late 40s
Native City: Beijing
Relevant Employment: Worked as secretary (1961–79) and as vice-director (1979–81) of a Beijing factory.
Arrived Hong Kong in 1981

26. Sex: Male
Age: 40 years old
Native Province: Guangdong
Education: Zhongshan University Political Economy Department
Relevant Employment: Worked in economic administrative offices of Guangzhou (1970–77).
Arrived Hong Kong in 1977

27. Sex: Male
Age: 46 years old
Native City: Beijing
Relevant Employment: Worked in management office of chemical factory in Beijing (1963–79).
Arrived Hong Kong in 1979

28. Sex: Male
Age: Early 60s
Native Province: Guangdong
Relevant Employment: Worked in planning office of a machinery and electric tool factory of Guangdong (1957–82).
Arrived Hong Kong in 1982

29. Sex: Male
    Age: 37 years old
    Native Province: Guizhou
    Relevant Employment: Worked as a teacher of political economy and later as head of the economics department of University of Guizhou (1971–1982). Also worked in provincial commerce departments.
    Arrived Hong Kong in 1982

30. Sex: Male
    Age: 30 years old
    Native Province: Guangdong
    Relevant Employment: Worked for military procurator's office. Also worked in factory office in Tianjin.
    Arrived in Hong Kong: (declined to answer)

31. Sex: Male
    Age: 46 years old
    Native Province: Guangdong
    Relevant Employment: Taught in finance department in school in Guangdong. Also worked in Guangdong economics department.
    Arrived in Hong Kong in 1978

B. *Beijing Interviews*. (Interview notes on file with the author.)

1. Interview with Wang Jiafu (Director), Liang Huixing (Researcher) at Legal Studies Research Institute, Chinese Academy of Social Studies, April 5, 1983. Xiao Mingping also attended.

2. Interview with Wu Lei (Vice-chairman, Law Dept.), Kang Jingcheng (Chairman, Economic Law Research Office), Liu Wenhua (Professor, Law Dept.), and Kang Baotian (Professor, Law Dept.) at Chinese People's University, April 6, 1983.

3. Interview with Wang Zhengming of Economic Laws and Regulations Research Center of State Council, April 6, 1983. Wang is an economist by training and formerly served in the State Economic Commission.

4. Interview with Rui Mu (International Law Section), Li Meiqin (Specialist on International Trade at Economic Law Research Office), and Wei Zhenying (Specialist on Civil Law and Economic Contracts) of Beijing University, April 9, 1983.

5. Meeting with Wang Xuezhen, vice-president of Beijing University, April 11, 1983. Wang was trained as a lawyer during the 1950s.

6. Interview with Yang Rongxin (Civil Procedure Law Research Office) and Xu Jie (Economic Law Research Office) of Beijing Political-Legal Institute, April 14, 1983.

Appendix 3. Table of Regulations

A. *1950–1965.*

"Provisional Methods for Signing Contracts and Charters By Organizations and State Enterprises and Cooperatives." Issued by Finance and Economic Committee of the Governmental Administrative Council (9/27/50), Guowuyuan jingji fa gui yanjiu zhongxin bangongshi (Office of the Economic Laws and Regulations Research Center of the State Council), *Jingji hetong fa gui xuanbian* (Compilation of Laws and Regulations on Economic Contracts) Beijing (1982) at 24.

"Decision on the Careful Signing and Strict Enforcement of Contracts." Issued by the Trade Ministry of the Central People's Government (10/3/50), *Jingji hetong fa gui xuanbian* (Compilation of Laws and Regulations on Economic Contracts), Beijing (1982) at 27.

Treasury Contract Standard Provisions. Issued by the People's Bank of China (1/2/51).

a. "Provisions of Treasury Contracts involving Trade."
b. "Provisions of Treasury Contracts involving Railroads."
c. "Provisions of Treasury Contracts involving Posts and Telecommunications."
d. "Provisions of Treasury Contracts involving Trade Unions."

Source: *Jinrong fa gui huibian 1948–1952* (Compilation of Finance Laws and Regulations 1949–1952), Beijing (1956) at 74 et seq.

"Basic Regulations for the Signing of Transport Contracts." Issued by Ministry of Railroads (10/20/54). *Jingji hetong fa gui xuanbian* (Compilation of Laws and Regulations on Economic Contracts), Beijing (1982) at 29.

"Directive on Signing Collective Contracts by Producing Factories and Mines." Issued by the Ministry for Heavy Industry and the National Congress of Chinese Heavy Industry Trade Unions (4/11/55). Source: *Zhonghua renmin gongheguo fa gui huibian* (Compilation of the Laws and Regulations of the PRC), Vol. 1, Beijing (1956) at 440.

"Provisional Basic Regulations of the Ministry of Heavy Industry for Products Supply Contracts." Issued by Ministry of Heavy Industry (7/1/56). Source: Zhongguo Renmin Daxue min fa jiao yan shi (Civil Law Teaching and Research Office of the Chinese People's University), *Zhonghua renmin gong-*

heguo minfa cankao ziliao (Reference Materials on PRC Civil Law), Beijing, 1956, at 243.

"Basic Special Regulations for Construction, Installation, and Engineering Projects Contracts" (Draft). Source: *Zhonghua renmin gongheguo minfa cankao ziliao* (Reference Materials on PRC Civil Law), Beijing, 1956, at 284.

"Model Regulations for an Agricultural Producer's Cooperatives." Issued by the Standing Committee of the National People's Congress (3/17/56). Source: Wang Enmao, *Selected Legal Documents of the People's Republic of China,* Arlington, Virginia: University Publications (1976) at 483.

"Joint Circular Concerning Several Present Questions Regarding the Linkage Between Industrial and Commercial Planning and the Fulfillment of Economic Contracts." Issued by Ministry of Commerce and the Ministry for Local Industry (4/13/56). Source: *Jingji hetong fa gui xuanbian* (Compilation of Laws and Regulations on Economic Contracts), Beijing (1982) at 32.

"Resolution on the Revamping of Rural Financial and Trade Control System to Adapt to the Situation of People's Communalization." Issued by the Central Committee (12/20/58). See Article 6. Source: Joint Publications Research Service, *Compendium of Laws and Regulations of the People's Republic of China,* Vol. 1 (1962) at 102 et seq.

"Regulations Concerning Certain Questions in the Work of the Credit Department of People's Communes and Concerning the Fluid Capital of State Enterprises." Issued by the State Council (12/20/58). See Article 7. Source: Joint Publications Research Service, *Compendium of Laws and Regulations of the People's Republic of China,* Vol. 1 (1962) at 325.

Joint Notice on the thorough Execution of Transaction Settlements." Issued by the Ministry of Commerce and the People's Bank of China (10/7/60). Source: Joint Publications Research Service, *Collection of Fiscal Laws and Regulations of the People's Republic of China 1958–1960* (1963) at 75.

"Regulations on the Work of State—Managed Industrial Enterprises—Draft" (Seventy Articles on Industry). (9/16/61) Source: Guojia jingji weiyuanhui jingji fa gui ju (Economic Laws and Regulations Bureau of the State Economic Commission) and Beijing Zheng Fa Xueyuan jingji fa min fa jiao yan shi (Teaching and Research Office for Economic and Civil Law of the Beijing Institute for Politics and Law), *Zhongguo gongye jingji fa gui huibian* (Compilation of Economic Laws and Regulations for Chinese Industry), (1961) at 545.

"Revised Draft Regulations on the Work of the People's Communes in Agricultural Villages." Published by Republic of China (1962). See Section 21.

"Circular Concerning the Strict Enforcement of Basic Construction Procedures and the Strict Enforcement of Economic Contracts." Issued by the Central Committee and the State Council (12/10/62). Source: *Jingji hetong fa gui xuanbian* (Compilation of Laws and Regulations on Economic Contracts), Beijing (1982) at 35.

"Provisional Regulations for the Basic Provisions of Contracts for the Ordering of Factory and Mining Goods." Issued by the State Economic Committee (8/30/63). Source: *Jingji hetong fa gui xuanbian* (Compilation of Laws and Regulations on Economic Contracts), Beijing (1982) at 53.

"Circular Amending the Provisions Concerning Penalties for Delayed Payment contained in the 'Provisional Regulations for the Basic Provisions of Contracts for the Ordering of Factory and Mining Goods'." Issued by the State Economic Committee (3/28/65). Source: *Jingji hetong fa gui xuanbian* (Compilation of Laws and Regulations on Economic Contracts), Beijing (1982) at 65.

"Circular Amending the Provisions Concerning Penalties for Delays in the Delivery and Acceptance contained in the 'Provisional Regulations for the Basic Provisions of Contracts for the Ordering of Factory and Mining Goods'." Issued by the State Economic Committee (12/14/65). Source: *Jingji hetong fa gui xuanbian* (Compilation of Laws and Regulations on Economic Contracts), Beijing (1982) at 66.

B. *1978–*

(1) Industrial and Commercial Contracts.

"Decision on Several Questions Concerning Accelerating Industrial Production", (4/20/78). Source: *Zhongguo gongye jingji fa gui huibian* (Compilation of Economic Laws and Regulations on China's Industrial Economy), Beijing (1979) at 36.

"Provisional Methods for the Management of Materials Cooperation Among Provinces, Centrally Administered Cities, and Autonomous Regions." (5/8/78). Source: *Jingji hetong fa gui xuanbian* (Compilation of Laws and Regulations on Economic Contracts), Beijing (1982) at 91.

"Opinion of the State Capital Construction Commission Concerning Broadening the Contract System in Capital Construction." (4/20/79). Source: *Jingji hetong fa gui xuanbian* (Compilation of Laws and Regulations on Economic Contracts), Beijing (1982) at 37.

"Provisional Regulations on Construction, Installation, and Engineering Contracts" (4/20/79). Source: *Jingji hetong fa gui xuanbian* (Compilation of Laws and Regulations on Economic Contracts), Beijing (1982) at 42.

"Provisional Regulations on Surveying and Design Contracts (4/20/79). Source: *Jingji hetong fa gui xuanbian* (Compilation of Laws and Regulations on Economic Contracts), Beijing (1982) at 49.

"Circular Concerning Grasping Well the Signing and Implementation of 1979 Ordering Contracts" (5/11/79). Source: *Jingji hetong ziliao* (Materials on Economic Contracts), Beijing (1980) at 28.

"Circular Concerning Methods of Handling Machinery and Electrical Goods Ordering Contracts Following Adjustment of the State Plan" (5/22/79).

Source: *Jingji hetong fa gui xuanbian* (Compilation of Laws and Regulations on Economic Contracts), Beijing (1982) at 96.

"Joint Circular on Several Issues in Managing Economic Contracts" (8/8/79). Source: *Jingji hetong fa gui xuanbian* (Compilation of Laws and Regulations on Economic Contracts), Beijing (1982) at 103.

"Opinion of the Ministry of Transport on Waterborne Shipment of Goods and Materials" (1979). Source: *Jingji fa gui huibian* (Compilation of Economic Laws and Regulations), Guangzhou (undated) at 511.

"Provisional Methods of the State Economic Commission and the Ministry of Finance Concerning the Retention of Profits by State Managed Industrial Enterprises" (1/22/80). Source: *Zhonghua renmin gongheguo guowuyuan gongbao* (PRC State Council Reports) (1980) at 7.

"Provisional Methods for All Around Management of Quality in Industrial Enterprises" (3/10/80). Source: *Zhonghua renmin gongheguo guowuyuan gongbao* (PRC State Council Reports) (1980) at 194.

"Provisional Regulations Concerning Several Issues in Expanding the Economic Management Autonomy of State Managed Building Enterprises" (5/4/80). Source: *Zhonghua renmin gongheguo guowuyuan gongbao* (PRC State Council Reports) (1980) at 219.

"Temporary Regulations Concerning the Basic Provisions in Contracts Between Industrial and Commercial Enterprises and Between Agricultural and Commercial Enterprises" (5/15/80). Source: *Jingji hetong fa gui xuanbian* (Compilation of Laws and Regulations on Economic Contracts), Beijing (1982) at 107.

"State Council Provisional Regulations Concerning Encouraging Economic Coordination" (7/1/80). Source: *Zhonghua renmin gongheguo guowuyuan gongbao* (PRC State Council Reports) (1980) at 227.

"Circular Concerning Continuing to Conscientiously Fulfill and Carry Out the Organization of Production of Machinery and Electrical Products According the Contracts" (11/11/80). Source: *Jingji hetong fa gui xuanbian* (Compilation of Laws and Regulations on Economic Contracts), Beijing (1982) at 100.

"Provisional Regulations for Factory and Mining Goods Contracts" (3/6/81). Source: *Jingji hetong fa gui xuanbian* (Compilation of Laws and Regulations on Economic Contracts), Beijing (1982) at 68.

"Circular Concerning Matters Related to the People's Bank of China Middle and Short Term Loans for Energy Conservation" (4/1/81). Source: *Zhonghua renmin gongheguo guowuyuan gongbao* (PRC State Council Reports) (1981) at 219.

"Provisional Methods for Completely Carrying Out the State Council's Documents on Expanding Autonomy and for Consolidating and Raising the Concrete Implementation of the Work of Expanding Autonomy" (5/20/81). Source: *Zhonghua renmin gongheguo guowuyuan gongbao* (PRC State Council Reports) (1981) at 440.

"State Council's Various Policy Regulations Regarding the Non-Agricultural

Individual Economy in Cities and Towns" (7/7/81). Source: *Zhonghua renmin gongheguo guowuyuan gongbao* (PRC State Council Reports) (1981) at 493.

"Provisional Regulations on Market Management of Materials for the Production of Industrial Goods" (8/8/81). Source: *Zhonghua renmin gongheguo guowuyuan gongbao* (PRC State Council Reports) (1981) at 551.

"Opinion of the State Economic Commission and the State Council Office for Reforming the Economic System Concerning Several Issues in Carrying Out the Industrial Responsibility System in Industrial Production" (8/8/81). Source: *Zhonghua renmin gongheguo guowuyuan gongbao* (PRC State Council Reports) (1981) at 757.

"Provisional Regulations Concerning Several Issues in the Economic Responsibility System in Industrial Production" (11/11/81). Source: *Zhonghua renmin gongheguo guowuyuan gongbao* (PRC State Council Reports) (1981) at 765.

Decision of the CPC Central Committee and the State Council Concerning Carrying Out Comprehensive Rectification by State Managed Industrial Enterprises" (1/2/82). Source: *Zhonghua renmin gongheguo guowuyuan gongbao* (PRC State Council Reports) (1982) at 647.

"Decision to Expand Commodity Circulation to Channels Between Urban and Rural Areas and Increase the Supply of Manufactured Goods to the Rural Areas" (6/17/82). Source: *FBIS (Daily Report): China,* June 23, 1982 at K13.

"For the Economic Responsibility System of Assumption of Tasks in Capital Construction" (3/3/83). Source: *Zhonghua renmin gongheguo guowuyuan gongbao* (PRC State Council Reports) (1982) at 292.

"Methods for Managing the Conduct of Production Materials Service Companies" (5/26/83). Source: *Zhonghua renmin gongheguo guowuyuan gongbao* (PRC State Council Reports) (1983) at 556.

"Regulations for Construction, Engineering, Surveying and Design Contracts" (8/8/83). Source: *Zhonghua renmin gongheguo guowuyuan gongbao* (PRC State Council Reports) (1983) at 772.

"Regulations for Construction and Installation Contracts" (8/8/83). Source: *Zhonghua renmin gongheguo guowuyuan gongbao* (PRC State Council Reports) (1983) at 775.

"Regulations of the PRC for Property Insurance Contracts" (8/22/83). Source: *Zhonghua renmin gongheguo jingji hetong fa ji you guan tiaoli* (The Economic Contract Law of the PRC and Related Regulations), Beijing, 1986 at 25.

"Notice of the Ministry of Hydroelectric Power Concerning Adjustment of Agreements for the Supply of Electricity and Implementation of 'Contracts for Planned Supply of Electricity' " (1/20/84). Source: Zhang Shouqiang (ed.), *Hetong fa gui yu hetong shiyang huibian* (Compilation of Contract Laws and Regulations and Contract Forms), Harbin, 1988 at 356.

"Regulations on Contracts for the Purchase and Sale of Factory and Mining

Goods" (1/23/84). Source: *Zhonghua renmin gongheguo guowuyuan gongbao* (PRC State Council Reports) (1984) at 37.

"State Council Provisional Regulations Concerning the Expansion of Autonomy of State Managed Industrial Enterprises" (5/10/84). Source: *Renmin ribao* (People's Daily), May 13, 1984 at 2.

"Opinion of the China National Petroleum Corporation Concerning How to Execute Contracts for the Purchase and Sale of Commodities" (August 9, 1984). Source: Shangye bu bangongting (Administrative Office of the Ministry of Commerce), *Shangye jingji hetong fa gui huibian* (Compilation of Laws and Regulations on Commercial Economic Contracts), Beijing (1982) at 54.

"Trial Implementation Methods for Contracts for Allocations of Fertilizer (8/15/84). Source: Zhang Shouqiang (ed.), *Hetong fa gui yu hetong shiyang huibian* (Compilation of Contract Laws and Regulations and Contract Forms), Harbin, 1988 at 86.

"Provisional Methods for Contracts for the Purchase and Sale of Hardware, Communications and Household Electrical Equipment and Chemical Commodities" (10/18/84; revised, 10/84). Source: Zhang Shouqiang (ed.), *Hetong fa gui yu hetong shiyang huibian* (Compilation of Contract Laws and Regulations and Contract Forms), Harbin, 1988 at 59.

"Provisional Methods for Contracts for the Purchase and Sale of Textiles, Knitted Goods and Clothing" (11/8/84). Source: Zhang Shouqiang (ed.), *Hetong fa gui yu hetong shiyang huibian* (Compilation of Contract Laws and Regulations and Contract Forms), Harbin, 1988 at 76.

"Provisional Regulations for Soliciting and Submitting Bids for Construction Engineering" (11/20/84). Source: Zhang Shouqiang (ed.), *Hetong fa gui yu hetong shiyang huibian* (Compilation of Contract Laws and Regulations and Contract Forms), Harbin, 1988 at 186.

"Regulations of the PRC on Processing Contracts" (12/24/84). Source: *Zhonghua renmin gongheguo jingji hetong fa ji you guan tiaoli* (The Economic Contract Law of the PRC and Related Regulations), Beijing, 1986 at 95.

"Regulations of the PRC on Loan Contracts" (2/28/85). Source: *Zhonghua renmin gongheguo jingji hetong fa ji you guan tiaoli* (The Economic Contract Law of the PRC and Related Regulations), Beijing, 1986 at 105.

"Regulations of the PRC on Warehousing and Storage" (10/15/85). Source: *Zhonghua renmin gongheguo jingji hetong fa ji you guan tiaoli* (The Economic Contract Law of the PRC and Related Regulations), Beijing, 1986 at 112.

"Detailed Regulations for Implementation of Contracts for Shipment of Goods by Public Roads" (12/1/86). Source: Zhang Shouqiang (ed.), *Hetong fa gui yu hetong shiyang huibian* (Compilation of Contract Laws and Regulations and Contract Forms), Harbin, 1988 at 240.

"Detailed Regulations for Implementation of Contracts for Shipment of Goods by Air" (12/1/86). Source: Zhang Shouqiang (ed.), *Hetong fa gui yu hetong shiyang huibian* (Compilation of Contract Laws and Regulations and Contract Forms), Harbin, 1988 at 247.

"Detailed Regulations for Implementation of Contracts for Shipment of Goods by Rail" (12/20/86). Source: Zhang Shouqiang (ed.), *Hetong fa gui yu hetong shiyang huibian* (Compilation of Contract Laws and Regulations and Contract Forms), Harbin, 1988 at 252.

"Detailed Regulations for Implementation of Contracts for Shipment of Goods by Water" (12/1/86). Source: Zhang Shouqiang (ed.), *Hetong fa gui yu hetong shiyang huibian* (Compilation of Contract Laws and Regulations and Contract Forms), Harbin, 1988 at 262.

"Technology Contract Law of the PRC (6/23/87). Source: Zhang Shouqiang (ed.), *Hetong fa gui yu hetong shiyang huibian* (Compilation of Contract Laws and Regulations and Contract Forms), Harbin, 1988 at 469.

"Methods for Trial Implementation for Loan Contract Guarantees by the Construction Bank" (7/15/87). Source: Zhang Shouqiang (ed.), *Hetong fa gui yu hetong shiyang huibian* (Compilation of Contract Laws and Regulations and Contract Forms), Harbin, 1988 at 419.

"Provisional Regulations of the PRC for Implementation of Technology Contracts" (3/2/88). Source: Zhang Shouqiang (ed.), *Hetong fa gui yu hetong shiyang huibian* (Compilation of Contract Laws and Regulations and Contract Forms), Harbin, 1988 at 495.

(2) Agriculture Contracts.

"Decision on the Acceleration of Agricultural Production" (9/28/79). Source: *FBIS Daily Report: China,* October 5, 1979 at 10.

"Several Issues Concerning the Progressive Strengthening and Perfecting of the Responsibility System in Agricultural Production" (9/14/80). Source: *Zhongguo nongye nianjian* (Yearbook of Chinese Agriculture), Beijing (1981) at 409.

"State Council Regulations Concerning the Implementation in Communes and Brigades of the Policy of National Economic Readjustment" (5/4/81). Source: *Zhonghua renmin gongheguo guowuyuan gongbao* (PRC State Council Reports (1981) at 263.

"Provisional Management Methods for Prices in the Negotiated Purchase and Sale of Agricultural Byproducts" (7/30/81). Source: *Zhonghua renmin gongheguo guowuyuan gongbao* (PRC State Council Reports) (1981) at 529.

"CPC Document No. 1 on Rural Economic Policies" (4/10/83). Source: *FBIS Daily Report: China,* April 13, 1983 at K1.

"Provisional Regulations Concerning Several Issues in Reforming the Circulation of Rural Commodities" (2/10/83). Source: *Zhonghua renmin gongheguo guowuyuan gongbao* (PRC State Council Reports) (1983) at 128.

"Regulation on the State Monopoly in Tobacco" (9/23/83). Source: *Zhonghua renmin gongheguo guowuyuan gongbao* (PRC State Council Reports) (1983) at 987.

"Report Concerning Adjustments in Policy for Procurement and Sale of Agricultural Byproducts and Organization of Many Channels of Management" (9/83). Source: *Zhonghua renmin gongheguo guowuyuan gongbao* (PRC State Council Reports) (1983) at 1053.

"Report of the Ministry of Commerce Concerning Doing a Good Job in Vegetable Supplies and Maintaining Basic Stability of Vegetable Prices" (12/28/83). Source: *Zhonghua renmin gongheguo guowuyuan gongbao* (PRC State Council Reports) (1984) at 74.

"CPC Central Committee Circular on Rural Work in 1984" (1/1/84). Source: *FBIS Daily Report: China,* June 13, 1984 at K1.

"Report Concerning Vegetable Supply Work and Maintaining Basic Stability in Vegetable Prices" (1/10/84). Source: *Zhonghua renmin gongheguo guowuyuan gongbao* (PRC State Council Reports) (1984) at 73.

"Regulations on Contracts for the Purchase and Sale of Agricultural Byproducts" (1/23/84). Source: *Zhonghua renmin gongheguo guowuyuan gongbao* (PRC State Council Reports), 1984 at 49.

"State Council Regulations on Several Issues Concerning the Transportation of Agricultural Byproducts by Cooperative Commercial Organizations and Individuals" (2/25/84). Source: *Zhonghua renmin gongheguo guowuyuan gongbao* (PRC State Council Reports), 1984 at 124.

"Implementation Methods for Contracts for the Allocation of Meat, Grain, Fowl and Eggs" (8/27/84). Source: Zhang Shouqiang (ed.), *Hetong fa gui yu hetong shiyang huibian* (Compilation of Contract Laws and Regulations and Contract Forms), Harbin, 1988 at 128.

"Implementation Methods for Contracts for the Purchase and Sale of Live Hogs, Fresh Eggs, Feed Cattle, Feed Mutton and Household Fowl" (8/28/84). Source: Zhang Shouqiang (ed.), *Hetong fa gui yu hetong shiyang huibian* (Compilation of Contract Laws and Regulations and Contract Forms), Harbin, 1988 at 123.

"Regulations for Implementation of Contracts for State Grain Plan Allocations" (9/5/84). Source: Shangye bu bangongting (Administrative Office of the Ministry of Commerce), *Shangye jingji hetong fa gui huibian* (Compilation of Laws and Regulations on Commercial Economic Contracts), Beijing (1986) at 82.

"Provisional Implementation Methods for Oils and Fats Allocation Contracts" (9/12/84). Source: Shangye bu bangongting (Administrative Office of the Ministry of Commerce), *Shangye jingji hetong fa gui huibian* (Compilation of Laws and Regulations on Commercial Economic Contracts), Beijing (1986) at 85.

"Implementation Methods for Contracts for the Purchase and Sale of Tea Leaves" (9/30/84). Source: Zhang Shouqiang (ed.), *Hetong fa gui yu hetong shiyang huibian* (Compilation of Contract Laws and Regulations and Contract Forms), Harbin, 1988 at 133.

"Provisional Draft Methods for Implementation of Contracts for Allocation of Cotton" (11/28/84). Source: Shangye bu bangongting (Administrative Office of the Ministry of Commerce), *Shangye jingji hetong fa gui huibian* (Compilation of Laws and Regulations on Commercial Economic Contracts), Beijing (1986) at 170.

(3) Implementation of the Economic Contract Law, Supervision of Contract Activity, Dispute Settlement.

"The Organization Law for the People's Courts of the PRC" (7/1/79). Source: *Fa gui xuanbian* (Compilation of Laws and Regulations), Beijing (1983) at 46.

"Experimental Methods for Contract Arbitration Procedures for Administrative Bureaux of Industry and Commerce" (5/15/80). Source: *Jingji hetong fa gui xuanbian* (Compilation of Laws and Regulations on Economic Contracts), Beijing (1982) at 15.

"Preliminary Opinion of the Economic Adjudication Chamber of the Supreme People's Court Concerning Methods for Accepting Cases by the Economic Adjudication Chambers of the People's Courts" (8/8/80). Source: *Jingji hetong fa gui xuanbian* (Compilation of Laws and Regulations on Economic Contracts), Beijing (1982) at 123.

"Preliminary Opinion of the Economic Adjudication Chamber of the Supreme People's Court Concerning the Scope for Accepting Cases by the Economic Adjudication Chambers of the People's Court" (8/8/80). Source: *Jingji hetong fa gui xuanbian* (Compilation of Laws and Regulations on Economic Contracts), Beijing (1982) at 126.

"Explanation of Several Points Regarding the 'Preliminary Opinion of the Economic Adjudication Chamber of the Supreme People's Court Concerning Methods for Accepting Cases by the Economic Adjudication Chambers of the People's Courts" (8/8/80). Source: *Jingji hetong fa gui xuanbian* (Compilation of Laws and Regulations on Economic Contracts), Beijing (1982) at 123.

"Provisional Regulations of the PRC for Lawyers" (8/26/80). Source: *Zhonghua renmin gongheguo guowuyuan gongbao* (PRC State Council Reports), 1980 at 283.

"Outline Report of the Central Bureau for Administration of Industry and Commerce" (3/81). Source: *Zhonghua renmin gongheguo guowuyuan gongbao* (PRC State Council Reports), 1981 at 464.

"Request for Instructions Concerning Opinion on Several Issues in Carrying Out the Economic Contract Law" (4/23/82). Source: *Zhongguo fazhi bao* (Chinese Legal System Gazette), 7/2/82 at 2.

"Provisional Regulations of the PRC on Notarization" (4/40/82). Source: *Zhonghua renmin gongheguo guowuyuan gongbao* (PRC State Council Reports), 1982 at 451.

"Regulations of the PRC on Arbitration of Economic Contracts" (8/22/83). Source: *Zhonghua renmin gongheguo guowuyuan gongbao* (PRC State Council Reports), 1983 at 803.

"Regulations of SAIC and the Ministry of Finance Concerning Standards and the Scope of Use for Economic Contract Arbitration and Certification

Fees" (1/18/84). Source: Shangye bu bangongting (Administrative Office of the Ministry of Commerce), *Shangye jingji hetong fa gui huibian* (Compilation of Laws and Regulations on Commercial Economic Contracts), Beijing (1986) at 149.

"Opinion of the Supreme People's Court Concerning Several Questions of Fully Implementing the «Economic Contract Law» (9/17/84). Source: Zhang Shouqiang (ed.), *Hetong fa gui yu hetong shiyang huibian* (Compilation of Contract Laws and Regulations and Contract Forms), Harbin, 1988 at 934.

"Provisional Regulations on Confirming and Handling Invalid Economic Contracts" (7/25/85). Source: Zhang Shouqiang (ed.), *Hetong fa gui yu hetong shiyang huibian* (Compilation of Contract Laws and Regulations and Contract Forms), Harbin, 1988 at 22.

"Opinion of the Supreme People's Court Concerning Several Questions of Adjudicating Cases of Disputes Over Agricultural Responsibility Contracts" (4/12/86). Source: Zhang Shouqiang (ed.), *Hetong fa gui yu hetong shiyang huibian* (Compilation of Contract Laws and Regulations and Contract Forms), Harbin, 1988 at 942.

"Answers From the Supreme People's Court Concerning Several Issues As to the Specific Application of the «Economic Contract Law» in Cases of Economic Contract Disputes" (7/21/87). Source: Zhang Shouqiang (ed.), *Hetong fa gui yu hetong shiyang huibian* (Compilation of Contract Laws and Regulations and Contracts Forms), Harbin, 1988 at 947.

"Implementation Methods for Administration of Economic Contracts by Commercial Departments" (9/1/87). Source: Zhang Shouqiang (ed.), *Hetong fa gui yu hetong shiyang huibian* (Compilation of Contract Laws and Regulations and Contract Forms), Harbin, 1988 at 25.

Notes

Introduction

1. The Third Plenum of the Eleventh Central Committee of the Chinese Communist party was held in November and December, 1978, and heralded the economic reform policies associated with Deng Xiaoping. The policies emerging from the Third Plenum emphasized the role of market forces in economic decision-making, supported material incentives in production management, and lent greater flexibility to the state planning process. Decentralization of economic decision-making was intended to permit economic enterprises to respond more flexibly to market conditions. Material incentives in agriculture and industry were intended to stimulate productivity. Permitting greater flexibility in performance of state plan directives was intended to maximize the initiative of local enterprises in obtaining production inputs needed for fulfillment of planning goals. These reforms were enacted to address the problems of overcentralization and inefficiency in the Chinese economy. For general discussion of the post-Third Plenum economic reform policies, *see* R. F. Dernberger, "Economic Policy and Performance," U.S. Congress, Joint Economic Committee, *China's Economy Looks Toward the Year 2000* (1986), at 15. Also *see* "Renmin ribao" lilun bu (Theoretical Department of People's Daily), *Jingji fazhan yu jingji gaige* (Economic development and economic reform) (Beijing, 1987). This volume addresses the post-Third Plenum economic reform policies through a series of articles collected by the Theory Department of *Renmin ribao* (People's Daily).

The Third Plenum also emphasized legal reforms, such that formalized laws and legal institutions were again permitted after the hiatus of the Cultural Revolution. The legal reforms were intended to curtail abuses of power that had become rampant during that period. In addition, legal reform provided a regulatory basis for economic reform. For general discussion of the interplay between legal and economic reform, *see* N. G. Lichtenstein, "Legal Implications of China's Economic Reforms," 1 *Foreign Investment Law Journal* 289 (1986).

2. *See* "Zhongguo gongchandang di shiyi jie zhongyang weiyuanhui di san ci quanti huiyi gongbao" (Communique of the Third Plenum of the Eleventh Central Committee of the CCP), *Hongqi* (Red Flag), no. 1, 1979, at 14, 17.

Also *see* "Decision on the Acceleration of Agricultural Production," in "CCP Central Committee's Decision on Agricultural Development," *FBIS Daily Report: China,* Oct. 5, 1979, at 10.

3. *See,* e.g., "Zhonggong zhongyang guanyu jiakuai gongye fazhan ruogan wenti de jueding (caoan)" (Draft decision of the Central Committee of the CCP concerning certain questions of accelerating industrial development), Guojia jingji weiyuanhui jingji fa gui ju (Economic Laws and Regulations Bureau of the State Economic Commission) and Beijing zheng fa xueyuan jingji fa min fa jiao yan shi (Teaching and Research Office for Economic and Civil Law of the Beijing Institute for Politics and Law), *Zhonghua renmin gongheguo gongye qiye fa gui xuanbian* (Compilation of laws and regulations for industrial enterprises of the PRC) (Beijing, 1981) at 73.

4. Further discussion of the changing aspects of contract regulations and practice are supplied in chapter 1 of this volume. For general discussion of Chinese economic policies during the period 1949–78, *see,* generally, A. Eckstein, *China's Economic Revolution* (1977); C. Howe, *China's Economy* (1978).

5. *See,* generally, D. Perkins, *Market Control and Planning in Communist China* (1966).

6. For discussion of the inconsistent effect of this policy, *see* C. Wong, "Material Allocation and Decentralization: The Impact of the Local Sector on Industrial Decentralization," in E. Perry and C. Wong, *The Political Economy in Post-Mao China* (1985).

7. For general discussion of the planning process, *see* Chu-yuan Cheng, *China's Economic Development: Growth and Structural Change* (1982), at 165 *et seq.* Also *see Jingji da cidian: gongye jingji juan* (Economic dictionary, volume on industrial economy) (Shanghai, 1983), at 107–9; Liu Longheng, *Jingji fa gailun* (Outline of economic law) (Beijing, 1985) at 87–116.

8. *See,* e.g., "Guojia jingji weiyuanhui guanyu gong kuang chanpin dinghuo hetong jiben tiaokuan de zanxing guiding" (Provisional regulations of the State Economic Commission on the basic provisions of contracts for ordering factory and mining goods), Article 4; Guowuyuan jingji fa gui yanjiu zhongxin bangongshi (Office of the Economic Laws and Regulations Research Center of the State Council), *Jingji hetong fa gui xuanbian* (Compilation of laws and regulations on economic contracts) (Beijing, 1982), at 53.

9. *See,* e.g. "Gongye bu, difang gongye bu dui muqian you guan gong shang jihua xianjie guanche jingji hetong zhong ruogan wenti guiding de lianhe tongzhi" (Joint directive of the Ministry of Commerce and the Ministry of Local Industry concerning the regulation of various issues in carrying out economic contracts linked to the commercial and industrial plan), *Jingji hetong fa gui xuanbian, supra* n. 8, at 32.

10. *See,* generally, "Zhongguo gongchandang di shiyi jie zhongyang weiyuanhui di san ci quanti huiyi gongbao" (Communique of the Third Plenum of the Eleventh Central Committee of the CCP), *Hongqi* no. 1, 1979. Also *see* Yin

Liangpei, *Jingji gaige yu jingji fazhi* (Economic reform and the economic legal system) (Shenyang, 1985); Lu Zhenyong, Luo Huanzhen, Huang Weiping, *Wo guo jingji tizhi gaige de huigu he zhanwang* (The review and the prospects of the reform of our economic system) (Beijing, 1987).

11. Article 1 of the ECL specifies that one of its purposes is to "protect the legal rights and interests of the parties to economic contracts." *See Zhonghua renmin gongheguo jingji hetong fa* (The Economic Contract Law of the People's Republic of China), Article 1. All references to the ECL are to the text as published by Law Publishing House, Beijing, 1981. In contrast, none of the contract regulations implemented from 1949–78 discussed the issue of the rights of the contracting parties. *See* appendix 3, Table of Regulations.

12. Schumpeter, for example, suggested that the recognition of private rights (implicit in grants of autonomy) works to dilute the power of "centrist socialism." *See,* e.g., J. Schumpeter, *Capital, Socialism, and Democracy* (1950), at 415 *et seq.*

13. *See,* generally, G. Roth, "Sociological Typology and Historical Explanation," in R. Bendix and G. Roth (eds.), *Scholarship and Partisanship* (1971), at 111 *et seq.*

14. For discussion of the process of "double institutionalization" by which social customs are converted into social norms, and then into legal rules, *see* P. Bohannon, "The Differing Realms of Law," in L. Nader, *The Ethnography of Law* (1965), at 34–37.

15. M. Weber, *Economy and Society* (G. Roth and C. Wittich, eds., 1978) at part 2, chap. 1, pp. 311 *et seq.* Also *see* S. Kalberg, "Max Weber's Types of Rationality: Cornerstones for the Analysis of Rationalization Processes in History," 85 *Am. J. of Soc.* 1145, at 1158.

16. *See,* generally, S. Lukes and A. Scull (eds.), *Durkheim and the Law* (1983).

17. Marx's most complete discussion of the function of law is found in *The German Ideology* (1932), although further discussion appears in the *Grundrisse* (M. Nicolaus, tr., 1973). *See,* generally, M. Rader, *Marx's Interpretation of History* (1979), at 35–41. For discussion of "hegemony," *see* A. Gramsci, *Selections From the Prison Notebooks* (Q. Hoare and G. N. Smith tr., eds., 1971), at 245–48. Also *see* E. Greer, "Antonio Gramsci and 'Legal Hegemony,' " in D. Kairys (ed.), *The Politics of Law: A Progressive Critique* (1982), at 304 *et seq.*

18. *See,* generally, M. Tigar and M. Levy, *Law and the Rise of Capitalism* (1977).

19. *See* M. Weber, *supra.* n. 15, at chap. 3, p. 2, pp. 217–23. Also *see* W. Schluchter, *The Rise of Western Rationalism: Max Weber's Developmental History* (1981), and R. Bendix, *Max Weber: An Intellectual Portrait* (1977), at 418–19.

20. I. Balbus, "Commodity Form and Legal Form: An Essay on the "Relative Autonomy of Law," 11 *Law and Society Rev.* 571 (1977).

21. D. Trubek, "Complexity and Contradiction in the Legal Order: Balbus and the Challenge of Critical Social Thought About Law," 11 *Law and Society Rev.* 529 (1977).

22. The difficulties of establishing a causal connection between formalization of law and economic growth in non-Western societies is discussed in J. Burns, "Civil Courts and the Development of Commercial Relations: The Case of North Sumatra," 15 *Law & Society Rev.* 347 (1980). For further critical discussion, *see* F. Snyder, "Law and Development in Light of Dependency Theory," 14 *Law & Society Rev.* 723 (1980).

23. For an interesting discussion of the passage of legal terminology from one culture to another, *see* D. F. Henderson, "Japanese Influences on Communist Chinese Legal Language," in J. A. Cohen (ed.), *Contemporary Chinese Law, Research Problems and Perspectives* (1970).

24. Roberto Unger uses the term *recognition* to describe the process of formation of the political community, as members of society recognize social values in the content of political doctrine. *See* R. M. Unger, *Knowledge and Politics* (1975).

25. This is the approach taken in J. Burns, "Civil Courts and the Development of Commercial Relations: The Case of North Sumatra," 15 *Law and Society Rev.* 347 (1980). Burns concluded that in North Sumatra, the perception of law's utility and function by the subjects of the law was the primary determinant of whether law is to serve a predictive function in the regulation of economic life.

26. *See,* generally, D. Bodde and C. Morris, *Law in Imperial China* (1967); S. Van Der Sprenkel, *Legal Institutions in Manchu China* (1962).

27. For example, the influential legal philosopher Wang Fuzhi (1619–92), whose career spanned the transition from the Ming to Qing dynasties, asserted that the essential aspect of law is its operation on public, society-wide, rather than private individualized activities. *See* Rao Xinxian, *Zhongguo falu sixiang shi gang* (Outline history of Chinese legal thought) (Lanzhou, 1987), at 223 *et seq.* For discussion of the role of public law in pre-Imperial China, *see* W. Alford, "The Inscrutable Occidental? Implications of Roberto Unger's Uses and Abuses of the Chinese Past," 64 *Texas Law Review* 915, 938 *et seq.* (1986).

28. For a brief discussion of salt monopoly laws in traditional China, *see,* generally, *Zhongguo jindai shi cidian* (Dictionary of modern Chinese history) (Shanghai, 1982), at 569.

29. For general discussion of contract practice in Imperial China, *see* R. Brockman, "Commercial Contract Law in Late Nineteenth Century Taiwan" in J. A. Cohen, R. Edwards, and F. M. Chen, *Essays on China's Legal Tradition* (1980). Also *see* F. M. Chen and R. Myers, "Customary Law and the Economic Growth of China during the Ch'ing Period," in *Ch'ing -shih wen-t'i* (Questions of Qing history) (1978).

30. For discussion of Mao Zedong's view that criminal law was to be used

to suppress class enemies, *see,* generally, Wang Zhangchang, "Mao Zedong tongzhi de xingfa lilun chutan" (Preliminary discussion of comrade Mao Zedong's theory of criminal law), in Zhongguo faxue hui (China Law Society), *Mao Zedong sixiang: Faxue lilun lunwen xuan* (Mao Zedong thought: Collection of articles on legal theory) (Beijing, 1985), at 98.

31. *See,* generally, P. Potter, "Peng Zhen: Evolving Views on Party Organization and Law," in C. Hamrin and T. Cheek, *China's Establishment Intellectuals* (1986), at 21, 25–31.

32. *See,* generally, Chu-yuan Cheng, *China's Economic Development: Growth and Structural Change* (1982).

33. *See,* generally, J. D. Calamari and J. M. Perillo, *Contracts* (1977), at 1–15 and sources cited.

34. For general discussion of the relationship between contracts and the plan in the 1950s and early 1969s, *see* R. Pfeffer, *Understanding Business Contracts in China* (1973) at 10 *et seq*.

35. For an introduction to the debates over the use of nonplan contracts, *see* A. Dicks, "A Legal Opinion," *China Trade Report,* April 1982 and April 1981.

36. *See* S. Lubman, "Mao and Mediation: Politics and Dispute Resolution in Communist China," 55 *California Law Review* 1284 (1967).

37. For a more complete discussion of the varying doctrinal views of political leadership groups and legal communities in Shanghai and Sichuan, *see* P. Potter, "Policy, Law and Private Economic Rights in China: The Doctrine and Practice of Economic Contracts" (Ph.D. diss., University of Washington, 1986).

38. Abstracts of the cases themselves are contained in the tables in appendix 1.

1. The Conflict of Norms

1. An earlier version of this chapter was published as *The Economic Contract Law of the People's Republic of China: An Exercise in Compilation and Reform* (Center for Contemporary Chinese Studies, Hong Kong, 1983).

2. The conventional Anglo-American definition of contract is "a promise or set of promises for the breach of which the law gives a remedy, or the performance of which the law in some way recognizes as a duty." S. Williston, *Contracts,* sec. 1 (3d ed., W. Jaeger, 1957); American Law Institute, *Restatement of Contracts,* sec. 1 (1932). This definition is predicated on a certain degree of freedom to contract. Since such freedom has largely been absent in China, application of this definition has its problems. Although contracts in China do contain the elements of promise, duty, and remedy, the administrative character of contracts in China's command economy has largely eliminated the freedom to contract that characterizes the Anglo-American model.

However, since this study addresses the capacity for Chinese economic actors to grant legitimacy to the PRC Economic Contract Law, the focus is on contracts within the Chinese meaning of the term. For the purposes of this study, I have used the term *contract* to refer to what the Chinese call *qiyue* or *hetong*, which are translated into the English as "contract."

3. "Jiguan, guoying qiye, hezuo she qianding hetong qiyue zanxing banfa" (hereafter, referred to as the Provisional Methods), Guowuyuan Jingji Fa Gui Yanjiu Zhongxin Bangongshi (Office of the Economic Laws and Regulations Research Center of the State Council), *Jingji hetong fa gui xuanbian* (Compilation of laws and regulations on economic contracts) (Beijing, 1982), at 24. Also *see* Shanghai Shi Zhexue Shehui Kexue Xuehui Lianhehui (Joint Society of Philosophy and Social Sciences of Shanghai Municipality), *Jingji fa cankao ziliao: gongye qiye guanli bufen* (Reference materials on economic law: Industrial enterprise management section) (Shanghai, 1980), at 12.

4. "Zhongyang renmin zhengfu maoyi bu guanyu renzhen dingli yu yange zhixing hetong de jueding" (Decision of the Central People's Government's Ministry of Trade on the careful signing and strict fulfillment of contracts), *Jingji hetong fa gui xuanbian, supra* n. 3, at 27.

5. "Zhonggong zhongyang guowuyuan guanyu yange zhixing jiben jianshe chengxu, yange zhixing jingji hetong de tongzhi," *Jingji hetong fa gui xuanbian, supra* n. 3, at 35.

6. "Guojia jingji weiyuanhui guanyu gong kuang chanpin dinghuo hetong jiben tiaokuan de zanxing guiding," *Jingji hetong fa gui xuanbian, supra* n. 3, at 53.

7. Article 2 of the Provisional Methods called for the use of contracts in a variety of transactions such as purchase and sale, manufacturing, transport, loans, agency, and leasing. *Jingji hetong fa gui xuanbian, supra* n. 3, at 24. The 1963 Ordering Contracts Regulations extended to contracts for supply of all industrial and mining goods and governed activities by a wide range of economic units. *Jingji hetong fa gui xuanbian, supra* n. 3, at 53.

8. Interviews in Beijing with Yang Rongxin and Xu Jie of the Beijing Political-Legal Institute (Apr. 14, 1983) and with Wang Zhengming of the Economic Laws and Regulations Research Center (Apr. 6, 1983). *See* appendix 2, Table of Interview Subjects. Notes from these meetings are on file with the author.

9. For an example of state intervention in contractual relationships within enterprises, *see* "Guanyu siying gong shang qiye lao zi shuangfang dingli jiti hetong de zanxing banfa" (Provisional methods concerning mutual signing of collective contracts between labor and capital in private industrial and commercial enterprises), *Renmin nianjian* (People's yearbook) (Hong Kong, 1950).

10. *See,* e.g., A. Eckstein, *China's Economic Revolution* (1977), at 166 *et seq*. Also *see* N. R. Chen, W. Galenson, *The Chinese Economy Under Communism* (1969), at 87 *et seq*.

11. The role of agricultural contracts as instruments of state planning is

discussed in "Zen yang tuixing hezuo she de hetong zhi" (How to carry out the contract system of the cooperatives), *Xin hua yue bao* (New China Monthly), no. 11, 1950, at 1082. The role of the cooperatives as the intermediary between the mutual aid teams and the state enterprises is discussed in "Jixu guanche hetong zhi, dali kaizhan cheng xiang jiaotong" (Continue to carry out the contract system, energetically open up the interchange between cities and towns) *Xin hua yue bao,* no. 5, 1951. Also *see* "Tuiguang hu bang zu he hezuo she de jiehe hetong" (Expand combined contracts between mutual aid teams and cooperatives), *Renmin ribao,* Apr. 10, 1952.

12. *See* "Hetong zhi zai zuzhi nongcun fuye chan xiao shang de zuoyong yu ying zhuyi de jige wenti" (The role of the contract system in organizing village sideline production and marketing and several questions which need attention), *Zhongguo nong bao* (China Agriculture Gazette), no. 6, 1950, at 109.

13. *Id.*

14. *See* "Zen yang kaizhan hetong jingying" (How to develop contract management), *Renmin ribao,* Apr. 1, 1950.

15. *See,* e.g., "Su bei hezuo she tuixing de hetong zhi" (The contract system carried out by cooperatives in northern Jiangsu), *Jiefang ribao* (Liberation Daily), Shanghai, Dec. 14, 1950.

16. *See* "Zen yang tuixing hezuo she de hetong zhi," *supra* n. 11.

17. *See,* e.g., "Zen yang kaizhan hetong jingying," *supra* n. 14.

18. "Jiguan, guoying qiye, hezuo she qianding hetong qiyue zanxing banfa," *supra* n. 3.

19. *Id.*

20. "Zhongyang renmin zhengfu maoyi bu guanyu renzhen dingli yu yange zhixing de jueding," *supra* n. 4.

21. *See* "Tuiguang hubang zu he hezuo she de jiehe hetong," *supra* n. 11.

22. *See* Preface to "Zhongyang renmin zhengfu maoyi bu guanyu renzhen dingli yu yange zhixing hetong de jueding," *supra* n. 4.

23. For general discussion of the role of local market forces in the "advance purchase contracts" used in agriculture during this period, *see* D. Perkins, *Market Control and Planning in Communist China* (1966).

24. "Jiguan, guoying qiye, hezuo she qianding hetong qiyue zanxing banfa," *supra* n. 3.

25. *See,* e.g., "Zen yang kaizhan hetong jingying," *supra* n. 14.

26. Article 10 of the Provisional Methods merely hinted at the mediation role of the management offices of the contracting parties: "If, after the contract or charter is signed, one party has a situation of nonfulfillment or harm to the contract or charter *without the agreement of the other party . . .*" (emphasis added). The Trade Ministry decision, on the other hand, was more specific in discussing the role of the management offices of the units involved. Article 4 states, "If there emerges the danger of nonfulfillment of the contract, the business offices of all levels of companies must immediately undertake discussion of the relevant matters so as to adopt effective remedies. . . ."

27. *See* "Jiguan, guoying qiye, hezuo she qianding hetong qiyue zanxing banfa," *supra* n. 3, at Article 10. Also *see* "Zhongyang renmin zhengfu maoyi bu guanyu renzhen dingli yu yange zhixing hetong de jueding," *supra* n. 4, at Article 4.

28. *See* "Jiguan, guoying qiye, hezuo she qianding hetong qiyue zanxing banfa," *supra* n. 3, at Article 10. Also *see* "Zhongyang renmin zhengfu maoyi bu guanyu renzhen dingli yu yange zhixing hetong de jueding," *supra* n. 4 at Article 5.

29. *See* "Taiyuan shi gong xiao she zhixing hetong cunzai wenti jingguo jiancha zhao dao yuanyin dingchu gaijin banfa" (Problems with the contracts carried out by supply and marketing cooperatives in Taiyuan City, through investigation find the causes and the methods for making amendments), *Da gong bao* (Impartial Daily), Tianjin, June 18, 1953.

30. The complacency toward contracts was exemplified by the phrase *wan shi da ji* (all is well) and by the belief that *jiehe hetong ding bu ding shi yi ge wei-er* (there is no difference between signing or not signing contracts). *See* "Ba jiehe hetong tigao yi bu" (Improve combined contracts a step), *Da gong bao*, Tianjin, July 30, 1954.

31. *See* "Jiji wenbu di tuiguang jiehe hetong shi cujin nongye shehui zhuyi gaizao de you li cuoshi zhi yi" (Positively and steadily popularizing combined contracts is one of the effective measures in promoting agricultural socialist transformation), *Renmin ribao*, June 28, 1954.

32. *See* "Wo dui shixing shucai chan xiao jiehe hetong de ganxiang" (My feelings regarding the implementation of vegetable production and marketing combined contracts), *Renmin ribao*, Sept. 12, 1954. The existence of this problem was confirmed by emigré interviews conducted in Hong Kong.

33. *Id.*

34. *See* "Ba jiehe hetong tigao yi bu," *supra* n. 30.

35. *See* "Taiyuan shi gongxiao she zhixing wenti . . . ," *supra* n. 29.

36. The fact that the courts were little used in the resolution of contract disputes can be traced to the long history of mediation in China. Resolution through the courts was often seen as bringing more harm than benefit to the plaintiff. The primacy of mediation was confirmed through interviews in Hong Kong and in Beijing. Also *see* S. Lubman, "Mao and Mediation: Politics and Dispute Resolution in Communist China," in 55 *California Law Review* 1284 (1967).

37. "Guoying gongye qiye gongzuo tiaoli (caoan)" (Draft regulations for the work of state-managed industrial enterprises), Guojia jingji weiyuanhui jingji fa gui ju (Economic Laws and Regulations Bureau of the State Economic Commission) and Beijing zheng fa xueyuan jingji fa min fa jiao yan shi (Teaching and Research Office for Economic and Civil Law of the Beijing Institute for Politics and Law), *Zhonghua renmin gongheguo gongye qiye fa gui xuanbian* (Compilation of laws and regulations for industrial enterprises of the PRC) (Beijing, 1981), at 45. For general discussion of the Seventy

Articles on Industry, *see* P. N. S. Lee, "The Post-Leap Policy of Enterprise Management and Its Impacts on the Current Economic Reforms in the PRC," unpublished paper presented at the China Regional Seminar held at the University of California, Berkeley, Nov. 13, 1982, copy on file with the author. The section on general principles of the Seventy Articles provided for the signing of contracts between state industrial enterprises and independent production and management units, and set forth other rules governing the use of contracts in formulating enterprise plans (Article 10); the apportionment of responsibility for losses (Article 41); and the required contents of contracts (Article 46).

38. *See,* generally, C. Howe, *China's Economy* (1978), at xxix.

39. These efforts were not fully successful, as is discussed in T. Bernstein, "Stalinism, Famine and Chinese Peasants: Grain Procurements During the Great Leap Forward," 13 *Theory and Society* 3 (1984). However, the state's attempts to extend control over economic activity deprived rural economic actors of economic motivations to insist on contract performance.

40. *See* "Lun gong nong ye chanpin jiaohuan de hetong zhidu" (On the contract system of exchange of goods by industrial and agricultural enterprises), *Renmin ribao,* Mar. 9, 1962.

41. *See* "Quan li cujin shengchan shixian shougou hetong" (Spare no effort in promoting production and implementing purchase contracts). *Da gong bao,* Beijing, Nov. 2, 1961. The effect of the human toll from the Great Leap also played a role in contract performance, as sympathetic local cadres permitted peasant producers to forego mandatory grain deliveries to make up local shortages.

42. *See* "Zhonggong zhongyang guowuyuan guanyu yange zhixing jiben jianshe chengxu, yange zhixing jingji hetong de tongzhi," *supra* n. 5.

43. *See* "Guojia jingji weiyuanhui guanyu gong kuang chanpin dinghuo hetong jiben tiaokuan de zanxing guiding," *supra* n. 6.

44. The Ordering Contracts Regulations were aimed specifically at industrial contracts. The 1962 circular purportedly covered all contracts, although the circular's treatment of basic construction procedures and the repeated references to merchandise suggested a focus on industry and commerce.

45. *See* "Guojia jingji weiyuanhui guanyu gong kuang chanpin dinghuo hetong jiben tiaokuan de zanxing guiding," *supra* n. 6, pt. 9, Articles 32–35.

46. *Id.,* at Articles 33, 34.

47. *See* Zhongyang zheng fa ganbu xuexiao min fa jiao yan shi (Teaching and Research Office of the Central Political and Legal Cadres School) *Zhonghua renmin gongheguo min fa jiben wenti* (Basic problems of Chinese civil law) (Beijing, 1958). This was a basic textbook for the study of law in China during the late 1950s, and emphasizes a preference for specific performance as the primary remedy for breach of contract. The book is discussed at length in Richard Pfeffer, *Understanding Business Contracts in China,* 1949–1963(1973), at 29–47.

48. *See* "Guojia jingji weiyuanhui guanyu gong kuang chanpin dinghuo hetong jiben tiaokuan de zanxing guiding," *supra* n. 6, Articles 5–10.

49. The relationship between vagueness in contract clauses and problems of enforceability was related by two informants in Hong Kong, both of whom worked in enterprise management offices. A third informant, who worked in a notarization office, stressed the relationship between clarity in contract clauses and enforceability of contracts.

50. For discussion of the organization of agricultural production following the Great Leap Forward, *see*, generally, R. J. Birrell, "The Centralized Control of the Communes in the Post-Great Leap Period," in A. D. Barnett, *Chinese Communist Politics in Action* (1969), at 400–443. Also *see* F. W. Crook, "The Commune System o the People's Republic of China 1963–74," in U.S. Congress Joint Economic Committee, *China: A Reassessment of the Economy* (1975), at 366–410.

51. *See* "Gou xiao jiehe hetong hao" (Purchase and sale combined contracts are good), *Da gong bao*, Beijing, Jan. 30, 1962. Also *see* "Zen yang cai neng shi gou xiao jiehe hetong duixian" (How do we have the ability to make good on purchase and sale combined contracts?), *Da gong bao*, Beijing, Mar. 30, 1962.

52. *Id.* Also *see* "Pan long gong xiao she jian chi yun yong hetong zhidu" (The Pan Long Supply and Marketing Cooperative upholds the use of the contract system), *Da gong bao*, Beijing, Feb. 15, 1962.

53. *See* "Zai suoshi shengchan de jichu shang qian ding shougou hetong" (Sign purchase contracts on the basis of achieving production), *Da gong bao*, Beijing, Mar. 30, 1962. Also *see* "Gou xiao jiehe hetong hao" (Purchase and sale combined contracts are good), *Da gong bao*, Beijing, Jan. 1, 1962.

54. Hong Kong emigré interviews. *See* appendix 2, Table of Interview Subjects. Notes on file with the author.

55. *Id.*

56. "Guojia jingji weiyuanhui guanyu gong kuang chanpin dinghuo hetong jiben tiaokuan de zanxing guiding," *supra* n. 6, at Article 36.

57. "Guojia jingji weiyuanhui guanyu yange zhixing jiben jianshe chengxu, yange zhixing jingji hetong de tongzhi," *supra* n. 5.

58. Hong Kong emigré interviews. *See* appendix 2, Table of Interview Subjects. Notes on file with the author.

59. *Id.*

60. Specific performance entails the issuance of an order that the party in breach carry out its contractual obligations. *See*, generally, J. D. Calamari and J. M. Perillo, *Contracts*, (1977), at 581 *et seq*. In China this remedy was often used, entailing an administrative or judicial order that the nonperforming party should resume performance of the contract.

61. Hong Kong emigré interviews. *See* appendix 2, Table of Interview Subjects. Notes on file with the author.

62. *Id.*

63. *Id.*

64. The role of personal *guanxi* as a primary feature in political and social life has long been noted by scholars. *See,* e.g., R. Solomon, *Mao's Revolution and the Chinese Political Culture* (1971), and L. Pye, *The Spirit of Chinese Politics: A Psycho-Cultural Study of the Crisis in Political Development* (1968). For discussion of the role of *guanxi* in an economic context, *see* A. Walder, *Communist Neo-Traditionalism: Work and Authority in Chinese Industry* (1986), at 181–85.

Informants in Hong Kong pointed out repeatedly that *guanxi* was a crucial determinant not only in the fulfillment of contracts but also in the resolution of disputes. The degree to which contracts were fulfilled depended primarily on the *guanxi* between officials in the contracting parties. Similarly, the manner in which a dispute was resolved depended on the personal relations between officials in the higher level units and the parties themselves.

65. Hong Kong emigré interviews. *See* appendix 2, Table of Interview Subjects. Notes on file with the author.

66. Overcoming the problems of rigidity and stagnation of the economy was noted by Professor Rui Mu of Beijing University as an important reason for developing economic legislation tailored to China's particular circumstances. Beijing interviews. *See* appendix 2, Table of Interview Subjects. Notes on file with the author.

67. For discussion of the subject-specific nature of Chinese regulations, *see,* generally, W. C. Jones, "An Approach to Chinese Law," in 4 *Review of Socialist Law* (1978), at 3–25.

68. "Zhongyang renmin zhengfu maoyi bu guanyu renzhen dingli yu yange zhixing hetong de jueding," *supra* n. 4.

69. "Guojia jingji weiyuanhui guanyu gong kuang chanpin dinghuo hetong jiben tiaokuan de zanxing guiding," *supra* n. 6.

70. ECL, Article 1.

71. "Jiguan, guoying qiye, hezuo she qianding hetong qiyue zanxing banfa," *supra* n. 3, at Article 1.

72. "Guojia jingji weiyuan hui guanyu gong kuang chanpin dinghuo hetong jiben tiaokuan de zanxing guiding," *supra* n. 6, at Article 2.

73. *See* ECL, Article 1.

74. "Jiguan, guoying qiye, hezuo she qianding hetong qiyue zanxing banfa," *supra* n. 3, at Article 5.

75. *See,* e.g., Bai Youzhong, Liu Qishan, *Jingji hetong fa zhishi wen da* (Questions and answers on knowledge of the Economic Contract Law) (Beijing, 1982), at 5–8.

76. *See* Shanxi sheng gong shang xingzheng guanli ju (Shanxi Provincial Bureau for Administration of Industry and Commerce), *Jingji hetong ying yong shouce* (Handbook for use with economic contracts) (Taiyuan, 1986), at 8–12; Guowuyuan jingji fa gui yanjiu zhongxin bangongshi (Office of the Economic Laws and Regulations Research Center of the State Council),

Zhonghua renmin gongeheguo jingji hetong fa: tiaowen shiyi (Interpretation of articles in the Economic Contract Law of the People's Republic of China) (Beijing, 1982), at 14.

77. The emphasis on the legal person contained in Article 5 of the 1950 Provisional Methods combined with the supervisory structure set forth in the Provisional Methods indicated a focus on central control.

78. *See,* e.g., Tao Xijin "Zai tiaozheng fangzhen zhidao xia jiji tuixing hetong zhi" (Actively carry out the contract system under the guidance of the policy of adjustment), in Guan Huai, *Jingji fa wen xuan* (Collection of articles on economic law) (Beijing, 1981), at 51–56. Also *see,* Sun Yaming, "Shiying xiandaihua jianshe xuyao de jingji hetong fa" (An economic contract law which is suitable to the needs of modernization construction), *Minzhu yu faxhi* (Democracy and the legal system), no. 9, 1982, at 20, 21.

79. *See,* e.g., Xiao Weiyun, "Wo guo de shehui zhuyi jingji zhidu" (Our country's socialist economic system), *Zhongguo fazhi bao* (Chinese Legal System Gazette), Jan. 14, 1983, at 3. Also *see* Zhao Ziyang, "Dangqian de jingji xingshi he jinhou jingji jianshe de fangzhen" (The present economic circumstances and the policy of economic construction in the future: Report on the work of the government to the fourth session of the Fifth National People's Congress), in *Zhonghua renmin gongheguo guowuyuan gongbao* (State Council reports) (1981), at 816–50. *See* particularly sec. 2, pt. 8 at 837–38.

80. *See* ECL, Article 1. Also *see* Guowuyuan jingji fa gui yanjiu zhongxin bangongshi (Office of the Economic Laws and Regulations Research Center of the State Council), *supra* n. 76, at 9, 10.

81. *See* "Jiguan, guoying qiye, hezuo she qianding hetong qiyue zanxing banfa," *supra* n. 3; "Zhongyang renmin zhengfu maoyi bu guanyu renzhen dingli yu yange zhixing hetong de jueding," *supra* n. 4; "Zhonggong zhongyang guowuyuan guanyu yange zhixing jiben jianshe chengxu, yange zhixing jingji hetong de tongzhi," *supra* n. 5; and "Guojia jingji weiyuanhui guanyu gong kuang chanpin dinghuo hetong jiben tiaokuan de zanxing guiding," *supra* n. 6.

82. *See* ECL, Article 7.

83. *See* nn 3–6 and accompanying text. Also *see,* e.g., "Zhengque di yunyong hetong zhidu" (Correctly utilize the contract system), *Da gong bao,* Beijing, Feb. 9, 1962.

84. *See* ECL, Article 35.

85. Article 35 cities liquidated damages as the first method of remedy. Although liquidated damages (*wei yue jin*) may be distinguished from penalty damages (*fa jin*) and from compensation (*pei chang*), liquidated damages embraced an element of penalty, and often are referred to as *fines.* Chapter 4 of the Economic Contract Law refers repeatedly to the use of liquidated damages. Also *see* Li Zhuguo, Bai Youzhong, *Hetong jiben zhishi* (Basic knowledge of contracts) (Beijing, 1981), at 41, 42.

86. *See* ECL, Article 35.

87. *See* ECL, Article 36.

88. The term *liquidated damages* refers to a remedy agreed upon by the parties in advance as an appropriate measure of compensation, and specified in the contract. *See* generally, J. D. Calamari and J. M. Perillo, *Contracts* (1977), at 564.

89. *See* "Guanyu gong kuang chanpin dinghuo hetong jiben tiaokuan de zanxing guiding," *supra* n. 6.

90. *See* "Jiguan, guoying qiye, hezuo she qianding hetong qiyue zanxing banfa," *supra* n. 3.

91. Under the method of "Four Investigations and Four Checkings" (*si cha si qing*), the first step in adjudication of a dispute is to investigate the legality of the contract, the fairness of rights and obligations set out in the contract, the background of the contract, and the nature of the issues regarding performance. *See* Bai Youzhong, Liu Qishan, *Jingji hetong fa zhishi wen da, supra* n. 75 at 112.

92. Several informants in Hong Kong who worked in management offices of enterprises described the investigation role played by mediating organizations. Since the remedy for nonperformance was to be based on these investigations, the disputing parties went to great lengths to ensure that the investigators found information that would lead to a favorable resolution. Hong Kong emigré interviews. *See* appendix 2, Table of Interview Subjects. Notes on file with the author.

93. The problem of determining compensatory damages is discussed in Liang Huixing, "Lun hetong zeren" (On contract responsibilities), *Xuexi yu tansuo* (Study and Inquiry), no. 1, 1982, at 58–61.

94. *See* ECL, Article 48.

95. "Zui gao renmin fayuan guanyu guanche zhixing 'Jingji hetong fa' ruogan wenti de yijian" (Sept. 17, 1984), *Zhonghua renmin gongheguo zui gao renmin fayuan gongbao* (PRC Supreme People's Court Bulletin), no. 3, 1985, at 3, 9.

96. The need for expanding the role of the courts in handling contract cases is discussed in Gong Zheng, "Jiaqiang guojia fazhi baozhang shehui zhuyi xiandaihua jianshe" (Strengthen the country's legal system, safeguard socialist modernization construction), *Hongqi,* no. 2, 1979, at 12, 13. By the end of 1980, more than 1002 economic chambers had been established in all levels of people's courts. Of these, 28 were in the higher level people's courts, 277 in intermediate level people's courts, and 697 in the basic level people's courts. *See* "Quan guo fayuan yi she jingji shenpan ting yi qian duo ge" (Courts throughout the country have already established more than one thousand economic chambers), *Zhongguo fazhi bao,* Mar. 27, 1981. By May 1981, Beijing alone had established 15 economic chambers, one at the higher level, one at the intermediary level, and 13 at the basic level. *See Selections From World Broadcasts,* July 16, 1981, at BII/6.

97. "Guanyu guanli jingji hetong ruogan wenti de lianhe tongzhi" (Joint

circular on several issues in managing economic contracts), *Jingji hetong fa gui xuanbian, supra* n. 3 at 103.

98. *See* ECL, Article 48. In 1980, the Economic Chamber of the Supreme People's Court indicated that arbitration should be used as a prerequisite to adjudication. *See* "Zui gao renmin fayuan jingji shenpan ting guanyu renmin fayuan jingji shenpan ting shou an banfa de chubu yijian" (Preliminary opinion of the Economic Adjudication Chamber of the Supreme People's Court concerning methods for accepting cases by the economic adjudication chambers of the people's courts), *Jingji hetong fa gui xuanbian, supra* n. 3, at 123. Also *see* "Zui gao renmin fayuan jingji shenpan ting guanyu renmin fayuan jingji shenpan ting shou an fanwei de chubu yijian" (Preliminary opinion of the Economic Adjudication Chamber of the Supreme People's Court concerning the scope of accepting cases by the economic adjudication chambers of the people's courts), *id.*, at 126. Although these opinions were technically superseded by the ECL's provisions for direct submission of contract cases to court, the practical result was strong encouragement for arbitration.

99. *See* ECL, Article 48. Also see Guowuyuan jingji fa gui yanjiu zhongxin bangongshi, *supra* n. 76, at 115, 116. During the three years after 1981 to 1983, some 89,494 economic disputes had been handled by the economic chambers. *See* "Jingji shenpan gongzuo pengbo fazhan" (Economic adjudication work develops vigorously), *Zhongguo fazhi bao,* Mar. 5, 1984. Between July 1983 and March 1984, some 37,000 cases, most of them involving contracts, had been handled by the economic chambers. *See* Zheng Tianxiang, "Report to the Sixth National People's Court," *FBIS Daily Report: China,* May 29, 1984, at K10.

100. *See,* e.g., Gu Ming, "Jingji hetong fa shi baozhang guojia jihua zhixing de youli gongju" (The Economic Contract Law is a powerful tool in ensuring implementation of the state plan), *Faxue zazhi* (Legal Studies Magazine), no. 3, 1982, at 7–9.

101. *See,* e.g., Liang Huixing, "Lun wo guo hetong falu zhidu de jihua yuanze yu hetong ziyou yuanze" (On the principles of planning and contractual freedom in our country's system of contract law), *Faxue yanjiu* (Legal Studies Research), no. 4, 1982, at 44–49.

102. This argument is in keeping with the phrase *yi jihua jingji wei zhu, yi shichang tiaojie wei fu* (Take economic planning as primary, take market adjustment as the supplement). *See* Guowuyuan jingji fa gui yanjiu zhongxin bangongshi, *supra* n. 76, at 11.

103. *See,* generally, Yan Ciqing, *Qiye jingji hetong yu hetong geshi* (Enterprise economic contracts and contract forms) (Beijing, 1987), at 66–71; *Jingji hetong ying yong shouce, supra* n. 76, at 16–22; Guojia gongshang xingzheng guanli ju jingji hetong si (Economic Contracts Office of the State Administration for Industry and Commerce), *Zen yang qianding jingji hetong* (How to execute economic contracts) (Beijing, 1985), at 19–23.

104. *See* Wang Zhong, Lin Ruifu, Song Haobo, Zhao Dengju, *Jingji fa xue*

(Studies in economic law) (Jilin, 1981), at 129–30. Also *see* Li Zhuguo, Bai Youzhong, *Hetong jiben zhishi* (Basic knowledge of contracts) (Beijing, 1981), at 45–48.

105. *See* "Zonghua renmin gongheguo gongzheng zanxing tiaoli" (Provisional regulations of the PRC on notarization), *Guowuyuan gong bao* (State Council reports) (1982), at 451. Also *see* "Si fa bu, guojia gongshang xingzheng guanli ju guangyu jingji hetong jianzheng yu gongzheng wenti de lianhe tongzhi (jie lu)" (Excerpt from joint notice of the Ministry of Justice and the State Administration for Industry and Commerce concerning issues of certification and notarization of contracts) (1983), *Jingji fa gui huibian* (Compilation of economic laws and regulations) (Guangzhou, n.d.), at 80. Also *see* Zhang Shouqiang, *Hetong fa gui yu hetong shiyang huibian* (Compilation of laws and regulations on contracts and contract forms) (Harbin, 1988).

106. *See* Gu Ming, "Guanyu 'Zhonghua renmin gongheguo jingji hetong fa caoan' de shuoming" (Explanation of the "Economic Contract Law of the People's Republic of China"), speech to fourth session of Fifth National People's Congress, *Zhonghua renmin gongheguo jingji hetong fa* (Economic Contract Law of the People's Republic of China) (Beijing, 1981), at 29.

107. *Id.* Also *see* Li Zhuguo, "Zhongshi hetong de jianzheng" (Emphasize the certification of contracts), *Renmin rabao,* Aug. 7, 1980.

108. *See* "Zonghua renmin gongheguo gongzheng zanxing tiaoli" and "Si fa bu, guojia gong shang xingzheng guanli ju guangyu jingji hetong jianzheng yu gongzheng wenti de lianhe tongzhi (jie lu)," *supra* n. 105.

109. *See,* generally, Zhang Sizhi, *Lushi, gongzheng yu tiaojie yewu* (The operations of lawyers, notarization and mediation) (Beijing, 1986), at 391 *et seq.*

110. *See,* e.g., "Shen me shi gong zheng" (What is notarization), *Guangming ribao* (Guangming Daily), May 5, 1981. However, since the notarization process is brought into force only at the request of the parties, the parties may choose not to undergo notarization if they are unaware of their differences in interpreting the meaning of either contract clauses or the contract law itself. In such an instance, differences in interpretation by the parties may not come to light until a dispute emerges—thus effectively nullifying the dispute-prevention purposes of the notarization process. *See,* e.g., Wang Runxuan, Xing Wenxin, "Zhubu kaizhan jingji hetong de gongzheng gongzuo" (Progressively open up the notarization work of economic contracts), *Guangming ribao,* Dec. 1, 1981.

111. *Id.* Also *see* Liu Longheng, *Jingji fa jian lun* (Elementary theory of economic law) (Beijing, 1981), at 115–16. In the past, it was this recordkeeping function that had been paramount. A Hong Kong informant who worked in a notary office during the 1950s maintained that aside from determining the validity of an agreement, the office did little to interpret the meaning of ambiguous terms.

112. *See,* e.g., Yan Weiqun, "Jiaqiang jingji sifa, baozhang jingji hetong" (Strengthen the economic judiciary and safeguard economic contracts), in

Guan Huai, *Jingji fa wen xuan* (Collection of articles on economic law) (Beijing, 1981), at 84–90. This was also recognized in the Supreme People's Court's 1980 opinions on accepting cases for the economic chambers, wherein it was conceded that these chambers were not fully equipped to handle large numbers of disputes. *See* "Zui gao renmin fayuan jingji shenpan ting guanyu renmin fayuan jingji shenpan ting shou an banfa de chubu yijian" and "Zui gao renmin fayuan jingji shenpan ting guanyu renmin fayuan jingji shenpan ting shou an fanwei de chubu yijian," *supra* n. 98.

113. The emphasis on use of the economic chambers for trial of economic crimes was underscored by the Request for Opinion issued in 1982 by the State Economic Commission, the State Administration for Industry and Commerce and the Economic Laws and Regulations Research Center of the State Council, in which the proposal was made that the people's courts should concentrate on cases involving use of contracts for criminal ends. *See* "Guowuyuan pizhuan guojia jing wei, guojia gong shang xingzheng guanli ju, guowuyuan jingji fa gui yanjiu zhongxin guanyu dui zhixing jingji hetong fa ruogan wenti de yijian de qingshi de tongzhi" (Notice of the State Council approving and circulating the request for opinion of the State Economic Commission, the State Administration for Industry and Commerce and the Economic Laws and Regulations Research Center of the State Council concerning implementation of the economic contract law), *Jingji fa gui huibian* (Compilation of economic laws and regulations) (Guangzhou, n.d.), at 19, 21. For instance, of the 6,132 economic cases brought to economic chambers at all levels between the time of their establishment and the end of 1980, 1,686 concerned economic crimes. While still in the minority of cases, economic crimes nonetheless took up a significant portion of the resources of the economic chambers. *See* "Quan guo fayuan yi she jingji shenpan ting yi qian duo ge" (Courts throughout the country have already established more than one thousand economic chambers), *Zhongguo fazhi bao,* Mar. 27, 1981. In 1986, the courts had handled some 78,133 cases of economic crimes as compared to 322,000 cases of civil economic disputes, suggesting that while the proportion of court time devoted to economic crime has declined, it is still substantial. *See* Zheng Tianxiang, "Zui gao renmin fayuan gongzuo baogao" (Report on the work of the Supreme People's Court), *Renmin ribao-hai wai ban* (Overseas ed.), Apr. 16. 1987, at 2.

114. *See* Wei Zhenying, Yang Zhenshan, "Lun weifan jingji hetong de peichang zeren" (On the responsibility for compensation for breach of economic contracts), in Guan Huai, *Jingji fa wen xuan* (Collection of Articles on Economic Law) (Beijing, 1981), at 83. Also *see Jingji hetong jiufen anli xuanbian,* (Compilation of cases of economic contract disputes) (Beijing, 1982). In this casebook, the majority of cases that go to court are sent back out for mediation.

115. The Economic Chamber of the Supreme People's Court had opined in 1980 that arbitration should be a prerequisite to court trial. *See* "Zui gao

renmin fayuan jingji shenpan ting guanyu renmin fayuan jingji shenpan ting shou an banfa de chubu yijian"; "Zui gao renmin fayuan jingji shenpan ting guanyu renmin fayuan jingji shenpan ting shou an fanwei de chubu yijian," *supra* n. 98.

116. *See,* e.g., "Gong shang guanli zong ju guanyu gong shang, nong shang jingji hetong jiben tiaokuan de shixing guiding" (Provisional regulations of the State Administration for Industry and Commerce on the basic provisions of industrial-commercial and agricultural-commercial economic contracts), *Jingji fa gui huibian* (Compilation of economic laws and regulations) (Guangzhou, n.d.), at 24.

117. For an example of a dispute that arose regarding the effect of articles in a contract, *see* case no. 2 in *Jingji hetong jiufen anli xuanbian, supra* n. 114, at 2–4. Also *see* R. MacNeil, "Contracts in China: Law Practice and Dispute Resolution," 38 *Stanford Law Review* 303 (1986).

118. The term *consideration* refers to the necessity of an exchange as the basis for the promise or promises that form a contract. *See,* generally, J. D. Calamari and J. M. Perillo, *Contracts* (1977), at 132 *et seq.*

119. For an example of a dispute arising over pricing, *see,* e.g., case no. 83 in *Jingji hetong jiufen anli xuanbian, supra* n. 114, at 126–130.

120. *See* Guowuyuan jingji fa gui yanjiu zhongxin bangong shi, *supra* n. 76, at 14–16.

121. Id.

122. *See* ECL, Article 3. Also *see* Guowuyuan jingji fa gui yanjiu zhongxin bangongshi, *supra* n. 76, at 16.

2. Doctrinal Norms

1. For further discussion on the doctrinal viewpoints of the political and legal communities in Shanghai and Sichuan, *see* P. Potter, "Policy, Law and Private Economic Rights in China: The Doctrine and Practice of Law on Economic Contracts" (Ph.D. diss., University of Washington, 1986).

2. Xue Muqiao, "Liyong jiazhi guilu wei jingji jianshe shiye fuwu" (Use the laws of value to serve the work of economic construction), *Hongqi,* no. 1, 1979, at 62.

3. Ma Hong, "Gaige jingji guanli tizhi yu kuoda qiye zizhuquan" (Reform the economic system and expand enterprise autonomy), *Hongqi,* no. 10, 1979, at 50.

4. *See,* generally, D. Solinger, "Marxism and the Market in Socialist China: The Reforms of 1979–1980 in Context," in V. Nee and D. Mozingo, *State and Society in Contemporary China* (1983), at 194, 210 *et seq.*

5. *See* Wang Renzhi, Gui Shiyong, Xu Jingan, "Lun wo guo jingji guanli tizhi gaige de jige wenti" (On several questions in the reform of our country's economic management system), *Hongqi,* no. 5, 1980, at 21.

6. "Xinhua Reports on National Work Conference on Production," *FBIS Daily Report: China,* Apr. 14, 1980, at L5; "National Production Work Conference Continues," *FBIS Daily Report: China,* Apr. 15, 1980, at L4.

7. "Gongye qiye quanmian zhiliang guanli zanxing banfa" (Provisional methods for all round management of quality in industrial enterprises), *Guowuyuan Gongbao,* 1980, at 193.

8. *See,* e.g., "Zhongguo gongchandang di shiyi jie zhongyang weiyuanhui di san ci quanti huiti baogao" (Communique of the third plenum of the eleventh central committee of the CCP), *Hongqi,* no. 1, 1979, at 17. "CCP Document no. 1 on Rural Economic Policies", *FBIS Daily Report: China,* Apr. 13, 1983, at K 1; "CCP Central Committee Circular on Rural Work in 1984," *FBIS Daily Report: China,* June 13, 1984, at K1, K6. Also *see* D. Zweig, K. Hartford, J. Feinerman, and J. Deng, "Law, Contracts and Economic Modernization: Lessons from the Recent Chinese Rural Reforms," 23 *Stanford Journal of International Law* 319 (1987).

9. *Id. See* chapter 1, n. 50, and accompanying text. Also *see* Chuyuan Cheng, *China's Economic Development: Growth and Structural Change* (1982), at 109.

10. *See,* generally, "Guowuyuan guanyu tuidong jingji lianhe de zanxing guiding" (Interim regulations of the state council concerning promoting economic coordination), *Guowuyuan gongbao,* 1980, at 227. These regulations permitted commercial enterprises to sign contracts with other enterprises both within and without their own administrative structure. Also *see* "Gong shang xingzheng guanli zongju guanyu gong shang, nong shang qiye jingji hetong jiben tiaokuan de shixing guiding" (Provisional regulations of the State Administration for Industry and Commerce concerning the basic provisions of contracts between industrial and commercial enterprises and between industrial and agricultural enterprises); Guowuyuan jingji fa gui yanjiu zhongxin bangongshi (Office of the Economic Laws and Regulations Research Center of the State Council), *Jingji hetong fa gui xuanbian* (Compilation of laws and regulations on economic contracts) (Beijing, 1982), at 107. These regulations were expressly aimed at improving the circulation of commodities through contracts rather than through the mechanism of state planning.

11. "Gong kuang chanpin hetong shixing tiaoli" (Provisional regulations on contracts for factory and mining goods), *Jingji hetong fa gui xuanbian, supra* n. 10, at 68; "Gong kuang chanpin gou xiao hetong tiaoli" (Regulations on contracts for the purchase and sale of factory and mining goods), *Guowuyuan gongbao,* 1984, at 37. Although regulations had been issued in 1979 concerning contracts, these entailed administrative directives under the state planning system. *See,* e.g., "Guanyu zhuhao qianding he zixing yi jiu qi jiu nian dinghuo hetong de tongzhi" (Circular on grasping well the signing and performance of 1979 ordering goods contracts); "Guanyu guojia jihua tiaozheng hou ji dian chanpin dinghuo hetong chuli banfa de tongzhi" (Circular on methods for handling contracts for ordering electrical and equipment

goods following adjustment to the state plan), in Guojia jingji weiyuanhui jingji fa gui ju (Economic Laws and Regulations Bureau of the State Economic Commission) and Beijing zheng fa xueyuan jingji fa min fa jiao yan shi (Teaching and Research Office for Economic and Civil Law of the Beijing Institute for Politics and Law), *Zhonghua renmin gongheguo gongye qiye fa gui xuanbian* (Compilation of industrial laws and regulations of the PRC) (Beijing, 1981), at 634, 636. The use of contracts in construction projects was encouraged in the State Capital Construction Commission's Opinion on Carrying out the Contract System in Capital Construction (1979) and regulations on related engineering and design services, *Jingji hetong fa gui xuanbian, supra* n. 10 at 37 *et seq.*, although the context involved providing construction services and thus was more akin to commercial contracting.

12. Part of the problem lay in the perception that increased autonomy for factory managers represented a threat to the political power of local party functionaries. Indeed, the issue of autonomy for industrial enterprise managers continued to be a sensitive issue up through 1987 and 1988, when debate delayed enactment of the enterprise law and the regulations on the authority of industrial managers. The PRC Law On State-Owned Industrial Enterprises was initially scheduled for enactment in early 1987, but the NPC Standing Committee decided at the last moment not to submit the law to the Fifth Session of the Sixth NPC for approval, due to continuing revisions. *See* "Law on Industry Not Ripe for NPC," *China Daily*, Mar. 20, 1987, at 1. The law was rescheduled for enactment at the 1988 NPC Session. "Qiye fa jiben chenglie jianyi tongguo shishi" (The enterprise law is basically ripe, suggestion is for implementation), *Fazhi ribao* (Legal System Daily), Mar. 7, 1988, at 2. The Regulations on the Work of Factory Managers in State-Owned Industrial Enterprises were initially enacted in September 1986 and granted substantial management autonomy to factory managers. *See* "Quan guo suoyouzhi gongye qiye gongzhang gongzuo tiaoli" (Regulations on the work of factory managers in state-owned industrial enterprises), *Zhongguo fazhi bao*, Oct. 22, 1986, at 2. However, the regulations were revised and reissued in January 1987 to incorporate suggestions that enterprise managers put priority on upholding state interests. *See* "New Rules Promote Factory Directors' Management Role," *China Daily*, Jan. 12, 1987, at 1.

13. *See*, e.g., Yang Shangkun's Standing Committee Report to the NPC," *FBIS Daily Report: China*, Dec. 18, 1981, at K10, K15; "Gu Ming xiang wu jie ren da si ci huiyi zuo guanyu 'zhongguo renmin gongheguo jingji hetong fa (caoan)' de shumian shuoming" (Gu Ming delivers written, explanation of the Economic Contract Law of the PRC (draft) to the Fourth Session of the Fifth National People's Congress), *Renmin ribao*, Dec. 9, 1981, at 1.

14. *Id.*

15. *See* ECL, Article 1.

16. *See*, e.g., Wang Jiafu, Shi Tanjing, Wang Baoshu, "Zhixing jingji hetong fa de jige zhishi wenti" (Several issues of knowledge in implementing the

economic contract law), *Renmin ribao,* Aug. 27, 1982, at 5. Although Wang and his colleagues are scholars at the Legal Studies Institute of the Chinese Academy of Social Sciences, the publication by *People's Daily* of their article indicates that the views expressed therein conformed to those of the central leadership.

17. "Jingji guanxi zhong de zhongyao zhunze" (An important standard in economic relationships), *Renmin ribao,* Dec. 17, 1981, at 1.

18. *See,* e.g., Wei Zhenying, Yu Nengbin, "Guanyu shixing he tuiguang hetong zhi de wenti" (Questions concerning implementing and expanding the contract system), *Faxue yanjiu,* no. 3, 1980, at 34; Ma Hong, "Gaige jingji guanli tizhi yu kuoda qiye zizhuquan" (Reform the economic system and expand enterprise autonomy), *Hongqi,* no. 10, 1979, at 50.

19. Li Zhuguo, "Tantan jingji tiaozheng yu jingji hetong de guanxi" (Discussion of the relationship between economic adjustment and economic contracts), *Faxue zazhi,* no. 5, 1981, at 15.

20. Bai Youzhong, Li Zhuguo, "Wo guo de shehui zhuyi hetong zhi de zuoyong" (The functions of our socialist contract system), *Zhongguo fazhi bao,* July 31, 1981, at 3. Although the actual publication work for the *Gazette* was done by an office within the Ministry of Justice, informants in Hong Kong and Beijing insisted that editorial policy during the early 1980s was dictated by the CCP legal committee. This view is underscored by the "Foreword" to the *Gazette*'s opening issues, which stressed the *Gazette*'s adherence to the Party's line, policies, and programs. *See* "Fakanci" (Foreword), in *Zhongguo fazhi bao* (Chinese legal system gazette), August 1, 1980.

21. Liang Huixing, "Lun wo guo hetong falu zhidu de jihua yuanze yu ziyou yuanze" (On the principle of planning and the principle of independence in our contract law system), *Faxue yanjiu,* no. 4, 1982, at 44.

22. *See,* e.g., Wang Nairong, "Shi lun chengbao hetong de falu xingshi" (Tentative discussion of the legal character of responsibility contracts), *Faxue yanjiu,* no. 5, 1983, at 40.

23. *See,* e.g., Gu Ming, "Jingji hetong fa shi baozhang jihua zhixing de youli gongju" (The Economic Contract Law is a powerful tool in ensuring implementation of the state plan), *Faxue zazhi,* no. 3, 1982, at 7. At the time of publication, Gu was a vice-chairman of the Commission on Legislative Affairs of the NPC Standing Committee. The publication of Gu's article reflected a convergence of interest and attitudes between the China Law Society and the conservatives among the central political leadership, represented in part by Peng Zhen.

24. Liu Baibi, "Buxu liyong jingji hetong jinxing weifa fanzui" (It is impermissible to use economic contracts to carry out illegal criminal activity), *Faxue zazhi,* no. 2, 1982, at 17; Xie Cichang, Bian Yaowu, "Jingji fa he keguan jingji guilu ziran guilu de guanxi" (The relationship between economic law and objective economic laws and natural law), *Faxue zazhi,* no. 5, 1982, at 22.

25. "Yao jiji xuanzhuan he shishi jingji hetong fa" (We must actively popularize and carry out the Economic Contract Law), *Zhongguo fazhi bao*, Dec. 18, 1981, at 1.

26. *See*, e.g., Wei Zhenying, Yu Nengbin, "Guanyu shixing he tuiguang hetong zhi de wenti" (Questions concerning implementation and expansion of the contract system), *Faxue yanjiu*, no. 3, 1980, at 4.

27. *See*, e.g., Wang Jiafu, Wang Baoshu, "Lun jiaqiang shehui zhuyi jingji fazhi jianshe" (On strengthening the building of the socialist economic legal system), *Faxue yanjiu*, no. 1, 1983, at 18, 20; Shi Tanjing, "Shilun jingji fa" (Tentative discussion of economic law), *Faxue yanjiu*, no. 3, 1983, at 44. It is worth noting that Wang Jiafu's support for the view that contracts were to serve planning priorities had been published previously in *People's Daily* (*see* n. 16, *supra*), reflecting that Wang's views were influenced by if not directed by the attitudes of the political leadership at the time.

28. *See*, e.g., Li Shirong, Wang Liming, "Jingji fa tiaozheng duixiang ruogan wenti tantao" (Exploratory discussion of certain questions of the objective of economic law adjustment), *Faxue yanjiu*, no. 5, 1983, at 33; Xie Huaishi, "Cong jingji fa da xingcheng kan wo guo de jingji fa" (Studying our economic law from the standpoiint of the formation of economic law), *Faxue yanjiu*, no. 2, 1984, at 16.

29. *See*, e.g., Jin Liqi, Cheng Shu, Gu Zhifang, "Shi xi hetong jiufen de yuanyin" (Tentative analysis of the reasons for contract disputes), *Faxue zazhi*, no. 3, 1981, at 20; Wang Yongfei, "Fa yu jingji" (Law and the economy), *Zhongguo fazhi bao*, Dec. 26, 1980.

30. Wang Jiafu, Liang Huixing, "Yong falu shouduan guanli jingji" (Usual legal methods to manage the economy), *Zhongguo fazhi bao*, July 15, 1983; Gu Ming, "Jingji fa lilun yanjiu gongzuo de jige wenti" (Several questions in theoretical and research work on economic law), *Zhongguo fazhi bao*, Dec. 16, 1983.

31. These differences stemmed in part from the respective influences of the Deng Xiaoping reformist coalition on the Academy of Social Sciences, and of conservative party elders such as Peng Zhen on the CCP's legal policies and on the Beijing legal establishment. Deng's influence at CASS was exercised during this period primarily through CASS President Ma Hong and General Secretary Mei Yi. Peng's influence on CCP legal affairs and on *Legal Studies Magazine* was exercised in part through long-term associates Cheng Zihua (senior member of the CCP Legal and Political Affairs Group) and Wang Hanbin (secretary general of the Legal Affairs Commission of the NPC Standing Committee). *See*, generally, P. Potter, "Peng Zhen: Evolving Views Toward Organization and Law," in C. Hamrin and T. Cheek, *China's Establishment Intellectuals* (1986).

32. *See* generally, N. Lardy, "Economic Planning in the People's Republic of China: Central-Provincial Fiscal Relations," U.S. Congress, Joint Economic Committee, *China: A Reassessment of the Economy* (1975), at 94; H. C. Ling,

The Petroleum Industry of the People's Republic of China (1975), at 49–53, 113–15; A. Eckstein, *China's Economic Revolution* (1977), at 110–58; and C. Howe, *China's Economy* (1978), at 30–65.

33. *See* "Jianzhu anzhuang gongzheng hetong shixing tiaoli" (Provisional regulations on construction, installation and engineering contracts), *Jingji hetong fa gui xuanbian, supra* n. 10, at 42.

34. "Guanyu zhuahao qianding he zhixing yi jiu qi jiu nian dinghuo hetong de tongzhi" (Circular on grasping well the signing and implementation of 1979 ordering contracts), Article 8, *Jingji hetong ziliao* (Materials on economic contracts) (1980), at 28. Also *see* "Guanyu guanli jingji hetong ruogan wenti de lianhe tongzhi" (Joint circular on several questions involving the administration of economic contracts), Article 1, *Jingji hetong ziliao* (Materials on economic contracts) (1980), at 47. Also *see Jingji hetong fa gui xuanbian, supra* n. 10, at 103.

35. "Jianzhu anzhuang gongzheng hetong shixing tiaoli," *supra* n. 33.

36. "Guanyu guanli jingji hetong ruogan wenti de lianhe tongzhi," *supra* n. 34, at 103.

See ECL, Article 51.

38. "National Meeting on Commerce, Industry Held in Beijing," *Xinhua* (New China News Agency) *Domestic Service,* Mar. 26, 1979, tr. in *FBIS Daily Report: China,* Mar. 28, 1979, at L4, L5. The SAIC bureaucracy had been inactive in the Cultural Revolution period but was re-established during 1978. The presence at the meeting of Vice-Premiers Li Xiannian, Yu Qiuli and Wang Renzhong indicated further the significance being attached to the role of the SAIC offices, including their role of supervising contracts. For general discussion of the revitalization of the SAIC, *see* Dong Jiuchang, Cai Lingcai, "Zhongguo gong shang xingzheng guanli xue gailun" (Introduction to the study of China's administration of industry and commerce) (Beijing, 1985).

39. "Gong shang xingzheng guanli zongju guanyu gong shang, nong shang qiye jingji hetong jiben tiaokuan de shixing guiding," Article 1, *supra* n. 10, at 107.

40. Under the provisions of the 1979 Joint Circular, the various levels of economic committees under the commission were charged with responsibility for managing economic contracts between different industrial departments and between industrial departments and materials, construction, and agricultural departments. *See* "Guanyu guanli jingji hetong ruogan wenti de lianhe tongzhi," Article 7, *supra* n. 34.

41. "Guowuyuan guanyu tuidong jingji lianhe de zanxing guiding," *supra* n. 10.

42. "Gong Shang Xingzheng Guanli Zongju xiang guowuyuan de huibao tigang" (Outline report of the Central Bureau for Administration of Industry and Commerce to the State Council), *Guowuyuan gongbao,* 1981, at 464. The report noted, "By means of contract management, we must increase the rate of

signing and fulfillment of contracts; study and summarize experiences in the certification of contracts; and cause contracts to play a greater role in strengthening the planning of production and sale, the coordination of the relations between production and sale, the reform of management, and the development of production." *Id.*, at 469.

43. Yang Shihong, "Jingji hetong fa de jige zhuyao wenti" (Several important questions of the Economic Contract Law), *Renmin ribao,* Dec. 25, 1981, at 5.

44. "Jiaqiang jingji hetong de tongyi guanli" (Strengthen unified administration of economic contracts), *Renmin ribao,* June 27, 1982, at 4.

45. "Wanshan guoxiao hetong zhi de zhongyao cuoshi" (Important measures for perfecting the system of purchase and sale contracts), *Renmin ribao,* Feb. 10, 1984, at 2.

46. "Guanyu jingji hetong jianzheng de zanxing guiding" (Interim regulations on the certification of economic contracts), *Zhongguo fazhi bao,* Sept. 6, 1985, at 2.

47. The word *jianzheng* is comprised of the words *jianding* (examination) and *zhengming* (verification).

48. "Sheng, shi, zizhiqu zhijian wu zi xiezuo guanli shishi banfa" (Methods for carrying out administration of cooperation in materials among provinces, centrally administered cities, and autonomous regions), *Jingji hetong fa gui xuanbian, supra* n. 10 at 91. Article 9 of the "Methods" provided that, "After a contract has gone through certification and becomes effective, the cooperating parties must carry it out in earnest." Article 10 provided that the shipping of materials and the financial accounting among provinces, centrally administered cities, and autonomous regions "must be done based on approved and certified contracts."

49. "Guanyu guanli jingji hetong ruogan wenti de lianhe tongzhi," *supra* n. 34, at 104. Article 3 of the circular stated "for the time being, we do not make unified regulations for certification of contracts," but went on to allow certification by the relevant contract management organs if the parties requested it.

50. *See,* e.g., Li Zhuguo, "Zhongshi hetong de jianzheng" (Emphasize the certification of contracts), *Renmin ribao,* Aug. 7, 1980. At the time of publication, Li was a legal scholar at the Shanghai Academy of Social Sciences. The printing of his article in *People's Daily* indicated central level political support for his views.

51. "Gong Shang Xingzheng Guanli Zongju xiang guowuyuan de huibao tigang," *supra* n. 42.

52. "Nong fu chanpin yi gou yi xiao jiage zanxing guanli banfa (caoan)" (Provisional methods for managing prices in the negotiated purchase and sale of agricultural byproducts), *Guowuyuan gongbao* (1981), at 562.

53. "Gu Ming xiang wu jie ren da si ci huiyi zuo guanyu 'Zhonghua renmin gongheguo jingji hetong fa (caoan)' de shumian shuoming" (Gu Ming delivers

written explanation of the 'Economic Contract Law of the PRC (Draft)' to the Fourth Session of the Fifth NPC), *Renmin ribao,* Dec. 9, 1981, at 1. For a complete text of Gu's report, *see* Gu Ming, "Guanyu 'Zhonghua renmin gongheguo jingji hetong fa (caoan)' de shuoming" (Explanation of the 'Economic Contract Law of the PRC [Draft]'), *Zhongguo fazhi bao,* Dec. 13, 1981, at 4.

54. "Guanyu jingji hetong qianzheng de zanxing guiding," *supra* n. 46. Virtually all types of contracts were subject to certification. In particular, certification was available for contracts that were formed outside normal ministerial channels, such as those between individual households or enterprises (*ge ti hu*) and state or collective enterprises or other legal persons.

55. "Sifa bu guanyu quanguo sifa xingzheng gongzuo zuotanhui de baogao" (Report of the Ministry of Justice on the national judicial administration work conference), *Guowuyuan gongbao,* 1980, at 639. "National Notarization Work Forum Held in Beijing," Beijing Domestic Service, Sept. 25, 1980, trans. in *FBIS Daily Report: China,* Sept. 29, 1980, at L 24. The conference report stated, "With respect to the notarization of economic contracts, at present the work of investigation and study can be carried out. In areas with the right conditions, experiments can also be carried out after ongoing consultation with the appropriate economic and SAIC offices."

56. "Gongzheng zhengming de haochu" (The advantages of notarization testimonials), *Guangming ribao,* May 15, 1980, at 3. This article urged that "in instances of illegal contract activities or non-performance of contracts, notarization organs have the authority through the relevant departments and their leading organs to push for the reformation of such activity or to act on their own to curb (such activity)." Also *see* Wang Runxuan, Xing Wenxin (last character indistinct), "Zhubu kaizhan jingji hetong de gongzheng gongzuo" (Progressively develop economic contract notarization work), *Guangming ribao,* Dec. 1, 1981, at 3.

57. "Zhonghua renmin gongheguo zanxing tiaoli" (Provisional regulations of the PRC on notarization), *Renmin ribao,* June 29, 1982.

58. *See,* e.g., "Xiahe Xian gongzheng chu jiji kaizhan jingji hetong gongzheng" (Xiahe County notary offices develop economic contract notarization), *Renmin ribao,* Feb. 7, 1983, at 3.

59. *See* "Longhua Xian shiban linye hetong gongzheng" (Longhua County experiments with notarization of forestry contracts), *Renmin ribao,* Apr. 10, 1983, at 4.

60. "Wo guo you gongzheng chu er qian duo ge" (Our country has more than 2,000 notary offices), *Renmin ribao,* Apr. 24, 1983, at 4.

61. *See,* e.g., "Pai you jie nan de gongzheng chu" (Notary offices which eliminate worries and resolve difficulties), *Renmin ribao,* July 6, 1984, at 4. "Gei zhuanye hu, jingji lianhe ti falu baohu" (Give legal protection to specialized households and cooperative groups), *Renmin ribao,* July 24, 1984, at 1.

62. *See,* e.g., Chen Liushu, "Zuo hao dui hetong de jianzheng, gongzheng

gong zuo" (Do good work in the certification and notarization of contracts), *Zhongguo fazhi bao,* Jan. 29, 1982, at 2.

63. *See* Wei Zhenying, Yu Nengbin, "Guanyu shixing he tuiguang hetong zhi de wenti" (Questions on implementing and expanding the contract system) *Faxue yanjiu,* no. 3, 1980, at 34. Although recognition was also given to the role of enterprise management offices, this reflected acquiescence in the existing norm, whereas references to bank supervision were an effort to posit an effective external alternative.

64. Xu Jie, Qi Tianchang, "Hetong jianzheng gongzuo he jige wenti" (Several questions in contract certification work), *Faxue yanjiu,* no. 5, 1980, at 29. The issues to be addressed through certification were to include: (1) the legal qualifications of the parties; (2) the legality of the rights and duties accruing from the contract and the scope of authority of the signatories; (3) the voluntariness, equality and mutual benefit of the contract; and (4) the completeness and adequacy of the contract's basic provisions.

65. *See,* e.g., Liang Huixing, "Lun wo guo hetong falu zhi du de jihua yuanze yu hetong zi you yuanze" (On the principle of planning and the principle of contract freedom in our contract law system), *Faxue yanjiu,* no. 4, 1982, at 44.

66. Chen Liushu, "Lun wo guo guojia gongzheng zhidu de jiben yuanze" (On the basic principles of our national notarization system), *Faxue yanjiu,* no. 1, 1983, at 66, 68.

67. Shi Tanjing, "Da bao gan hetong de shengchan he fazhan" (The emergence and development of the contract system for comprehensive assumption of tasks), *Faxue yanjiu,* no. 4, 1983, at 1.

68. Sun Rulin, "Shi lun jingji hetong gongzheng" (Tentative comments on the notarization of economic contracts), *Faxue yanjiu,* no. 6, 1984, at 62.

69. *Id.,* at 65. The evidentiary role of notarization has more significance as a matter of conceptual theory than in practice, since very few contract disputes were resolved through the courts, and the evidentiary rules in arbitration and mediation proceedings are very flexible, accepting as evidence virtually any facts (including certification documents) brought forth by the parties.

70. *See,* e.g., Liu Zhongya, Su Yang "Guanyu zhiding he zhunbei shishi jingji hetong fa de jige wenti" (Several questions concerning enacting and preparing to carry out the Economic Contract Law), *Faxue yanjiu,* no. 3, 1982, at 46, 47.

71. *See* Jin Liqi, Cheng Shu, Gu Zhifang, "Shi xi hetong jiufen de yuan yin" (A tentative analysis of the reasons for contract disputes), in *Faxue zazhi,* no. 3, 1981, at 20. Certification was presented as important in preventing contract disputes, by ensuring the legality of the contract; the completeness and concreteness of contract provisions; the formalizing of procedures for signing the contract; the qualifications of the parties; and the inclusion of specific provisions for economic responsibility in the event of nonperformance. These were much the same virtues as were ascribed to notarization.

72. Gu Ming, "Jingji hetong fa shi baozhang jihua zhixing, de youli gongju" (The Economic Contract Law is a powerful tool in ensuring implementation of the state plan), *Faxue zazhi,* no. 3, 1982, at 7.

73. Also *see* Li Zhuguo, "Tantan jingji tiaozheng yu jingji hetong de guanxi" (Discussion of the relationship between economic adjustment and economic contracts), *Faxue zazhi,* no. 5, 1981, at 15.

74. *See* Wen Zhongying, "Tan tan gongzheng dui jingji hetong de zuoyong" (A discussion of the role of notarization for economic contracts), *Faxue zazhi,* no. 3, 1983, at 43. Wen's article discussed the impact of notarization on contract performance in Liaoning, noting that in some counties the contract performance rate approached 100 percent due to the use of notarization. And in an oblique criticism of reliance on certification, the article contended that contract management required more than just administrative methods of contract management. In the same issue, the legal adviser column for *Legal Studies Magazine* asserted that certification offices were to override notarized documents, or to require certification thereof. *See* "Gongzheng jiguan shi fou keyi gongzheng jingji hetong" (Can't notary organs notarize economic contracts?), *Faxue zazhi,* no. 3, 1983, at 62. Also *see* Chen Liushu, "Banli jingji hetong gongzheng wenti chu tan" (Elementary exploration of questions on carrying out notarization of economic contracts), *Faxue zazhi,* no. 4, 1983, at 47.

75. Liu Baibi, "Buxu liyong jingji hetong jinxing weifa fanzui" (It is impermissible to use economic contracts to carry out illegal criminal activity), *Faxue zazhi,* no. 2, 1982, at 17. Liu's assertions that contracts be subjected to "legal supervision" suggested support for the notaries that, as organs under the Ministry of Justice, were to carry out contract supervision according to the requirements of "socialist public law." This emphasis on public law suggested that notarization should not, as CASS had suggested, be a mechanism for asserting autonomy, but rather should ensure that contracts were in compliance with state policies.

76. *See* Sun Bosheng, "Hetong bixu jinxing jianzheng" (Contracts must undergo certification), *Zhongguo fazhi bao,* Mar. 20, 1981.

77. Even preceding the national work conference on notarial work held in September 1980, the *Gazette* expressed support for the role of notarization of both foreign and domestic contracts. *See,* e.g., "Quan guo gongzheng gongzuo zai pengpo fazhan zhong" (National notarization work is in flourishing development), *Zhongguo fazhi bao,* Aug. 15, 1980, at 1.

78. *See,* e.g., "Beijing shi gongzheng gongzuo xunsu fazhan" (Beijing's notarial work is developing rapidly), *Zhongguo fazhi bao,* Apr. 10, 1981; "Kaifeng shi gongzheng chu kaizhan jingji hetong gongzuo" (The Kaifeng notarial office begins economic contract work), *Zhongguo fazhi bao,* June 26, 1981. "Wei nongye chengbao ban hetong gongzheng" (Notarization of agricultural responsibility contracts), *Zhongguo fazhi bao,* July 17, 1981.

79. The *Gazette* did give limited attention to the role of SAIC certification, particularly in the context of the SAIC Arbitration Regulations issued in Au-

gust 1983. *See,* e.g., "Jianchi yi fa banshi, jiaqiang hetong guanli" (Insist on doing things according to law, strengthen contract administration), *Zhongguo fazhi bao,* Nov. 18, 1983.

80. Compensation for losses and straight fines also were possible in theory. However, since as a rule enterprise losses would be made up by the state, there was little concern with compensating such losses. *See,* e.g., "Guojia jingji weiyuanhui guanyu gong kuang chanpin dinghuo hetong jiben tiaokuan de zanxing guiding" (Provisional regulations of the State Economic Commission concerning the basic provision of contracts for ordering factory and mining Goods), Articles 23–25, *Jingji hetong fa gui xuanbian supra* n. 10, at 61–63.

81. "Guanyu guanli jingji hetong ruogan wenti de lianhe tongzhi *supra* n. 34, at 105, 106. While the *wei yue jin* was intended in part to compensate losses, it was generally payable regardless of whether it exceeded actual damages caused by nonperformance, and thus was more in the nature of a fine. The Thirty Articles on Industry (1978) also emphasized certainty of remedies for nonperformance, "Those who carry out contracts not in accordance with their terms or who arbitrarily break off cooperative relations must affix responsibility and compensate for losses. *See* "Zhonggong zhongyang weiyuanhui guanyu jiakuai gongye fazhan ruogan wenti de jueding" (Decision of the CCP Central Committee concerning several issues in accelerating industrial production), Article 10, *Zhonghua renmin gongheguo gongye qiye fa gui xuanbian, supra* n. 11, at 73.

82. "Gong Shang Xingzheng Guanli Zongju, guanyu gong shang, nong shang qiye jingji hetong jiben tiaokuan de shixing guiding," *supra* n. 10, at 111–13.

83. *Id.,* Articles 16 and 17.

84. *Id.,* Article 17.

85. *See,* e.g., "Lun weifa jingji hetong de peichang zeren" (On the responsibility of compensation for breach of contract), *Renmin ribao,* Oct. 16, 1980, at 1.

86. *See* ECL, Article 35.

87. *See,* e.g., Stanley Lubman, "Mao and Mediation: Politics and Dispute Resolution in Communist China," 55 *California Law Review* 1284 (1967).

88. "Guanyu guanli jingji hetong ruogan wenti de lianhe tongzhi," Article 6, *supra* n. 34, at 105.

89. *See* ECL, Article 48.

90. For general discussion of arbitration procedure, *see Jingji hetong zhongcai shouce* (Handbook on economic contract arbitration) (Beijing, 1984). Also *see* Jingji hetong fa qicao xiaozu bangongshi (Office of the small group for drafting the ECL), *Zhonghua renmin gongheguo jingji hetong fa wenti jieda* (Questions and answers on the Economic Contract Law of the PRC) (Beijing, 1983), at 108 *et seq.;* Zhang Chengquan, *Jingji hetong de dingli he zhongcai* (Execution and arbitration of economic contracts) (Beijing, 1985); Zhou Shijie, *Jingji zhongcai jiben zhishi* (Basic knowledge of economic

arbitration) (Beijing, 1986); Wang Cunxue, *Jingji zhongcai yu jingji sifa* (Economic arbitration and economic judicature) (Beijing, 1987).

91. "Jianzhu anzhuang gongzheng hetong shixing tiaoli" (Provisional regulations for construction, installation and engineering contracts), Article 30 and "Kancha sheji hetong shixing tiaoli" (Provisional regulations for surveying and design contracts), Article 17, both in *Jingji hetong fa gui xuanbian, supra* n. 10, at 48, 52.

92. "Guanyu zhua hao qianding he zhixing yi jiu qi jiu nian dinghuo hetong de tongzhi", *supra* n. 34.

93. "Guanyu guanli jingji hetong ruogan wenti de lianhe tongzhi," *supra* n. 34.

94. *Id.*, Article 6, at 105.

95. "Guanyu gong shang xingzheng guanli bumen hetong zhongcai chengxu de shixing banfa" (SAIC provisional methods for contract arbitration procedures), *Jingji hetong fa gui xuanbian, supra* n. 10, at 115. The regulations were intended for use in disputes involving state industrial and agricultural procurement contracts. The regulations were divided into seven chapters addressing, respectively, the issues of (1) the institutions and organizations charged with arbitration; (2) the acceptance of cases; (3) investigation and proof in arbitrations; (4) first-level arbitration; (5) second-level arbitration; (6) the coming into effect and implementation of arbitration decisions; and (7) re-examination and case filing.

96. *See* ECL, Article 49. The two levels of arbitration both involved appealability of the initial arbitral decision. *See* "Guanyu gong shang xingzheng guanli bumen hetong zhongcai chengxu de shixing banfa," *supra,* n. 95, Article 22. Criticism of this approach appeared in "Lun weifan jingji hetong de peichang zeren" (On the responsibility for compensation for breach of contract), *Renmin ribao,* Oct. 16, 1980, at 1.

97. "Zhonghua renmin gongheguo jingji hetong zhongcai tiaoli" (Regulations of the PRC on contract arbitration), *Guowuyuan gongbao,* 1983, at 803. The regulations contained many of the same provisions as the 1980 SAIC arbitration regulations. Thus, Articles 4 and 32 imposed on arbitration organs the duties of investigation and written explanation of the final decision. In Article 33, the new regulations reaffirmed the right of appeal to the people's courts. The binding character of the arbitration decision, and the elimination of the two-level system of arbitration were reaffirmed in Article 3.

98. *Id.*, at Article 14.

99. *Id.*, at Article 24.

100. "Arbitration Committees to Handle Contract Disputes," *Xinhua Domestic Service,* Sept. 1, 1983, trans. in *FBIS Daily Report: China,* Sept. 2, 1983, at K3.

101. "Wo guo jingji hetong guanli ri zhen wanshan" (Our economic contract administration is becoming more perfect day by day), *Jingji cankao* (Economic reference), Sept. 23, 1987, at 1. Also *see* "Jingji hetong fa shishi wu

nian zuoyong jueda" (The effects of five years of implementation of the Economic Contract Law are great), *Zhongguo fazhi bao,* June 30, 1987, at 1.

102. *See,* e.g., Gong Zheng, "Jiaqiang guojia fazhi, baozhang shehui zhuyi xiandaihua jianshe" (Strengthen the country's legal system, safeguard socialist modernization construction), *Hongqi,* no. 2, 1979, at 12, 13.

103. "Guanyu guanli jingji hetong ruogan wenti de lianhe tongzhi," Article 6, *supra* n. 34, at 105.

104. "Zui gao renmin fayuan jingji shenpan ting guanyu renmin fayuan jingji shenpan ting shou an banfa de chubu yijian" (Preliminary opinion of the Economic Adjudication Chamber of the Supreme People's Court concerning methods of accepting cases by the economic adjudication chambers of the people's courts), *Jingji hetong fa jui xuanbian, supra* n. 10, at 123. Under these Methods, the economic chambers were only to accept cases that had already undergone the two levels of arbitration specified in the 1980 SAIC arbitration regulations. The economic chambers could also accept disputes concerning contracts with respect to which arbitration was not an option. This foreshadowed, and presumably qualified, the subsequent ECL provision that disputants could bring their cases directly to court. Under the Supreme Court's Methods, adjudication without prior effort to arbitrate applied to contracts *within* the administration systems of the Ministries of Industry, Materials, or Commerce that might not have been eligible for arbitration by SAIC. The 1980 SAIC arbitration regulations pertained only to contracts *between* industrial and commercial departments and *between* agricultural and commercial departments. *See* "Guanyu gong shang xingzheng guanli bumen hetong zhongcai chengxu de shixing banfa," Article 1, *supra* n. 95, at 115.

105. "Zui gao renmin fayuan jingji shenpan ting guanyu renmin fayuan jingji shenpan ting shou an fanwei de chubu yijian" (Preliminary opinion of the Economic Adjudication Chamber of the Supreme People's Court concerning the scope of accepting cases by the economic adjudication chambers of the people's courts), *Jingji hetong fa gui xuanbian, supra* n. 10, at 126. This opinion listed three categories of domestic contract disputes as appropriate for court adjudication: (1) disputes involving contracts for production, supply, shipment, and sale between socialist, publicly owned enterprises (i.e., state managed enterprises); (2) disputes involving contracts for capital construction and repair; and (3) disputes involving contracts for achievements in scientific research or which require the use of patented technology. The explanatory addendum to the Opinion indicated that the disputes over contracts for production, supply, shipment, and sales (category 1) were to be limited further to contracts signed by factory and mining enterprises. "Dui 'Guanyu renmin fayuan jingji shenpan ting shou an fanwei de chubu yijian' de ji dian shuoming" (Explanation of several points regarding the 'preliminary opinion concerning the scope of accepting cases by the economic adjudication chambers of the people's courts'), *Jingji hetong fa gui xuanbian, supra* n. 10, at 128.

106. "Dui 'Guanyu renmin fayuan jingji shenpan ting shou an fanwei de

chubu yijian' de ji dian shuoming" (Explanation of several points regarding the 'preliminary opinion concerning the scope of accepting cases by the economic adjudication chambers of the people's courts'), *Jingji hetong fa gui xuanbian, supra* n. 10 at 131.

107. *See,* e.g., "Lun weifan jingji hetong de peichang zeren" (On the responsibility of compensation for breach of contract), *Renmin ribao,* Oct. 16, 1980, at 1. Also *see* Gao Jingwen, "Jiji kaizhan jingji shenpan gongzuo" (Actively develop economic adjudication work), *Renmin ribao,* Apr. 23, 1981, at 5.

108. "Economic Sections Established in the People's Courts," *FBIS Daily Report: China,* Mar. 26, 1981, at L2.

109. Of the some 6,132 cases before the economic chambers through the end of 1980, 4,382 had been handled through administrative mediation. *Id.*

110. Some 37,000 cases were handled by the economic chambers between July 1983 and March 1984, the bulk of which involved economic contracts. Zheng Tianxiang, "Report to the Sixth National People's Congress on the Work of the Supreme People's Court," *FBIS Daily Report: China,* May 29, 1984, at K10. In 1985, 220,000 economic cases were handled by the economic chambers. This figure increased to 320,000 cases in 1986, and to 640,000 during the first half of 1987. "Renmin fayuan jingji shenpan gongzuo zai kaituo zhong qianjin" (The economic adjudication work of the people's courts advances during the period of development), *Zhongguo fazhi bao,* Nov. 11, 1987, at 1.

111. "National Meeting on Trying Economic Cases Ends," *FBIS Daily Report: China,* Apr. 9, 1984, at K8. The presence at the meeting of Zheng Tianxiang, chief justice of the Supreme People's Court indicated the importance which the central leadership place on this issue.

112. *See* Zheng Tianxiang, "Zui gao renmin fayuan gongzuo baogao" (Report on the work of the Supreme People's Court), *Renmin ribao-hai wai ban* (Overseas ed.), Apr. 16, 1987, at 2.

113. *See* Wei Zhenying, Yu Nengbi, "Guanyu shixing he tuiguang hetong zhi de wenti" (Questions on the implementation and expansion of the contract system), *Faxue yanjiu,* no. 3, 1980, at 34.

114. *See* ECL, Article 36.

115. *See* Chu Si, Da Bang, "Lun fanwei hetong de minshi zeren" (On civil liability for breach of contract), *Faxue yanjiu,* no. 3, 1982, at 51. The penalty payment was to be paid at the point when nonperformance occurred and was not to be a substitute for compensation for losses unless the amount of penalty payment exceeded the amount of loss. Compensation was to be paid to redress actual harm caused by nonperformance. Compensation could be required to make up for lost benefits that would reasonably have accrued had the contract been performed. While state regulations were seen as available for measuring the value of the loss caused directly by nonperformance, the opinions of disinterested experts were also to be solicited to determine the value of indirect damages.

116. This view was reiterated in a discussion of the rule that where the breaching party was not at fault, the liability for nonperformance could be lessened. *See* Zhang Yulin, "Wo guo jingji hetong fa wu guoshi zeren yuanze chu tan" (Exploratory discussion of the principle of lack of fault in our economic contract law), *Faxue yanjiu,* no. 6, 1984, at 41.

117. *See* Zhang Yulin, "Shi lun jingji hetong de danbao" (Tentative discussion of guarantees for economic contracts), *Faxue yanjiu,* no. 4, 1983, at 8.

118. *See* Wang Weiguo, "Lun hetong de qiangzhi shiji luxing" (On the compulsory actual performance of contracts), *Faxue yanjiu,* no. 3, 1984, at 46. Economic remedies were to be used in addition to specific performance in instances such as those where the flaws in performance could not be corrected and the aggrieved party could be made whole by payment of money or reduction of price and in cases of market-based contracts, where the supply exceeded demand and it was the seller who has not performed. These included most circumstances to which the ever expanding scope of contract activity might apply.

119. *See* Jin Liqi, Cheng Shu, Gu Zhifang, "Shixi hetong jiufen de yuanyin" (A tentative analysis of the reasons for contract disputes), *Faxue zazhi,* no. 3, 1981, at 20. Although reference was made to the duty to pay fines and compensation in the event of nonperformance, this was discussed in the broader context of the origins of contract disputes, and thus did not constitute a ringing endorsement for the use of economic remedies.

120. *See* Liu Baibi, "Buxu liyong jingji hetong jinxing weifa fanwei" (It is impermissible to use economic contracts to carry out illegal criminal activities), *Faxue zazhi,* no. 2, 1982, at 17. This article's emphasis on the potential criminal aspects of contract activities indicated a preoccupation with the collectivist public law aspects of contract practice, rather than the autonomous contract relationships that reliance on economic remedies is intended to foster.

121. "Weifan hetong de zeren—1" (Responsibility for breach of contract—1), *Zhongguo fazhi bao,* Nov. 27, 1981; "Weifan hetong de zeren—2" (Responsibility for breach of contract—2), *Zhongguo fazhi bao,* Dec. 4, 1981. Also *see* Bai Youzhong, Li Zhuguo, *Hetong jiben zhishi* (Basic knowledge of contracts) (Beijing, 1981).

122. For specific citations to discussions in the legal adviser column, *see* Appendix 1(c), Table of Case Citations.

123. *See* Wei Zhenying, Yu Nengbi, "Guanyu shixing he tuiguang hetong zhi de wenti" (Questions on the implementation and expansion of the contract system), *Faxue yanjiu,* no. 3, 1980, at 34.

124. *See* Xue Enqin, Chen Zhangming, "Shenli jingji jiufen anjian yao renzhen zhixing zhengce he yi fa ban shi" (Adjudication cases of economic disputes must conscientiously enforce policy and do things according to law), *Faxue yanjiu,* no. 4, 1982, at 50. Also *see* Bei Zhongjing, "Yi fa shi shi qiu shi di panming zeren" (Determining responsibility by relying on law and seeking truth from facts), *Faxue yanjiu,* no. 1, 1983, at 37; Chen Qinyi, "Dui fayuan

tiaojie ruogan wenti de tantao" (An exploratory discussion of several questions concerning court mediation), *Faxue yanjiu*, no. 1, 1984, at 34.

125. *See* Liu Zhongya, Su Yang, "Guanyu zhiding he zhunbei shishi jingji hetong fa de jige wenti" (Several issues in enacting and preparing to carry out the Economic Contract Law), *Faxue yanjiu*, no. 3, 1982, at 46. This was proposed as an alternative to the "two arbitration—two adjudication system," under which parties to a dispute first had to seek administrative arbitration and only after going through two rounds of arbitration could the issue be brought before a court. *See* n. 96, *supra*, and accompanying text.

126. *See* Yin Tian, "Wo guo jingji hetong zhongcai jiguan de xingzhi ji qi falu diwei" (The character and legal status of our economic contract arbitration organs), *Faxue yanjiu*, no. 1, 1985, at 25.

127. *See* Jin Liqi, Cheng Shu, Gu Zhifang, "Shixi hetong jiufen de yuanyin" (A tentative analysis of the reasons for contract disputes), *Faxue zazhi*, no. 3, 1981, at 20.

128. "Yi qi wu zhiliang biaozhen de hetong jiufen shi zen yang dedao yuanman jiejue de" (How a contract dispute over the lack of quality standards is resolved satisfactorily), *Faxue zazhi*, no. 2, 1982, at 44.

129. *See* Shen Guangsheng, Zhu Zhongming, "Tan tan dui jingji hetong jiufen anjian de shenli" (Discussion of the adjudication of cases of economic contract disputes), *Faxue zazhi*, no. 6, 1982, at 39. Noting that the economic chambers of the people's courts had handled some 14,600 contract cases during 1980–82, the article went on to stress the role of judicially sponsored mediation and arbitration.

130. *See* Zong Xiaoyou, Yan Yangxian, "Guanyu jingji jiufen anjian anyou queding de tan lun" (Exploratory discussion on determining the causes of economic dispute cases), *Faxue zazhi*, no. 6, 1983, at 50.

131. *See*, e.g., "Yi fa tiaojie jiufen, gong zheng caijue hetong" (Rely on law in mediation disputes, impartially adjudicate contracts), *Zhongguo fazhi bao*, Apr. 22, 1983. Prior to this, *China Legal System Gazette* had pointedly downplayed the role of SAIC arbitration, as evidenced in part by the failure to include in the reprints of Bai Youzhong and Li Zhuguo's book on contracts not including references to SAIC arbitration, despite the inclusion of such references in the original text. *See* "Hetong jiufen de chuli—xieshang" (The handling of contract disputes—negotiation), *Zhongguo fazhi bao*, Jan. 1, 1982, at 3; "Hetong jiufen de chuli—tiaojie" (The handling of contract disputes—mediation), *Zhongguo fazhi bao*, Jan. 8, 1982, at 3; "Hetong jiufen de chuli—zhongcai" (The handling of contract disputes—arbitration), *Zhongguo fazhi bao*, Jan. 15, 1982 at 3; "Hetong jiufen de chuli—shenli" (The handling of contract disputes—adudjication), *Zhongguo fazhi bao*, Jan. 29, 1982, at 3. Also *see* Bai Youzhong, Li Zhuguo, *Hetong jiben zhishi*, *supra* n. 121.

132. *See* Zhang Chengquan, "Zhongcai shi jiejue jingji hetong jiufen de zhongyao falu zhidu" (Arbitration is an important legal system for resolving

economic contract disputes), *Zhongguo fazhi bao,* Sept. 16, 1983. SAIC arbitration was presented as a legal method of dispute settlement, in contrast to the view expressed elsewhere that SAIC certification of contracts constituted administrative activity that was less preferable than judicial supervision through notarization. *See,* e.g., Sun Rulin, "Shi lun jingji hetong gongzheng," *supra* n. 68. This position was qualified somewhat by subsequent assertions that while arbitration constituted a legal system, it was neither a purely legal nor a purely administrative method of dispute resolution. *See,* e.g., Zhang Chengquan, "Shen me shi jingji hetong zhongcai" (What is arbitration of economic contracts), *Zhongguo fazhi bao,* Oct. 21, 1983.

133. *See,* e.g., "Jianchi yi fa ban shi, jiaqiang hetong guanli" (Insist on doing things according to law, strengthen contract management), *Zhongguo fazhi bao,* Nov. 18, 1983.

134. *See* "Jiaqiang jingji shenpan gongzuo de yi xiang zhongyao cuoshi" (An important measure in strengthening economic adjudication work), *Zhongguo fazhi bao,* Oct. 7, 1983.

135. *See* Ren Jianxin, "Renmin fayuan jingji shenpan gongzuo de renwu he shou an fanwei" (The duties and the scope of accepting cases in the work of the economic chambers of the people's court), *Zhongguo fazhi bao,* Apr. 23, 1984. In early 1984, the *Gazette* noted that some 89,494 economic disputes had been handled by the economic chambers in the past three years. *See* "Jingji shenpan gongzuo pengbo fazhan" (Economic adjudication work develops vigorously), *Zhongguo fazhi bao,* Mar. 28, 1984. This contrasted with reports that the SAIC departments had handled 12,700 disputes in the past year. *See* "Quan guo jingji hetong guanli gongzuo chengji xianzhe" (The accomplishments in national economic contract management work are obvious), *Zhongguo fazhi bao,* Mar. 5, 1984.

136. For citations to the contract case reports in *Zhongguo fazhi bao, see* Appendix 1(c), Table of Case Citations.

137. *See* nn. 104–106, *supra,* and accompanying text.

138. *See* discussion of legitimation based on legitimacy of the lawmaking process in Introduction at n. 15 and accompanying text.

3. Operational Aspects of Contract Formation

1. The operational characteristics of contracts in China are identified through examination of actual contract disputes, as reported in Chinese newspapers and legal journals. Although the cases reported in the Chinese press are published primarily for their pedagogical value, nonetheless they supply important data on contract practice unavailable elsewhere. The cases discussed in this chapter were taken from the periodicals listed in the bibliography. These materials were reviewed for each day from January 1, 1979 through June 30, 1985, in an effort to collect every reported case from this period. The case

reports consist of either responses to reader inquiries to legal advice columns, or reports of formal judicial or administrative dispute settlement processes. Both of these types of reports contain information on the formation of contracts, and in dispute resolution. The responses to reader inquiries often were reported prior to the final resolution of the dispute, in which case the result reported in appendix 1 is a "recommended result." The reports on formal dispute settlement processes generally contain final results, which are listed as such in Appendix 1. Whether in the form of a response to a specific inquiry, or as the formal resolution of a dispute, all of the reports may be termed "cases" since they represent actual individual disputes as to which specific solutions are either suggested or imposed. Tables containing information on each of the cases are set forth in Appendixes 1(a) and 1(b). The cases are organized chronologically according to the July 1, 1982, date of the Economic Contract Law going into effect. This chronological approach is useful to ascertain the effect of the ECL on contract autonomy.

2. *See* Introduction at 16, *et seq.*

3. *See* Appendix 1.

4. *See* chapter 2, at 96, *et seq.*

5. Hereafter, all case references are to Appendix 1, Table of Cases.

6. This new authority was based in part on the State Capital Construction Commission's "Opinion on Carrying out the Contract System in Capital Construction" (1979), Guowuyuan jingji fa gui yanjiu zhongxin bangongshi (Office of the Economic Laws and Regulations Research Center of the State Council), *Jingji hetong fa gui xuanbian* (Compilation of Laws and Regulations on Economic Contracts) (Beijing, 1982), at 37, *et seq.*

7. This included parties from within and without the centrally administered cities of Beijing, Shanghai, and Tianjin.

8. *See* "CCP Issues Minutes of 1981 Rural Work Conference," *FBIS Daily Report: China*, Apr. 7, 1982, at K1. Also *see* "Guanyu jin yi bu jiaqiang he wanshan nongye shengchan zerenzhi de jige wenti" (Several issues concerning the progressive strengthening and perfecting of the responsibility system in agricultural production), *Zhongguo nongye nianjian* (Yearbook of Chinese agriculture) (1981), at 409.

9. *See* ECL, Article 54. The effect of the Communist party directives on agriculture were also a contributing factor. *See* n. 8, *supra*, and accompanying text.

10. While the arbitral organ was not named, in all likelihood it would have been the appropriate branch of the State Administration for Industry and Commerce (SAIC). As discussed in chapter 2, the SAIC had been recognized as the primary contract arbitration organ in the 1979 Joint Circular on contract management and this role was confirmed in the SAIC's provisional regulations on arbitration issued in 1982, and in the PRC arbitration regulations issued in August 1983. *See* "Guanyu guanli jingji hetong ruogan wenti de lianhe tongzhi" (Joint circular on several questions of administration of economic

contracts) and "Guanyu gong shang xingzheng guanli bumen hetong zhongcai chengxu de shixing banfa" (SAIC provisional methods for contract arbitration), *Jingji hetong fa gui xuanbian, supra,* n. 6, at 103, 115; "Zhonghua renmin gonghe guo jingji hetong zhongcai tiaoli" (Regulations of the PRC on arbitration of economic contracts), *Guowuyuan gongbao* (State Council Reports), 1983, at 803.

11. Also see case no. 128. The use of guarantors had been recognized in PRC contract regulation as early as 1950. *See* "Jiguan, guoying qiye, hezuo she qianding hetong qiyue zanxing banfa" (Provisional methods for signing contracts and charters by organizations and state enterprises and cooperatives," *Jingji hetong fa gui xuanbian, supra,* n. 6, at 24.

4. Dispute Resolution

1. According to a 1982 circular issued by the State Council, the ECL was not to be applied to contracts formed prior to its effective date of July 1, 1982. *See* "Guanyu dui zhixing jingji hetong fa ruogan wenti de yijian de qingshi" (Request for opinion on several issues concerning implementing the economic contract law), *Zhongguo fazhi bao,* July 2, 1982.

2. *See* case citations accompanying Appendix 1b: Table of Cases, Issues Related to Dispute Resolution. Also *see* Appendix 3: Table of Regulations.

3. *See* ECL, Article 48.

4. Although peasant producers were also the cause of nonperformance (*see,* e.g., case no. 18), in thirteen of fifteen cases reported, the local political authority or state organ was the party in breach. In response to these continuing problems, and the threat they posed to legitimation of the ECL as a basis for the agricultural contract system, the CPC's Document no. 1 of 1984 took as its major theme the protection of the interests of peasants—particularly those belonging to the key households (*zhong dian hu*) and the specialized households (*zhuan ye hu*)—who entered into responsibility contracts. *See* "CCP Central Committee Circular on Rural Work in 1984," *FBIS Daily Report: China,* June 13, 1984, at K1.

5. Indeed, as indicated in case nos. 8, 79, and 115, the courts had been unable to resolve a number of contract disputes, sometimes because of refusal of the parties to comply with decisions.

Conclusion

1. "Guanyu guanche zhixing 'Jingji hetong fa' ruogan wenti de yijian" (Opinion on various issues of thorough implementation of the "Economic Contract Law"), Zhang Shouqiang, *Hetong fa gui yu hetong shiyang huibian* (Compilation of laws and regulations on contracts and contract forms) (Harbin, 1988), at 934. The bulk of the Opinion was devoted to issues of

determining the legal effectiveness of contracts, indicating continued problems with maintaining control over contract activity in the face of policy recognition of broader contract authority for economic actors.

2. "Guanyu zai shenli jingji hetong jiufen anjian zhong juti shiyong jingji hetong fa de ruogan wenti de jieshi" (Explanation of various issues concerning the concrete use of the Economic Contract Law in the adjudication of cases of economic contract disputes), *Zhonghua renmin gongheguo zuigao renmin fayuan gongbao* (PRC Supreme Court Reports), no. 3, 1987, at 3. This Explanation was founded in part on an earlier Opinion of the Supreme Court concerning enforcing agricultural responsibility contracts. *See* "Opinion of the Supreme People's Court Concerning Several Questions of Adjudicationg Cases of Disputes Over Agricultural Responsibility Contracts" (4/12/86), Zhang Shouqiang (ed.), *Hetong fa gui yu hetong shiyang huibian, supra* n. 1, at 942.

Selected Bibliograpy

English Language Sources

Books

American Law Institute. *Restatement (2d) of Contracts*. St. Paul, Minn.: American Law Institute, 1981.

Barnett, A.D., ed. *Chinese Communist Politics in Action*. Seattle and London: University of Washington Press, 1969.

Baum, R. *Scientism and Bureaucratism in Chinese Thought: Cultural Limits of the "Four Modernizations."* Lund, Sweden: Research Policy Institute, 1981.

Beirne, P., and R. Sharlet, eds. *Pashukanis: Selected Writings on Marxism and Law*. New York: Academic Press, 1980.

Bendix, R. *Max Weber: An Intellectual Portrait*. Berkeley and Los Angeles: University of California Press, 1977.

———, and G. Roth. *Scholarship and Partisanship*. Berkeley and Los Angeles: University of California Press, 1971.

Bodde, D., and C. Morris. *Law in Imperial China*. Philadelphia: University of Pennsylvania Press, 1967.

Bulletin of Concerned Asian Scholars. *China from Mao to Deng: The Politics and Economics of Socialist Development*. Armonk, N.Y.: M. E. Sharpe, 1983.

Calamari, J.D., and J.M. Perillo. *Contracts*. 2d ed. St. Paul, Minn.: West Publishing Co., 1977.

Chang, Y. *Functional and Coalition Politics in China: The Cultural Revolution and Its Aftermath*. New York: Praeger Publishers, 1976.

Chen, N., and W. Galenson. *The Chinese Economy Under Communism*. Chicago: Aldine Atherton, 1969.

Cheng, C. Y. *China's Economic Development: Growth and Structural Change*. Boulder, Colo.: Westview Press, 1982.

China Council for the Promotion of International Trade. *30th Anniversary Bulletin*. Beijing, 1982.

Chu, G., and F. Hsu. *China's New Social Fabric*. London: Kegan Paul International, 1983.

Chu Tung-tsu. *Law and Society in Traditional China.* Paris: Mouton Press, 1961.

Cohen, J. A., ed. *Contemporary Chinese Law: Research Problems and Perspectives.* Cambridge, Mass.: Harvard University Press, 1970.

———, R. R. Edwards, and F. M. Chen, eds. *Essays on China's Legal Tradition.* Princeton: Princeton University Press, 1980.

Durkheim, E. *The Division of Labor in Society.* Translated by G. Simpson. New York: Free Press, 1964.

Eckstein, A. *China's Economic Revolution.* Cambridge: Cambridge University Press, 1977.

Friedman, L. M., and S. Macaulay. *Law and the Behavioral Sciences.* 2d ed. Indianapolis: Bobbs-Merrill, 1977.

Frolic, B. M. *Mao's People.* Cambridge, Mass.: Harvard University Press, 1983.

Fryer, B., et al., eds. *Law, State and Society.* London: Croon Helm, 1981.

Gluckman, M. *The Judicial Process Among the Barotse of Northern Rhodesia.* Manchester, England: Manchester University Press, 1955.

Goldman, M. *China's Intellectuals: Advice and Dissent.* Cambridge, Mass.: Harvard University Press, 1981.

Gramsci, A. *Selections from the Prison Notebooks.* Translated by Q. Hoare and G. N. Smith. New York: International Publishers, 1971.

Hamrin, C., and T. Cheek, eds. *China's Establishment Intellectuals.* Armonk, N.Y.: M. E. Sharpe, 1986.

Harding, H. *Organizing China: The Problems of Bureaucracy, 1949–1976.* Stanford: Stanford University Press, 1981.

Howe, C. *China's Economy.* New York: Basic Books, 1978.

Joint Publications Research Service. *Compendium of Laws and Regulations of the People's Republic of China.* Washington, D.C.: Joint Publications Research Service, 1962.

———. *Collection of Fiscal Laws and Regulations of the People's Republic of China.* Washington, D.C.: Joint Publications Research Service, 1963.

Kairys, D. *The Politics of Law: A Progressive Critique.* New York: Pantheon, 1982.

Lardy, N. *Economic Growth and Distribution in China.* Cambridge: Cambridge University Press, 1978.

Lee, P. N. "The Post-Leap Policy of Enterprise Management and Its Impacts on the Current Economic Reforms in the PRC." Unpublished monograph. Chinese University of Hong Kong, 1982.

Li, V. *Law Without Lawyers.* Boulder, Colo.: Westview Press, 1978.

Lieberthal, K. *Central Documents and Politburo Politics in China.* Ann Arbor: University of Michigan Press, 1978.

———. *Chinese Politics in 1978: Modernization and the Ghost of Mao.* New York: China Council of the Asia Society, 1978.

Ling, H. C. *The Petroleum Industry of the People's Republic of China.* Stanford: Stanford University Press, 1975.

Lukes, S., and A. Scull, eds. *Durkheim and the Law.* New York: St. Martin's Press, 1983.

MacFarquar, R. *The Origins of the Cultural Revolution: Contradictions Among the People, 1955–1957.* New York: Columbia University Press, 1974.

Maine, H. *Ancient Law.* London: J. Murray, 1861.

Marx, K. *Grundrisse.* Translated by M. Nicolaus. Harmondsworth, England: Penguin, 1973.

———. *The German Ideology.* Translated by Ryazanskaya. Moscow: Foreign Languages Press, 1932.

Miller, L. *Chinese Political Debate Since the December Third Plenum.* Washington, D.C.: Foreign Broadcast Information Service, 1979.

Morse, R. *The Limits of Reform in China.* Boulder, Colo.: Westview Press, 1983.

Nader, L., ed. *The Ethnography of Law.* Menasha, Wis.: American Anthropological Association, 1965.

Naquin, S., and E. R. Rawski. *Chinese Society in the Eighteenth Century.* New Haven and London: Yale University Press, 1987.

Nee, V., and D. Mozingo, eds. *State and Society in Contemporary China.* Ithaca, N.Y.: Cornell University Press, 1983.

Parish, W. L., and M. K. Whyte. *Village and Family in Contemporary China.* Chicago: University of Chicago Press, 1978.

Peng, S. T. *The Chinese Communist Part in Power.* New York: Monad Press, 1980.

Perkins, D., ed. *Rural Small Scale Industry in the People's Republic of China.* Berkeley and Los Angeles: University of California Press, 1977.

———. *Market Control and Planning in Communist China.* Cambridge, Mass.: Harvard University Press, 1966.

Perry, E., and C. Wong, eds. *The Political Economy of Post-Mao China.* Cambridge, Mass.: Harvard University Press, 1985.

Pfeffer, R. *Understanding Business Contracts in China.* Cambridge, Mass.: Harvard University Press, 1973.

Pye, L. *The Dynamics of Chinese Politics.* Cambridge, Mass.: Delgeschlager, Gunn & Haine, 1981.

———. *The Spirit of Chinese Politics: A Psycho-Cultural Study of the Crisis in Political Development.* Cambridge, Mass.: MIT Press, 1968.

Rader, M. *Marx's Interpretation of History.* New York: Oxford University Press, 1979.

Renner, K. *Institutions of Law and Their Social Functions.* Translated by A. Schwarzschild. London: Routledge and Kegan Paul, 1949.

Schluchter, W. *The Rise of Western Rationalism: Max Weber's Developmental History.* Berkeley and Los Angeles: University of California Press, 1981.

Schumpeter, J. *Capitalism, Socialism and Democracy.* New York: Harper & Brothers, 1950.

Sit, V., ed. *Commercial Laws and Business Regulations of the People's Republic of China.* Hong Kong: Tai Dao Publishing, 1983.

Solomon, R. *Mao's Revolution and the Chinese Political Culture.* Berkeley and Los Angeles: University of California Press, 1971.

The Twelfth National Congress of the CCP. Beijing: Foreign Languages Press, 1983.

Szabo, I., and Z. Peters. *A Socialist Approach to Comparative Law.* Leyden: A. W. Suthoff, 1977.

Tigar, M., and M. Levy. *Law and the Rise of Capitalism.* New York: Monthly Review Press, 1977.

Tucker, R. C., ed. *The Marx-Engels Reader.* 2d ed. New York: W. W. Norton, 1978.

Unger, R. M. *Law in Modern Society.* New York: Free Press, 1976.

———. *Knowledge and Politics.* New York: Free Press, 1975

U. S. Congress, Joint Economic Committee. *China's Economy Looks Toward the Year 2000.* Washington, D.C.: U.S. Government Printing Office, 1986.

———. *China Under the Four Modernizations.* Washington, D.C.: U.S. Government Printing Office, 1978.

———. *China: A Reassessment of the Economy.* Washington, D.C.: U.S. Government Printing Office, 1975.

Van Der Sprenkel, S. *Legal Institutions in Manchu China.* New York: Athlone Press, 1962.

Wang, E., ed. *Selected Legal Documents of the People's Republic of China.* Arlington, Va.: University Publications, 1976.

Weber, M. *Economy and Society.* Edited by G. Roth and C. Wittich. Berkeley and Los Angeles: University of California Press, 1974.

Whyte, M. K. *Small Groups and Political Rituals in China.* Berkeley and Los Angeles: University of California Press, 1974.

Williston, S. *Contracts.* 3d ed., edited by W. Jaeger. Mt. Kisco, N.Y.: Baker Voorhis, 1957.

Yu M., ed. *Criminal Law Code and Three Other Codes of the People's Republic of China.* Hong Kong: Great Earth Book Co., 1980.

Periodicals

American Journal of Legal History
American Journal of Sociology
American Political Science Review
American Journal of Comparative Law
Asian Survey
Beijing Review
California Law Review
China Business Review

China Daily
China Directory
China Law Reporter
China Trade Report
Chinese Law and Government
Columbia Journal of Transnational Law
Contemporary China
Foreign Broadcast Information Service (FBIS) China Report: Agriculture
FBIS China Report: Economy
FBIS China Report: Political, Sociological, Military
FBIS China Report: Red Flag
FBIS Daily Report: China
Harvard International Law Journal
International and Comparative Law Quarterly
International Legal Materials
Journal of Asian Studies
Law and Society Review
Problems of Communism
Review of Socialist Law
Selections from Mainland Chinese Magazines
Selections from World Broadcasts
Stanford Journal of International Law
Stanford Law Review
Texas Law Review
The China Quarterly
The International Lawyer
Theory and Society
U.C.L.A. Law Review
Washington University Law Quarterly
Yale Law Journal

Chinese Language Sources

Books

Bai Youzhong, Li Qishan. *Jingji hetong fa zhishi wen da* (Questions and answers on knowledge of the economic contract law). Beijing, 1982.

Beijing cai mao xueyuan (Beijing Institute of Finance and Trade). *Jingji hetong guanli gailun* (Introduction to the administration of contracts). Beijing, 1989.

Beijing nongye daxue (Beijing Agriculture University). *Jingji da cidian: nongye jingji juan* (Economic dictionary: Volume on the agricultural economy). Shanghai, 1983.

Beijing zheng fa xue yuan jingji fa jiao yan shi (Office of Teaching and Research on Economic Law of the Beijing Institute for Politics and Law). *Jingji hetong ziliao* (Materials on economic contracts). Beijing, 1980.

Chen Guangwei, Liu Zhipeng, Zhu Suibin, "*Zhonghua renmin gongheguo jingji hetong fa*" *jianghua* (Lectures on the Economic Contract Law of the PRC). Zhengzhou, 1986.

Chen Xulu, Fang Shiming, Wei Jianyou, eds. *Zhongguo jindai shi cidian* (Dictionary of modern Chinese history). Shanghai, 1982.

Dong Jiuchang, Ding Yaotang. *Jingji hetong fa gailun* (Introduction to the Economic Contract Law). Beijing, 1985.

Dong Jiuchang, Cai Liangcai. *Zhongguo gong shang xingzheng guanli xue gailun* (Introduction to the study of China's administration for industry and commerce.) Beijing, 1985.

Faxue jiao cai bianji bu ziliao shi (Materials Office of the Legal Education and Materials Editorial Department). *Fa gui xuanbian* (Compilation of Laws and Regulations). Beijing, 1983.

Guan Huai, ed. *Jingji fa wen xuan* (Collection of articles on economic law). Beijing, 1981.

Guangzhou shi gong shang xingzheng guanli xueyuan, Guangzhou shi zhong shan jingji jishu zixun fuwu zhongxin (Guangzhou Municipal Industrial and Commercial Administrative Institute and the Zhong Shan Economic and Technical Consultative Service Center of Guangzhou Municipality). *Jingji fa gui huibian* (Compilation of economic laws and regulations). Guangzhou, n.d.

Guo Ouyi. *Jingji hetong jichu zhishi* (Fundamental knowledge of economic contracts). Beijing, 1985.

Guojia gongshang xingzheng guanli ju jingji hetong si (Economic Contracts Office of the State Administration for Industry and Commerce). *Zen yang gianding jingji hetong* (How to execute economic contracts). Beijing, 1985.

Guojia jihua weiyuanhui tiao fa bangongshi (Office of Treaties and Law of the State Planning Commission). *Zhongyao jingji fa gui ziliao xuanbian* (Compilation of important economic laws and regulations). Beijing, 1987.

Guowuyuan jingji fa gui yanjiu zhongxin bangongshi (Office of the Economic Laws and Regulations Research Center of the State Council). *Jingji hetong fa gui xuanbian* (Compilation of laws and regulations on economic contracts). Beijing, 1982.

———. *Zhonghua renmin gongheguo jingji hetong fa tiaowen shiyi* Interpretation of articles of the Economic Contract Law of the PRC). Beijing, 1982.

Guojia jingji weiyuanhui jingji fa gui ju (Economic Laws and Regulations Bureau of the State Economic Commission). *Zhonghua renmin gongheguo jingji fa gui he zhengce wenjian* (Compilation of economic laws and regulations and policy documents of the PRC). Beijing, 1987.

———. *Changzhang chang yong jingji fa gui shouce* (Handbook of economic laws and regulations used by factory directors). Beijing, 1983.

———. *Zhonghua renmin gongheguo yi jiu ba yi nian gongye jiaotong jingji fa gui xuanbian* (Compilation of economic laws and regulations of the PRC for industry and transport, 1981). Beijing, 1982.

———, and Beijing zheng fa xueyuan jingji fa min fa jiao yan shi (Teaching and Research Office for Economic Law and Civil Law of the Beijing Institute for Politics and Law), eds., *Zhonghua renmin gongheguo gongye giye fa gui xuanbian* (Compilation of industrial enterprise laws and regulations of the PRC). Beijing, 1981.

Guowuyuan fa zhi ju (State Council Bureau on the Legal System). *Zhonghua renmin gongheguo fa gui huibian* (Compilation of laws and regulations of the People's Republic of China). Beijing, yearly.

———. *Zhonghua renmin gongheguo xianxing fa gui huibian* (Compilation of current laws and regulations of the PRC). Beijing, 1987.

He Ke, Bai Zhongyao, Zhao Ying, Zhou Diankun. *Nong shang jingji hetong gailun* (Introduction to agricultural and commercial contracts). Beijing, 1986.

Huang Zhenqi. *Shehui zhuyi jingji guilu jianghua* (Lectures on the economic laws of socialism). Beijing, 1980.

Jin Shi, Bing Yi, eds. *Jingji fa lunwen xuan* (Collection of articles on economic law). Nanjing, 1986.

Jingji hetong zhongcai shouce bianji zu (Editorial Group for "Handbook on Economic Contract Arbitration"), ed. *Jingji hetong zhongcai shouce* (Handbook of economic contract arbitration). Beijing, 1984.

Jingji hetong fa qicao xiao zu bangongshi (Office of the Small Group for Drafting the Economic Contract Law). *Zhonghua renmin gongheguo jingji hetong fa jieda* (Answers to the Economic Contract Law of the PRC). Beijing, 1983.

Jingji hetong jiufen anli xuanbian bianji zu (Editorial Group for "Compilation of Cases of Economic Contract Disputes"), ed. *Jingji hetong jiufen anli xuanbian* (Compilation of cases of economic contract disputes). Beijing, 1982.

Li Fang, ed. *Jingji fa shouce* (Handbook on economic law). Shenyang, 1988.

Li Rongsheng. *Jingji hetong gailun* (Introduction to economic contracts). Harbin, 1983.

Li Zhuguo. *Jingji hetong de jiandu yu guanli* (Supervision and administration of economic contracts). Beijing, 1985.

———. *Jingji hetong ti jie jiu shi jiu* (Ninety-nine questions and answers on economic contracts). Tianjin, 1985.

———, and Bai Youzhong. *Hetong jiben zhishi* (Basic knowledge of contracts). Beijing, 1981.

Lin Wenken, Guan Shaobing, Zhao Mingfei, Song Yanghua, Kang Yunsheng, eds. *Zhong wai shiyong jingji hetong geshi daquan* (Encyclopedia of domestic and foreign practical economic contract forms). Shenyang, 1988.

Liu Longheng. *Jingji fa jian lun* (Elementary theory of economic law). Beijing, 1981.

———. *Jingji fa gailun* (Introduction to economic law). Beijing, 1984.

———. *Jingji fa gailun xiuding ben* (Introduction to economic law. Rev. ed.). Beijing, 1987.

Lu Feng, Luo Huanzhen, Huang Weiping. *Wo guo jingji tizhi gaige de huigu yu zhanwang* (Review and prospects for the reform of our country's economic system). Beijing, 1987.

Lu Zhenyong. *Fasheng hetong jiufen zen me ban* (What is to be done when a contract dispute arises). Beijing, 1986.

Pan Haimin, Huang Peijian, eds. *Jingji hetong chang zhi ji cankao geshi* (Common knowledge and reference forms on economic contracts). Beijing, 1989.

Pi Chunxie, He Shiying. *Jingji hetong fa jian shuo* (Elementary introduction to the Economic Contract Law). Taiyuan, 1982.

Qin Youshi, Wang Gen. *Wo guo jingji hetong de lilun he shixian* (Theory and practice of our country's economic contracts). Beijing, 1986.

Quan guo renmin daibiao da hui changwu weiyuanhui fa zhi gongzuo weiyuanhui (Committee on the Work of the Legal System of the National People's Congress Standing Committee). *Zhonghua renmin gongheguo falu ji you guan fa gui huibian, 1985–1986* (Compilation of laws of the PRC and related laws and regulations, 1985–1986). Beijing, 1987.

———. *Zhonghua renmin gongheguo falu ji you guan fa gui huibian, 1979–1984* (Compilation of laws of the PRC and related laws and regulations, 1979–1984). Beijing, 1986.

Rao Xinxian. *Zhongguo falu sixiang shi gang* (Outline history of Chinese legal thought). Lanzhou, 1987.

"Renmin ribao" lilun bu (Theory department of "People's Daily"). *Jingji fazhan yu jingji gaige* (Economic development and economic reform). Beijing, 1987.

Shanghai shehui kexue yuan bumen jingjisuo (Institute of Departmental Economics of the Shanghai Academy of Social Sciences). *Jingji da cidian: gongye jingji juan* (Economic dictionary: Volume on the industrial economy). Shanghai, 1983.

Shanghai shi zhexue shehui kexue xuehui lianhehui (Joint Society of Philosophy and Social Sciences of Shanghai Municipality). *Jingji fa cankao ziliao: gongye qiye guanli bufen* (Reference materials on economic law: Industrial enterprise management section). Shanghai, 1980.

Shangye bu bangongting (Administrative Office of the Ministry of Commerce). *Shangye jingji hetong fa gui huibian* (Compilation of laws and regulations on commercial economic contracts). Beijing, 1986.

———. *Jingji changyong jingji fa gui shouce* (Handbook of laws and regulations used by managers). Beijing, 1983.

Shanxi sheng gong shang xingzheng guanli ju (Shanxi Provincial Administration for Industry and Commerce). *Jingji hetong ying yong shouce* (Handbook for use with economic contracts). Taiyuan, 1986.

Sun Beinan, Ji Haibo. *Jingji hetong zhongcai anli pingxi* (General analysis of economic contract arbitration cases). Jiangsu, 1989.

Tian Jiang, Guo Zhiming, Yuan Jianmin. *Jishu hetong de dingli yu luxing* (Execution and performance of technology contracts). Beijing, 1989.

Wang Cunxue. *Jingji zhongcai yu jingji sifa* (Economic arbitration and economical judicature). Beijing, 1987.

———, Tian Shuqing, Wei Ning. *Zen yang jiejue jingji hetong jiufen* (How to resolve disputes over economic contracts). Beijing, 1987.

Wang Jiafu, ed. *Jingji fa yaoyi* (Significance of economic law). Beijing, 1988.

———, and Wang Baoshu, eds., *Jingji falu zhishi shouce* (Handbook of knowledge of economic law). Beijing, 1988.

Wang Jiafu, Xie Huaishi, Yu Xinru, Wang Baoshu, Liang Huixing, Yu Nengbin. *Hetong fa* (Contract law). Beijing, 1986.

Wang Jingan. *Xukezheng hetong* (Licensing contracts). Beijing, 1987.

Wang Ling, ed. *Jingji hetong fa gui shiyong daquan* (Practical encyclopedia of economic contract laws and regulations). Beijing, 1989.

Wang Zhong, Liu Ruifu, Song Haobo, Zhao Dengju. *Jingji fa xue* (Studies in economic law). Jilin, 1981.

Xu Demin, Li Jingmin. *Zen yang ding hetong* (How to execute contracts). Xian, 1986.

Yan Ciqing, ed. *Qiye jingji hetong yu hetong geshi* (Enterprise economic contracts and contract forms). Beijing, 1987.

Yang Bingzhi. *Jingji hetong fa lilu yu shiwu* (Theory and application of the Economic Contract Law). Beijing, 1988.

Yang Kaidong. *Jingji hetong* (Economic contracts). Jinan: 1982.

Yang Peng, Luo Shirun, Zhou Shunlan, Chen Jiansen. *Jingji hetong fa jian jie* (Elementary introduction to the Economic Contract Law). Fuzhou, 1982.

Yang Xueqi, Zhang Yulin. *Jingji hetong fa gailun* (Introduction to the Economic Contract Law). Dalian, 1986.

Yin Liangpei. *Jingji gaige yu jingji fa zhi* (Economic reform and economic legal system). Shenyang, 1985.

Yunnan sheng gaoji renmin fayuan (Yunnan Provincial Higher Level People's Court). *Jingji sifa gongzuo shouce* (Handbook of economic adjudication work). Kunming, 1985.

Zhang Chengquan. *Jingji hetong de dingli he zhongcai* (Execution and arbitration of economic contracts). Beijing, 1985.

Zhang Dean, Ma Zhiguo. *Jishu hetong qianding zhinan* (Guide to the execution of technology contracts). Xian, 1988.

Zhang Shouqiang, ed. *Hetong fa gui yu hetong shiyang huibian* (Compilation of laws and regulations on contracts and contract forms). Harbin, 1988.

Zhang Sizhi, ed. *Lushi gongzheng yu tiaojie yewu* (The operations of lawyers, notarization and mediation). Beijing, 1986.

Zhongguo fa xue hui (Law Society of China). *Mao Zedong sixiang: Faxue lilun lunwen xuan* (Mao Zedong thought: Collection of articles on legal thought). Beijing, 1985.

Zhongguo renmin yinhang zonghang (Central branch of the People's Bank of China). *Jinrong fa gui huibian: 1949–52* (Compilation of finance and banking laws and regulations). Beijing, 1956.

Zhongguo shehui kexue yuan gongye jingji yanjiusuo qingbao ziliao shi (Information and Materials Office of the Institute on the Industrial Economy of the Chinese Academy of Social Sciences). *Zhongguo gongye jingji fa gui xuanbian* (Compilation of laws and regulations on China's industrial economy). Beijing, 1979.

Zhongguo renmin daxue min fa jiao yan shi (Civil Law Teaching and Research Office of Chinese People's University). *Zhonghua renmin gong he guo min fa cankao ziliao* (Reference materials on civil law of the PRC). Beijing, 1956.

Zhongguo shehui kexue yuan faxue yanjiusuo (Legal Research Institute of the Chinese Academy of Social Sciences). *Zhonghua renmin gongheguo jingji fa gui xuanbian* (Compilation of Economic Laws and Regulations of the People's Republic of China). Beijing, 1980.

Zhonghua renmin gongheguo jingji hetong fa (The Economic Contract Law of the People's Republic of China). Beijing, 1981.

Zhonghua renmin gongheguo jingji hetong fa ji you guan tiaoli (The Economic Contract Law of the PRC and Related Regulations). Beijing, 1986.

Zhonghua renmin gongheguo sifa bu falu zhengce yanjiu shi (Laws and Regulations Research Office of the PRC Ministry of Justice). *Heng xiang jingji lianhe falu fa gui zhengce huibian* (Compilation of laws, statutes, and regulations, and policies of horizontal economic integration). Beijing, 1987.

Zhongyang zheng fa ganbu xuexiao min fa jiao yan shi (Teaching and Research Office of the Central Political and Legal Cadres School). *Zhonghua renmin gongheguo min fa jiben wenti* (Basic problems of Chinese civil law). Beijing, 1958.

Zhou Dawei. *Jishu hetong fa daolun* (Guide to the Technology Contracts Law). Beijing, 1988.

Zhou Min, Wang Wenhua, Li Minghua. *Jingji hetong de dingli yu guanli* (Signing and administration of economic contracts). Hubei, 1981.

Zhou Shijie, ed. *Jingji zhongcai jiben zhishi* (Basic knowledge of economic arbitration). Beijing, 1985.

Periodicals

Beijing daxue xuebao (Bulletin of Beijing University)

Ch'ing-shih wen t'i (Issues of Ching history)

Da gong bao (Impartial Daily)

Faxue (Legal Studies)

Faxue jikan (Legal Studies Quarterly)

Faxue yanjiu, (Legal Studies Research)
Faxue zazhi (Legal Studies Magazine)
Faxue shenghuo (Legal Studies and Life)
Fa zhi ribao (Legal System Daily)
Gongren ribao (Worker's Daily)
Guangming ribao (Guangming Daily)
Hongqi (Red Flag)
Jiefang ribao (Liberation Daily)
Jingji cankao (Economic Reference Materials)
Jingji ribao (Economic Daily)
Liaoning daxue xuebao (Bulletin of Liaoning University)
Minzhu yu fazhi (Democracy and the Legal System)
Renmin ribao (People's Daily)
Shehui kexue (Social Sciences)
Shichang (The Market)
Sichuan ribao (Sichuan Daily)
Wen hui bao (Literary Gazette)
Xinan zheng fa xueyuan xuebao (Journal of the Southwest Political-Legal Institute)
Xinhua yue bao (New China Monthly)
Xuexi yu tansuo (Study and Inquiry)
Zheng fa hongqi (Politics and Law Red Flag)
Zhengzhi yu falu (Politics and Law)
Zongguo caimao bao (Chinese Finance and Trade Journal)
Zhongguo fazhi bao (Chinese Legal System Gazette)
Zhongguo nong bao (China Agricultural Gazette)
Zhongguo nongye nian jian (Yearbook of Chinese Agriculture)
Zhonghua renmin gongheguo guowuyuan gongbao (PRC State Council Reports)
Zhonghua renmin gongheguo zui gao renmin fayuan gongbao (PRC Supreme Court Reports)

Index

PITMAN B. POTTER is Professor of Law and Director of Chinese Legal Studies at the University of British Columbia Law Faculty. He received his Ph.D. (political science) and Juris Doctor (law) degrees from the University of Washington. He conducted field research in China and Hong Kong during 1980, 1981, and 1983. Prior to joining UBC, Professor Potter practiced law for five years, including three years in Beijing, where he also taught law at Peking University. He continues to travel regularly to China and Taiwan and is working on research in Chinese legal culture.

www.ingramcontent.com/pod-product-compliance
Lightning Source LLC
LaVergne TN
LVHW050249080826
844660LV00012B/615

* 9 7 8 0 2 9 5 9 7 1 2 7 8 *